*Voices
at the Door*

Voices
at the Door

An Anthology of Favourite Poems

Edited by

Owen Burt and Christine Jones

Published on behalf of Shelter Cymru
by the University of Wales Press

CARDIFF
1995

British Library Cataloguing in Publication Data

A catalogue record for this book is available from the British Library.

ISBN 0-7083-1316-7

**Published with the financial support of
NatWest Cymru Wales**

**All proceeds from this book will be donated to
Shelter Cymru, the Welsh Campaign for Homeless
People (Registered Charity Number 515902)**

Illustrations in this volume by members of the Printmakers of Wales

Cover design by John Garland, Pentan Partnership, Cardiff
Cover illustration by Paul Peter Piech

Typesetting at the University of Wales Press
Printed in Great Britain by Bookcraft, Midsomer Norton, Avon

To those who never give up . . .

Contents

Foreword

Two persistent themes run through this unique anthology. One is Welshness, the other compassion.

This is only proper. The purpose of the book is to support the institution of kindness called Shelter; its contributors are a wide range of Welsh people, or people linked with Wales, to nearly all of whom some feeling of *Cymreictod* (Welshness), is essential to existence, and is more or less co-terminous with the idea of poetry. The world, of course, loves to call Wales 'The Land of Song', when it is not indulging in some less flattering epithet, and is generally thinking of male-voice choirs, rugby crowds and the tremulous parlour tenors of our grandparents' day, with Geraint Evans and Bryn Terfel thrown in for politeness's sake. The true Welsh song, though, from medieval times to the present day, has been poetry, and especially perhaps lyric poetry of the kind which, in the Welsh way, not only wears its heart on its sleeve but is inclined to be laughing up it, too.

Not all the poems in this book are by Welsh poets, but most of them fit these criteria anyway. They are kind, they are melodious, they are disrespectful, they are often funny in a sly and self-deprecatory way – they have the very qualities, in short, which characterize the greatest of all our poets, Dafydd ap Gwilym himself. Even the holiest of them (and though the collection is nothing if not ecumenical, still a good many are Christian poems) are alive with paradox and familiarity: if George Herbert likens his Lord and Saviour to the perfect host at a dinner table, Saunders Lewis addresses the Good Thief as a brother and an intermediary. It is a friendly assembly of literature: nothing pompous about it, nothing hectoring. The most eminent of its academic contributors explain their choices most amiably – not always a characteristic of eminent academics.

When the collection first reached me, in typescript, I was astonished by the full-blooded scope of it. Anthologies are more usually restrained. Honest bawdy is the one category of poetry missing from this book (surprising in a Welsh selection, but perhaps the contributors were inhibited by the work's high-minded intent). Otherwise, almost everything is here: poems haunting and poems provocative, poems old and new, poems of childhood and of maturity, poems of love and poems if not of hate exactly, at least of mockery. There are a few poems that might be regarded by critics of austere preferences as a trifle sentimental, but there is hardly a one that they would dare dismiss as worthless.

I wish I could say that all this merely reflects the habits of Wales itself – that given a choice of pleasures, we would all plump for reading Gerard Manley Hopkins and Caradog Prichard, R. Williams Parry and Vaughan the Silurist. There was certainly a time when most Welsh people, I think it is safe to say, would be able to quote some verse or other from one of the great hymn-writers. However in Wales, as everywhere else, the world's corrosion oozes in, and if ours remains a land of poetry-writers, I fear it is scarcely a land of poetry-readers: only in its Welsh-speaking areas will the pith of an *englyn*, the flow of a *pryddest*, still find a knowledgeable popular audience.

But if we cannot honestly say the contents of this book represent the taste of Wales, I think we can still claim that its purpose properly reflects the spirit of the place. This is still, on the whole, a very kind country – still the country where Hopkins found that 'comforting smell breathed at very entering'. It is a paradox that in an age of violence, there is perhaps more compassion around than ever before, and the beauty, the fun, the gentleness, the dedication that are the hallmarks of this collection still find their echoes, thank God, in the every-day relationships of the Welsh. They are too often masked, as every poet knows, by hypocrisy, Philistinism, malicious gossip, backbiting and avarice: but they are there, and they are the best song of Wales.

Jan Morris

Rhagair

Peth rhyfedd ar un olwg ydi hel ynghyd docyn mawr o gerddi er mwyn y rhai sydd heb do uwch eu pennau. Be' mae cân yn dda, neno'r dyn, a chithau heb dŷ? Ond mae barddoniaeth yn arf rymus iawn hyd heddiw yn ein gwlad ni, waeth be' mae neb yn ei ddweud. Mae Talwrn y Beirdd bob wythnos yn berwi o anniddigrwydd gwleidyddol. Ac yn Nhalwrn Mawr yr Eisteddfod Genedlaethol, pan fydd bardd yn adrodd rhyw englyn mawr, a si yn mynd drwy'r dyrfa o un peth i'r llall, fel gwynt drwy'r dail crin, a'r meuryn yn fud am funud fach, mi fyddaf yn meddwl weithiau mai'r Babell Lên ydi'r peth agosa' sy gynnon ni i Senedd, a'r areithiau bach cynnil yn fwy cofiadwy o beth coblyn na dim byd glywch chi yn Nhŷ'r Cyffredin.

Doedd y beirdd ers talwm yn poeni dim oll am bobl ddigartref, wrth reswm. Pobl oedd yn byw mewn llysoedd mawr ysblennydd a mynachlogydd, a'u byrddau'n gwegian gan gig a gwin, oedd eu diddordeb nhw. A bydd rhai beirniaid heddiw yn leicio dweud mai peth elitaidd dosbarth-canol ydi gwneud cerddi, yn enwedig cerddi caeth. Ŵyr neb pwy piau'r Hen Benillion, ond merched tlawd cefn gwlad, a'u henwau wedi mynd dros go' ers talwm, wnaeth lawer ohonyn nhw. Mae rhai o'r cerddi hynny yn y gyfrol hon, a cherddi gan grwydriaid a glowyr a phobol gyffredin eraill hefyd, yn ogystal â chanu beirdd mawr enwog.

Pan oeddwn i flynyddoedd maith yn ôl yn clera yn Abertawe, a 'nhelyn yn gynhaliaeth, mi fyddwn i'n cychwyn i lawr Allt Constitution yn fore iawn, a'r delyn ar fy nghefn, a'r byd i gyd heb godi, er mwyn bod yn fy hoff lecyn, lle'r oedd y mur yn taflu fy llais, cyn i fyddin y bysgwyr ddeffro. A bob bore, mi fyddai 'na hen wreigen flêr iawn yr olwg yn cerdded heibio'r fan ar ei ffordd i'r farchnad. A bob bore yn gofyn yr un peth: 'Cana'r Deryn Pur, fy machgen i.' A bob bore'n gwrando'r un fath, a bob tro'n dweud: 'Fe fyddai'n ddiflas iawn heb gân.'

Twm Morys

Editors' Preface

In order to compile this anthology we wrote to a large number of people who in our view represented a reasonable cross-section of contemporary Welsh society. They were asked to choose a favourite poem and give reasons for their selection. We are very grateful to everyone who responded. The contributions have been included in the language in which they were supplied. In all cases Welsh-language comments by contributors are accompanied by an English translation. However, Welsh-language poems have not been translated into English.

We would like to thank Jan Morris and Twm Morys for writing the Foreword, and Paul Peter Piech and the Printmakers of Wales for the illustrations.

Many other people have provided invaluable help. In particular we must thank Ned Thomas, Ceinwen Jones and staff of the University of Wales Press for advice on content and production, Professor M. Wynn Thomas for comments on the typescript and Anne Dahne and Alison Jones for clerical assistance.

The anthology provides some unusual perspectives on poems both old and new, made all the more interesting by the variety in style and character of the contributors' comments. We hope you enjoy it. By buying a copy you are making a direct contribution to Shelter Cymru and its work to prevent homelessness in Wales. Thank you.

Owen Burt
Christine Jones
1995

Like so many of today's charitable organizations, Shelter Cymru is reliant on donations and the fund-raising efforts of its supporters. NatWest has supported Shelter Cymru for many years and I am delighted that we have been given the opportunity to be associated with this selection of poetry, in this, the UK Year of Literature.

I am sure that readers will enjoy the anthology and take pleasure from the thought that in doing so they have helped to raise funds to assist the homeless and those in need of help with their housing situation.

Thank you for supporting Shelter Cymru.

Denis Larmer
Regional Managing Director
NatWest Cymru Wales

The Anthology

Dannie Abse

I have just come back from holiday in Cyprus and on the way to the airport in Paphos I saw a sign to Platres. At once I remembered one of my favourite poems, 'Helen' by George Seferis. It begins 'The nightingales will never let you go to sleep in Platres.' 'They certainly won't,' said our Cypriot taxi-driver. 'There are masses of them there.'

I had come across 'Helen' in Rex Warner's translation in 1960 and, ever since, lines from it have stayed with me. Seferis, in this wonderful anti-war poem, speaks with the voice of Teucer, one of Helen's suitors who fought at Troy. He was the best archer among the Greeks. Later Teucer retired to Cyprus and here, in the poem, he wonders whether all the suffering of the Trojan war had been for nothing, 'for an empty garment', – like, perhaps, all wars to come.

Helen

Teucer: *. . . towards sea surrounded Cyprus, where Apollo said*
I was to settle down and call my city's name
Salamis, in memory of my old island home . . .

Helen: *I never went to Troy. Only a phantom went . . .*

Messenger: *What's this? Then did we toil in vain there simply for a cloud?*

Euripedes, Helen

'The nightingales will never let you go to sleep at Platres.'

Shy nightingale, in the shuddering breath of the leaves,
Giver of the dewy music, the dew of the forest,
To bodies parted each from each, to the souls
Of those who know that they will not come back again.
Blind voice, in the darkened memory turning over
Footsteps, gestures of hands, I'd not dare say kisses,
And the bitter heave of the heart, the heart of a slave grown savage.

'The nightingales will never let you go to sleep at Platres.'

2

Platres, what is it? Who is it knows this island?
I have lived my life hearing names heard for the first time;
New places and new madnesses
Whether of men or gods.
                              My own fate which wavers
Between the final sword of an Ajax
And another Salamis
Has brought me to this shore; here the moon
Has risen from the sea like Aphrodite,
Has blotted out the Archer, and now she goes,
To the Heart of the Scorpion, changing everything.
O truth, where are you?
I also was an archer in the war;
My fate that of a man who missed the mark.

Melodious nightingale,
On such a night as this the Spartan slave girls
Heard you on Proteus's beach and lifted their lament.
And among them there was – who could have thought it? – Helen!
She, our pursuit for years beside Scamander.
She was there, at the desert's edge. I touched her. She spoke to me.
'It is not true, it is not true', she cried.
'I never went aboard that coloured ship;
I never trod the ground of manly Troy.'

Deep-girdled, the sun in her hair, with that way of standing,
The print of shadows and the print of smiles
On shoulders, thighs and knees,
The lively skin, the eyes and the great eyelids,
She was there, on the banks of the Delta.
                              And at Troy?

Nothing. At Troy a phantom.
So the gods willed it.
And Paris lay with a shadow as though it were solid flesh:
And we were slaughtered for Helen ten long years.

Great pain had fallen on Greece.
So many bodies thrown
To jaws of the sea, to jaws of the earth;
So many souls
Given up to the mill-stones to be crushed like corn.

And the muddy beds of the rivers sweated with blood
For a wavering linen garment, a thing of air,
For a butterfly's jerk, for a swan's down, for a Helen.
And my brother?
                    O nightingale, nightingale,
What is god? What is not god? What is in-between?

'The nightingales will never let you go to sleep at Platres!'

Tearful bird,
            at sea-kissed Cyprus,
Ordained for me to remind me of my country,
I moored alone and brought this fairy story,
If it is true that it is a fairy story,
If it is true that man will not set in motion once more
The old deceit of the gods;
                            if it is true
That after many years some other Teucer,
Some Ajax, maybe, or Priam or Hecuba,
Or someone quite unknown, nameless, yet one who saw
The corpses crown the banks of a Scamander,
Were not so fated as this – fated to hear
The steps of the messengers, who come to tell him
That so much suffering, so much of life
Fell into the abyss
For the sake of an empty garment, for a Helen.

George Seferis

Poems, translated by Rex Warner (Bodley Head, 1960)

Leo Abse

These are seasons of political disenchantment; and in such seasons, as at all times when ideals seem vanities, and scepticism and cynicism rule, we re-learn that nothing matters except personal relationships. Public clamour and our conceits, our bitter-sweet successes and our humiliating defeats, our fulfilled and unfulfilled ambitions, all can be relegated if we truly love; for on this darkling plain only our loves and friendships have significance; these days the rest is trash. By mourning with Arnold the loss of our dreams, we are strangely comforted.

Dover Beach

The sea is calm tonight.
The tide is full, the moon lies fair
Upon the straits; on the French coast the light
Gleams and is gone; the cliffs of England stand,
Glimmering and vast, out in the tranquil bay.
Come to the window, sweet is the night-air!
Only, from the long line of spray
Where the sea meets the moon-blanched land,
Listen! you hear the grating roar
Of pebbles which the waves draw back, and fling,
At their return, up the high strand,
Begin, and cease, and then again begin,
With tremulous cadence slow, and bring
The eternal note of sadness in.

Sophocles long ago
Heard it on the Aegean, and it brought
Into his mind the turbid ebb and flow
Of human misery; we
Find also in the sound a thought,
Hearing it by this distant northern sea.

The Sea of Faith
Was once, too, at the full, and round earth's shore
Lay like the folds of a bright girdle furled.

But now I only hear
Its melancholy, long, withdrawing roar,
Retreating, to the breath
Of the night-wind, down the vast edges drear
And naked shingles of the world.

Ah, love, let us be true
To one another! for the world, which seems
To lie before us like a land of dreams,
So various, so beautiful, so new,
Hath really neither joy, nor love, nor light,
Nor certitude, nor peace, nor help for pain;
And we are here as on a darkling plain
Swept with confused alarms of struggle and flight,
Where ignorant armies clash by night.

Matthew Arnold

The Poems of Matthew Arnold, ed. Kenneth Allott (Longmans, 1965)

Donald Anderson

It has not been very easy to select a single poem. I rejected the politically correct solution for a Swansea boy of Dylan Thomas and decided to adopt the Desert Island Discs test of eight poems I could take with me and then face the choice – 'and if there were only one?'

The eight would certainly include Milton, perhaps 'On his blindness', and Du Bellay's 'Heureux Qui Comme Ulysse', an almost Welsh essay in *hiraeth* from marbled Rome for his slated village of Liré.

There would be no video and I love Westerns. The nearest equivalent in poetry is surely Macaulay's 'Horatius'; I would boo the assembling baddies and cheer the ultimate triumph of our wounded hero, in company with the Romans, 'the ranks of Tuscany' and perhaps John Wayne.

And so to 'the one'. For a poem which illumines our contemporary human condition it must be Cavafy's 'Waiting for the Barbarians'. Like all great poems it speaks to us on several levels. Some will relate it to our confusion after the 'certainties' of the wasted years of the Cold War. I read into it a challenge to face the real issues of our day and avoid escapist diversions.

Waiting for the Barbarians

What are we waiting for, assembled in the forum?

    The barbarians are due here today.

Why isn't anything going on in the senate?
Why are the senators sitting there without legislating?

    Because the barbarians are coming today.
    What's the point of senators making laws now?
    Once the barbarians are here, they'll do the legislating.

Why did our emperor get up so early,
and why is he sitting enthroned at the city's main gate,
in state, wearing the crown?

Because the barbarians are coming today
and the emperor's waiting to receive their leader.
He's even got a scroll to give him,
loaded with titles, with imposing names.

Why have our two consuls and praetors come out today
wearing their embroidered, their scarlet togas?
Why have they put on their bracelets with so many amethysts,
rings sparkling with magnificent emeralds?
Why are they carrying elegant canes
beautifully worked in silver and gold?

    Because the barbarians are coming today
    and things like that dazzle the barbarians.

Why don't our distinguished orators turn up as usual
to make their speeches, say what they have to say?

    Because the barbarians are coming today
    and they're bored by rhetoric and public speaking.

Why this sudden bewilderment, this confusion?
(How serious people's faces have become.)
Why are the streets and squares emptying so rapidly,
everyone going home lost in thought?

    Because night has fallen and the barbarians haven't come.
    And some of our men just in from the border say
    there are no barbarians any longer.

Now what's going to happen to us without barbarians?
Those people were a kind of solution.

C. P. Cavafy

Collected Poems, translated by Edmund Keely and Philip Sherrard
(Hogarth Press, 1984)

The Marquess of Anglesey

My favourite poem (at t'moment) is 'Whole Duty of Children'. I like it especially because the last line comes as a surprise – *a very witty surprise* and it *smashes* in eight words all vestiges of pompous preaching contained in the previous three lines!

Whole Duty of Children

A child should always say what's true
And speak when he is spoken to,
And behave mannerly at table:
At least as far as he is able.

Robert Louis Stevenson

A Child's Garden of Verses (Oxford University Press, 1966)

Graham Benfield

I have found it impossible to choose my all-time favourite poem so I have opted for the poem that has had most impact on me in the last year. It is entitled 'Persecution' by Pastor Niemoeller, who was a victim of the Nazis.

I value the poem because it is powerful, direct and unambiguous as it brings home to me the sense of personal responsibility for what happens to others. The poem is particularly relevant during a year when persecution again surfaced in Europe and when 'ethnic cleansing' became a new way of describing policy and action which had been prematurely confined to the history book.

Speaking out can take many forms and I was conscious of Pastor Martin Niemoeller's words when watching the brilliant film adaptation of Thomas Keneally's book *Schindler's Ark*, where individual action in the face of seemingly overwhelming odds had a fundamental effect in securing future generations.

Finally the poem also helps square the circle of the conflicting political and moral dilemma of the twentieth century – individualism versus collectivism – by demonstrating how concern for the collective welfare of others ultimately determines the fate of oneself.

Persecution

First they came for the Jews,
and I did not speak out,
because I was not a Jew.

Then they came for the communists,
and I did not speak out,
because I was not a communist.

Then they came for trade unionists,
and I did not speak out,
because I was not a trade unionist.

Then they came for me,
and there was no one left
to speak out for me.

Martin Niemoeller

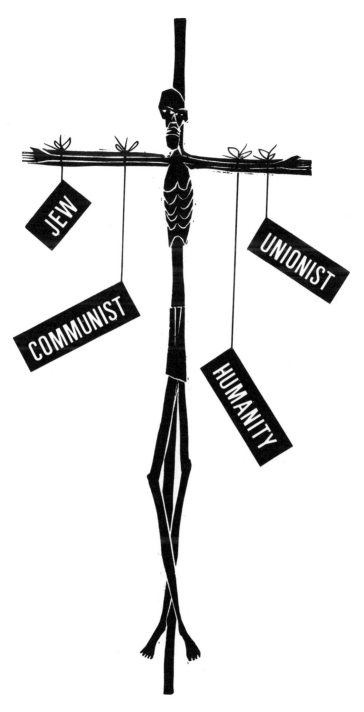

'Persecution'. Graphics by Paul Peter Piech.

Clive Betts

It would have been easier to find a favourite piece of music, as I frequently listen to records (and attend concerts) for enjoyment and relaxation. I can hardly say the same about poetry.

But there have been over the years a number of poems which I can easily recall to my memory. 'The Bard' by Thomas Gray was one of my A-Level texts when I was a sixth-former in Acton. At that time, I knew little about Wales. It would be silly and wrong to say the poem about the mountain-top bard challenging the might of Edward I's army awakened my interest in Wales. Some sort of interest should, surely, exist within the breast of any cultured Englishman. The poem's importance is, rather, as a reminder that the relationship between Wales and England is not, as some would try to argue, inevitably purely one of conflict. That conflict certainly exists, but alongside that can be found the intelligent-English wish to understand the neighbour. Sometimes, such English people can teach the Welsh a point or two: Gray, professor of modern history at Cambridge, was one of the first to appreciate the wild beauty of Wales, almost unparalleled throughout the world but ignored by too many of the natives, even today.

Another, again by Thomas Gray, is 'Ode on the Death of a Favourite Cat'. I suppose I like this because of its light-hearted, but so delicately crafted, contrast to 'The Bard'. In addition, I don't like cats, despite my daughter's recent acquisition of a (neutered) tom.

Harri Webb's 'Synopsis of the Great Welsh Novel' lies at the other extreme of the craft, where poetry stands close to prose. Harri loved his nation more than most, but he was far from blind to its weaknesses and follies. I could almost liken his attitude to that of the Jews, who are so capable of laughing at their own race's follies from a position of deep love. Or even the (non-Northern) Irish. I suppose if Harri wrote the Synopsis today, his characters would be different. But in a volume bought for 15s., he paints a picture which, in its essentials, has not changed.

Synopsis of the Great Welsh Novel

DAI K lives at the end of the valley. One is not quite sure
Whether it has been drowned or not. His Mam
Loves him too much and his Dada drinks.
As for his girlfriend Blodwen, she's pregnant. So
Are all the other girls in the village – there's been a Revival.
After a performance of Elijah, the mad preacher
Davies the Doom has burnt the chapel down.
One Saturday night after the dance at the Con Club,
With the Free Wales Army up to no good in the back lanes,
A stranger comes to the village; he is, of course,
God, the well known television personality. He succeeds
In confusing the issue, whatever it is, and departs
On the last train before the line is closed.
The colliery blows up, there is a financial scandal
Involving all the most respected citizens; the Choir
Wins at the National. It is all seen, naturally,
Through the eyes of a sensitive boy who never grows up.
The men emigrate to America, Cardiff and the moon. The girls
Find rich and foolish English husbands. Only daft Ianto
Is left to recite the Complete Works of Sir Lewis Morris
To puzzled sheep, before throwing himself over
The edge of the abandoned quarry. One is not quite sure
Whether it is fiction or not.

Harri Webb

The Green Desert: Collected Poems, 1950–1969 (Gwasg Gomer, 1969)

13

'Politics'. Graphics by Keith Bayliss.

Michael Boyce

I do not know what Yeats had in mind when he wrote this poem – but perhaps what matters is how his message is received and not how it was sent. I have spent my working life alongside the practitioners of politics yet outside politics: an apolitical life immersed in the politics of hard-working, committed, brilliant, ignorant, despotic, corrupt councillors; amongst self-important, arrogant, caring, sensitive Members of Parliament. Ministers: cold, clever, conceited, sincere and honest; politicians who advance policies to further their own interests and their careers, their egos, their constituents; politicians who help the disadvantaged, the deprived, the unemployed, the sick, the uneducated, the homeless. And their power, bank balances and status. Virtues and vices shared by all parties because people are people first. Not Tories, Socialists, Nationalists or even Feminists, Environmentalists, Racists. The message I receive from Yeats and the view I share is that what drives or touches people is love; being in love or searching for love or mourning the loss of love. And for me 'Politics' is about the importance of romantic love and how it beats politics any day!

Politics

'In our time the destiny of man presents its meaning in political terms.'
Thomas Mann

How can I, that girl standing there,
My attention fix
On Roman or on Russian
Or on Spanish politics?
Yet here's a travelled man that knows
What he talks about,
And there's a politician
That has read and thought,
And maybe what they say is true
Of war and war's alarms,
But O that I were young again
And held her in my arms!

W. B. Yeats

The Poems, ed. Richard J. Finnerman (Macmillan, 1983)

15

Noreen Bray

It has been a very difficult task choosing just one favourite poem. In the end I've chosen William Blake's 'The Tyger'. This is probably one of the first poems we learnt by heart at school. The English teacher used to demonstrate how poetry really comes into its own when read or spoken out loud. These days I can only remember the first couple of lines but I've chosen it because it can be enjoyed by every reader from nine to ninety. It's got something for everyone and its powerful imagery and hammering rhythm makes this beautiful and dangerous animal spring off the page right into our living rooms.

Born in 1757, Blake was a self-taught man and some of his poetry can be a little odd but 'The Tyger' shows how poetry can speak from one age to another because the human emotions expressed – fear and awe – are common to us all.

The Tyger

Tyger! Tyger! burning bright
In the forests of the night,
What immortal hand or eye
Could frame thy fearful symmetry?

In what distant deeps or skies
Burnt the fire of thine eyes?
On what wings dare he aspire?
What the hand dare seize the fire?

And what shoulder, and what art,
Could twist the sinews of thy heart?
And when thy heart began to beat,
What dread hand? And what dread feet?

What the hammer? What the chain?
In what furnace was thy brain?
What the anvil? What dread grasp
Dare its deadly terrors clasp?

'Tyger, Tyger'. Graphics by Paul Peter Piech.

When the stars threw down their spears,
And water'd heaven with their tears,
Did he smile his work to see?
Did he who made the Lamb make thee?

Tyger! Tyger! burning bright
In the forests of the night,
What immortal hand or eye
Dare frame thy fearful symmetry?

William Blake

Poetry and Prose of William Blake, ed. Geoffrey Keynes (Nonesuch Library, 1961)

Rachel Bromwich

Hopkins's poetry has meant a great deal to me over a great many years. Although 'In the Valley of the Elwy' is one of his simpler sonnets, I think that it has a unique quality of its own. I think also that it summarizes a great deal about Hopkins himself. In it the poet gives memorable expression to his belief in a hard-won reconciliation between his agonizing internal conflict and his deep awareness of a divinely ordered and supremely beautiful creation, manifested here in his immediate, sensitive response to the Welsh countryside which lay around him. The poem was composed while Hopkins was in training as a Jesuit priest at St Beuno's College near St Asaph (Llanelwy) in Clwyd. During his time there he became greatly attracted to the Welsh language and to Welsh poetry. He learned to speak a little Welsh (though he admits to having found the local dialect difficult to comprehend). He was interested and intrigued by the metrical complexities of Welsh poetry, and he made several attempts at composing *cywyddau* in Welsh. Although alliteration is an innate feature in both Welsh and English poetry, and appears even earlier in both than does rhyme, the combination of alliteration and internal rhyme in Welsh *cynghanedd* attains a degree of complexity which is almost impossible to achieve in English – not least because of the absence from English of the Welsh system of initial mutations. This gives all the greater interest to Hopkins's occasional attempts to reproduce the complex harmony of *cynghanedd*. This poem offers two impressive examples, in the lines 'All the air things wear that build this world of Wales' and 'Being mighty a master, being a father and fond'.

In the Valley of the Elwy

I remember a house where all were good
    To me, God knows, deserving no such thing:
    Comforting smell breathed at very entering,
Fetched fresh, as I suppose, off some sweet wood.
That cordial air made those kind people a hood
    All over, as a bevy of eggs the mothering wing
    Will, or mild nights the new morsels of spring:
Why, it seemed of course; seemed of right it should.

Lovely the woods, waters, meadows, combes, vales,
All the air things wear that build this world of Wales;
   Only the inmate does not correspond:
God, lover of souls, swaying considerate scales,
Complete thy creature dear O where it fails,
   Being mighty a master, being a father and fond.

Gerard Manley Hopkins

The Poetical Works of Gerard Manley Hopkins, ed. Norman Mackenzie
(Oxford University Press, 1990)

Lord Callaghan

One of the poems that I always like to read is Gray's 'Elegy Written in a Country Churchyard'. I particularly like the verse:

> Full many a gem of purest ray serene,
> The dark unfathom'd caves of ocean bear:
> Full many a flower is born to blush unseen,
> And waste its sweetness on the desert air.

This verse seems to me to illustrate the truth about the life of many of our people in south Wales who, in the heat of the Industrial Revolution, were never given a full opportunity for their talents to blossom. Today the situation is of course better, but we should not be complacent. There are still those, especially among the ethnic minorities, whose capacity and talents remain unrecognized.

Elegy Written in a Country Churchyard

The Curfew tolls the knell of parting day,
The lowing herd wind slowly o'er the lea,
The plowman homeward plods his weary way,
And leaves the world to darkness and to me.

Now fades the glimmering landscape on the sight,
And all the air a solemn stillness holds,
Save where the beetle wheels his droning flight,
And drowsy tinklings lull the distant folds;

Save that from yonder ivy-mantled tow'r
The mopeing owl does to the moon complain
Of such, as wand'ring near her secret bow'r,
Molest her ancient solitary reign.

Beneath those rugged elms, that yew-tree's shade,
Where heaves the turf in many a mould'ring heap,
Each in his narrow cell for ever laid,
The rude Forefathers of the hamlet sleep.

The breezy call of incense-breathing Morn,
The swallow twitt'ring from the straw-built shed,
The cock's shrill clarion, or the echoing horn,
No more shall rouse them from their lowly bed.

For them no more the blazing hearth shall burn,
Or busy housewife ply her evening care:
No children run to lisp their sire's return,
Or climb his knees the envied kiss to share.

Oft did the harvest to their sickle yield,
Their furrow oft the stubborn glebe has broke;
How jocund did they drive their team afield!
How bow'd the woods beneath their sturdy stroke!

Let not Ambition mock their useful toil,
Their homely joys, and destiny obscure;
Nor Grandeur hear with a disdainful smile,
The short and simple annals of the poor.

The boast of heraldry, the pomp of pow'r,
And all that beauty, all that wealth e'er gave,
Awaits alike th' inevitable hour.
The paths of glory lead but to the grave.

Nor you, ye Proud, impute to These the fault,
If Mem'ry o'er their Tomb no Trophies raise,
Where thro' the long-drawn isle and fretted vault
The pealing anthem swells the note of praise.

Can storied urn or animated bust
Back to its mansion call the fleeting breath?
Can Honour's voice provoke the silent dust,
Or Flatt'ry sooth the dull cold ear of Death?

Perhaps in this neglected spot is laid
Some heart once pregnant with celestial fire;
Hands, that the rod of empire might have sway'd,
Or wak'd to extasy the living lyre.

But Knowledge to their eyes her ample page
Rich with the spoils of time did ne'er unroll;
Chill Penury repress'd their noble rage,
And froze the genial current of the soul.

Full many a gem of purest ray serene,
The dark unfathom'd caves of ocean bear:
Full many a flower is born to blush unseen,
And waste its sweetness on the desert air.

Some village-Hampden, that with dauntless breast
The little Tyrant of his fields withstood;
Some mute inglorious Milton here may rest,
Some Cromwell guiltless of his country's blood.

Th' applause of list'ning senates to command,
The threats of pain and ruin to despise,
To scatter plenty o'er a smiling land,
And read their hist'ry in a nation's eyes,

Their lot forbad: nor circumscrib'd alone
Their growing virtues, but their crimes confin'd;
Forbad to wade through slaughter to a throne,
And shut the gates of mercy on mankind,

The struggling pangs of conscious truth to hide,
To quench the blushes of ingenuous shame,
Or heap the shrine of Luxury and Pride
With incense kindled at the Muse's flame.

Far from the madding crowd's ignoble strife,
Their sober wishes never learn'd to stray;
Along the cool sequester'd vale of life
They kept the noiseless tenor of their way.

Yet ev'n these bones from insult to protect
Some frail memorial still erected nigh,
With uncouth rhimes and shapeless sculpture deck'd,
Implores the passing tribute of a sigh.

Their name, their years, spelt by th' unletter'd muse,
The place of fame and elegy supply:
And many a holy text around she strews,
That teach the rustic moralist to die.

For who to dumb Forgetfulness a prey,
This pleasing anxious being e'er resign'd,
Left the warm precincts of the chearful day,
Nor cast one longing ling'ring look behind?

On some fond breast the parting soul relies,
Some pious drops the closing eye requires;
Ev'n from the tomb the voice of Nature cries,
Ev'n in our Ashes live their wonted Fires.

For thee, who mindful of th' unhonour'd Dead
Dost in these lines their artless tale relate;
If chance, by lonely contemplation led,
Some kindred Spirit shall inquire thy fate,

Haply some hoary-headed Swain may say,
Oft have we seen him at the peep of dawn
Brushing with hasty steps the dews away
To meet the sun upon the upland lawn.

There at the foot of yonder nodding beech
That wreathes its old fantastic roots so high,
His listless length at noontide would he stretch,
And pore upon the brook that babbles by.

Hard by yon wood, now smiling as in scorn,
Mutt'ring his wayward fancies he would rove,
Now drooping, woeful wan, like one forlorn,
Or craz'd with care, or cross'd in hopeless love.

One morn I miss'd him on the custom'd hill,
Along the heath and near his fav'rite tree;
Another came; nor yet beside the rill,
Nor up the lawn, nor at the wood was he;

The next with dirges due in sad array
Slow thro' the church-way path we saw him born.
Approach and read (for thou can'st read) the lay,
Grav'd on the stone beneath yon aged thorn.'

The EPITAPH

Here rests his head upon the lap of Earth
A Youth to Fortune and to Fame unknown.
Fair Science frown'd not on his humble birth,
And Melancholy mark'd him for her own.

Large was his bounty, and his soul sincere,
Heav'n did a recompence as largely send:
He gave to Mis'ry all he had, a tear,
He gain'd from Heav'n ('twas all he wish'd) a friend.

No farther seek his merits to disclose,
Or draw his frailties from their dread abode,
(There they alike in trembling hope repose,)
The bosom of his Father and his God.

Thomas Gray

The Poems of Thomas Gray, William Collins and Oliver Goldsmith,
ed. Roger Lonsdale (Longmans, 1969)

Wyn Calvin

The poem 'Cartref' was composed by my late brother, Bryn Calvin-Thomas, and is one that has proved very popular over the years. It relates to times past – but only by one generation – and recalls the real meaning of 'family' in the Welsh culture.

Whenever this was broadcast on radio it created a huge reaction and requests for copies – especially from Welsh folk who had left their own 'cartref' to live and work in England or even, in some cases, other parts of Europe.

Cartref

Why did they call it 'Pleasant View'?
For the description is hardly true.
It faces no scenes of the flower decked hedges
But a mud choked river with coal blackened edges
And beyond, no trees with their varying greens
Instead, a colliery with its ugly machines.
Perhaps for the glimpse of the mountain side
That wheels and walls just fail to hide

But step through the doorway off the street
There's a dear old lady I'd like you to meet.
By the fading picture on the wall
You'll guess she was belle at many a ball
But time and toil, and worries untold
Have crowned her with silver in place of gold,
Of money bought pleasures she's had few
But a smile will light those eyes of blue
As she boasts that she has found all her joys
In the care of her home and the love of her boys
And if ever a fellow was proud then I am
For the picture I'm painting is that of my Mam.

There's a pair of hands I'd like you to see,
They're hands that have meant very much to me.
Hands that have bled through cutting coal,
Hands stretched out to draw the dole.

Hands that have set the Joy Bells ringing
Cos they're hands that have led Bethania's singing.
Hands that have touched down many a goal,
Hands clasped in prayer for many a soul.
Hands that have helped the weak and old,
Hands that children love to hold.
Hands worked hard to make a living,
Yet hands that never grow tired of giving
And if you shake these hands you'll know you've had
The pleasure of meeting my old Dad.

So, if you're up our way any time at all
Just go and tell them I told you to call.
There's a cup of tea and a welcome for you
If you knock at the door of 'Pleasant View'.

Bryn Calvin-Thomas

Alex Carlile

'The Ghost' by Walter de la Mare is one of my favourite poems. It is eerie yet somehow not frightening, just sad. I love the strange dignity of the conversation and the bitter-sweet taste that the poem leaves. Is it better that he had not imagined his wife there at all, or was it too sweet a reunion to have missed? This poem belongs to a world I could never hope to inhabit, only occasionally visit. Perhaps that is why I find it so magnetizing.

The Ghost

'Who knocks?' 'I, who was beautiful,
  Beyond all dreams to restore,
I, from the roots of the dark thorn am hither.
  And knock on the door.'

'Who speaks?' 'I – once was my speech
  Sweet as the bird's on the air,
When echo lurks by the waters to heed;
  'Tis I speak thee fair.'

'Dark is the hour!' 'Ay, and cold.'
  'Lone is my house,"Ay, but mine?'
'Sight, touch, lips, eyes yearned in vain.'
  'Long dead these to thine . . .'

Silence. Still faint on the porch
  Break the flames of the stars.
In gloom groped a hope-wearied hand
  Over keys, bolts, and bars.

A face peered. All the grey night
  In chaos of vacancy shone;
Nought but vast sorrow was there –
  The sweet cheat gone.

Walter de la Mare

Complete Poems of Walter de la Mare (Faber & Faber, 1969)

Phil Carradice

'Raiders' Dawn' by Alun Lewis is a deceptively simple statement about the effects of war. The lyrical nature and quality of the poem contrast sharply with the subject matter – that, for me, is what makes it such an effective piece of writing. I don't need (or even want) a graphic description about the horror of an air raid, about its tragic aftermath or even the effect it has on people's lives. The implication is enough – something should be left to the readers' imagination.

The poem is less well known than others by Alun Lewis – 'All Day It Has Rained' or some of his Indian pieces. Yet in its deliberate understatement, in its haunting rhythms and imagery, it is, in my opinion, one of the finest anti-war poems to come out of the Second World War. Every time I read it the shattering effect of conflict – its pain, terror and destruction – is brought home to me. The poem should, I believe, be essential reading for anybody intending to study either history or literature.

Raiders' Dawn

Softly the civilized
Centuries fall,
Paper on paper,
Peter on Paul.

And lovers waking
From the night –
Eternity's masters,
Slaves of Time –
Recognize only
The drifting white
Fall of small faces
In pits of lime.

Blue necklace left
On a charred chair
Tells that Beauty
Was startled there.

Alun Lewis

Raiders' Dawn and Other Poems (Allen & Unwin, 1942)

Harold Carter

Cerdd yw hon sy'n crynhoi teimladau llawer o bobl sydd yn ymwneud â Chymru, ei hiaith a'i diwylliant, mewn ffordd syml ond hollol sylfaenol. Wrth imi ymchwilio trwy'r blynyddoedd ynglŷn â dosbarthiad daearyddol yr iaith, y newidiadau a ddigwyddodd a'r rhesymau drostynt, fe fu'r gerdd hon yno yn fy meddwl trwy gydol yr amser rywsut, megis rhyw ymdeimlad yn y cefndir o hyd. Yn wir fe'm temtiwyd ar un adeg i roi dyfyniad ohoni ar dudalen flaen un gyfrol o'm gwaith.

Y mae yna stori adnabyddus iawn a adroddir am Almaenwr, Ffrancwr a Chymro y gofynnwyd iddynt wneud ymchwiliad i mewn i fywyd yr eliffant. Ysgrifennodd yr Almaenwr am gymeriad ffisiolegol y creadur mewn deg cyfrol; canolbwyntiodd y Ffrancwr ar fywyd carwriaethol yr anifail; ysgrifennodd y Cymro ar 'Yr Eliffant a'r Iaith Gymraeg'! Ar adegau o wasgedd a galwadau am bennod o un cyfeiriad, am sylwadau o gyfeiriad arall, am bennu dyddiad cyfleus ar gyfer cyfarfod neu bwyllgor a phan geir y cyfryngau'n sydyn yn rhedeg allan o syniadau am raglen neu erthygl ac yn awgrymu un arall eto ar yr iaith, fe ddaw'r temtasiwn yn gryf weithiau i wfftio'r iaith a'i phroblemau. Oni byddai ein bywyd gymaint yn fwy syml a didrafferth hebddi? Ond yn y bôn rhywbeth arwynebol a thros dro yn unig yw hwn, rhyw ewyn ar wyneb y dyfnder, heb sylwedd na pharhad iddo. Odditano ceir y gwir ymdeimlad o hunaniaeth, o fod yn perthyn, sef yn syml, o'r sylfaen sicr i fywyd ei hun.

I'r daearyddwr mae'r teimladau hyn yn cynrychioli cred sylfaenol mewn lle a diwylliant, rhyw argyhoeddiad yn arwyddocâd y *genus loci*, nid fel tir yn unig ond tir wedi ei lunio gan holl elfennau'r diwylliant a'r profiadau sydd ynghlwm wrtho. Fe all fod wrth gwrs, fel y dengys y byd ohoni yn ddigon clir, yn ffynhonnell gwrthdaro ac arswyd, ond y mae hefyd yn ffynhonnell y syniad o fod yn perthyn, sydd yn llunio ac yn rhoi ystyr i hunaniaeth a thrwy hynny i fywyd ei hun. 'Duw a'm gwaredo, ni allaf ddianc rhag hon.'

~

This is a poem which summarizes, in a simple but totally basic way, the feelings of many people involved with Wales, her language and her culture. As I've researched through the years on the geographical distribution of the language, the changes that occured and the reasons for them, this poem has always been there in the back of my mind somehow. Indeed I was tempted at one point to quote an extract from it on the front page of one of my books.

There is a well-known story about a German, a Frenchman and a Welshman who were asked to research the life of the elephant. The German wrote ten volumes on the physiological character of the elephant; the Frenchman concentrated on the love life of the elephant; the Welshman wrote on 'The Elephant and the Welsh Language'! During times of pressure and calls for a chapter from one direction, comments from another, requests to arrange a convenient date for a meeting or committee and when suddenly the media runs out of ideas for a programme or article and suggests yet another one on the language, the temptation to flout it and its problems is sometimes strong. Wouldn't our life be so much simpler and easier without the language? But basically this is something superficial and temporary, like the crest of a wave, without substance or continuation. Underneath it is the real feeling of identity, of belonging, namely simply of the firm foundation of life itself.

To the geographer these feelings represent a basic belief in place and culture, some conviction in the significance of the *genus loci*, not as land only but land formed by all the elements of the culture and the experiences that are part of it. It can be of course, as the present world shows clearly enough, a source of conflict and fear, but it is also the source of the idea of belonging, which shapes and gives meaning to identity and through that to life itself. 'God deliver me, I cannot escape from this.'

Hon

Beth yw'r ots gennyf i am Gymru? Damwain a hap
Yw fy mod yn ei libart yn byw. Nid yw hon ar fap

Yn ddim byd ond cilcyn o ddaear mewn cilfach gefn.
Ac yn dipyn o boendod i'r rhai sy'n credu mewn trefn.

A phwy sy'n trigo'n y fangre, dwedwch i mi,
Pwy ond gwehilion o boblach? Peidiwch, da chwi,

Â chlegar am uned a chenedl a gwlad o hyd:
Mae digon o'r rhain, heb Gymru, i'w cael yn y byd.

'R wyf wedi alaru ers talm ar glywed grŵn
Y Cymry, bondigrybwyll, yn cadw sŵn.

Mi af am dro, i osgoi eu lleferydd a'u llên,
Yn ôl i'm cynefin gynt, a'm dychymyg yn drên.

A dyma fi yno. Diolch am fod ar goll
Ymhell o gyffro geiriau'r eithafwyr oll.

Dyma'r Wyddfa a'i chriw; dyma lymder a moelni'r tir;
Dyma'r llyn a'r afon a'r clogwyn; ac, ar fy ngwir,

Dacw'r tŷ lle'm ganed. Ond wele, rhwng llawr a ne'
Mae lleisiau a drychiolaethau ar hyd y lle.

'R wy'n dechrau simsanu braidd; ac meddaf i chwi,
Mae rhyw ysictod fel petai'n dod drosof i;

A mi glywaf grafangau Cymru'n dirdynnu fy mron.
Duw a'm gwaredo, ni allaf ddianc rhag hon.

T. H. Parry-Williams

Ugain o Gerddi (Gwasg Aberystwyth, 1949)

As an English choice I would like to nominate 'Poem XXXV' by A. E. Housman. No one should go through adolescence without immersion in the poems of A. E. Housman. They were part of my youth and have remained with me ever since. This is an absolutely characteristic example; a universal emotion simply expressed. To quote from another poet, it brings the eternal note of sadness in – the sadness inherent in living where dreams and aspirations become meaningless against the passing of time and the accumulation of experience. Things which are so strongly desired, when achieved quickly relapse into the stuff of everyday living. To quote from Housman again:

> Ten thousand times I have done my best
> And all's to do again.

It is, of course, the very heart of cliché – to journey hopefully is better than to arrive: there is no crock of gold at the end of the rainbow, only the dross of disillusion.

The real strength of the poem is that a universal feeling is so simply yet effectively encapsulated. There are some eighty-two words in the poem, and eighty of them are monosyllabic. The expression of the depth of feeling needs no abstruse vocabulary nor complexity. That is where the real genius of poetry lies.

Perhaps I should add a point of criticism. I do wonder if the last verse is necessary. The first two lines of it are a somewhat banal interpretation of inevitability. All that is needed is said in the first two verses.

XXXV

When first my way to fair I took
    Few pence in purse had I,
And long I used to stand and look
    At things I could not buy.

Now times are altered: if I care
    To buy a thing, I can;
The pence are here and here's the fair,
    But where's the lost young man?

– To think that two and two are four
    And neither five nor three
The heart of man has long been sore
    And long 'tis like to be.

A. E. Housman

The Collected Poems of A. E. Housman (Jonathan Cape, 1939)

'The Gnarlysnork'. Graphics by William Brown.

Pat Chown

This is a 'pome' written for me by my Dad when I was about eight or nine. He was a strange man who was very difficult to know. He was a somewhat distant and stern figure throughout my childhood and 'The Gnarlysnork' is a tiny glimpse of the warm, funny man who lived inside him. Unfortunately he died in 1987 before I really got to know him well.

The Gnarlysnork

A fearsome beast is the Gnarlysnork
With ears as big as a Charleyfork
It lurks in the shade of a Bong Bong tree
Looking for someone to eat for tea
So take good care
Beware, beware . . .
It loves little girls – you'll see.

Harry Tarr

Joseph P. Clancy

It may seem strange that after all the years of reading, teaching, reviewing and translating poetry, I can name my favourite poem with not a moment's hesitation. But George Herbert's 'Love' is a poem that is always with me, one of the few poems I know by heart, though I never consciously tried to memorize it.

As I speak it to myself now, Herbert's artistry again delights and astonishes; the easy movement of conversational style within a strict and subtle stanza, the spareness of language for action and dialogue. Above all, the lucidity: we look *through* rather than *at* the words.

What we see in this fictive encounter between self-conscious guest and generous host is what Christians believe (or with some of us, at least hope) actually happens here and now at communion time and will actually happen for good at the moment of death.

Ask me what Christianity is all about and I would recite not the Nicene creed but this poem. Herbert has simply (*simply!*) imagined what it means to believe in a God who *is* Love.

Love (III)

Love bade me welcome: yet my soul drew back,
    Guilty of dust and sin.
But quick-eyed Love, observing me grow slack
    From my first entrance in,
Drew nearer to me, sweetly questioning
    If I lacked anything.

'A guest,' I answered, 'worthy to be here.'
    Love said, 'You shall be he.'
'I, the unkind, ungrateful? Ah, my dear,
    I cannot look on thee.'
Love took my hand, and smiling did reply,
    'Who made the eyes but I?'

'Truth, Lord; but I have marred them; let my shame
    Go where it doth deserve.'
'And know you not,' says Love, 'who bore the blame?'
    'My dear, then I will serve.'
'You must sit down,' says Love, 'and taste my meat.'
    So I did sit and eat.

George Herbert

The Works of George Herbert (Clarendon Press, 1941)

Hafina Clwyd

Yr wyf yn cofio'r tro cyntaf erioed i mi fwyta eirin gwlanog. Yn Sioe Flodau Rhuthun y digwyddodd pan oeddwn tua phymtheg oed. Aeth eu blas â 'ngwynt. Yn fuan wedyn deuthum ar draws englyn Saunders Lewis ar y pwnc a chefais fy ngwefreiddio gan impiad y seiniau a'r synhwyrau. Aeth yr englyn hefyd â 'ngwynt.

Y mae'n uned berffaith o synhwyrau wedi'u pentyrru nes cyrraedd uchafbwynt lle y teimlaf fy mod yn boddi yn y sudd a'r gwawl. 'Melfed yr haf' meddai – a dyma fi'n medru teimlo croen yr eirin yn gynnes dan fy llaw ac yn ailfyw'r teimlad a geir wrth anwylo cefn porchell neu glustiau cath. Y mae'r geiriau 'pêr ias blas' yn creu dincod melys ac wrth ymhyfrydu yn yr atgof am flas y ffrwyth fe'm gorfodir wedyn i ymgolli yn y disgrifiad o'i ffurf – yn llawn a chrwn ac esmwyth a siapus – yn wledd i'r llygad megis ffiol risiant neu ysgrif Othig. I goroni'r cyfan ceir y trosiad 'gwaed Awst'. Gwaed sydd yn rhoi lliw a bywyd. Awst sydd â'i ramant ei hun.

Awst yw'r Eisteddfod a sŵn y Maes. Awst plentyndod pan oedd yr ŷd yn ffraeth wrth ddadlwytho yn y gadlas. Awst aeron a thrydar gwybed a phelmynt poeth. Ac Awst yr eirin gwlanog beichiog a Sioe Flodau Rhuthun pan oedd pedair cenhedlaeth o'r teulu'n cyfarfod am eu sgwrs flynyddol fawr.

~

I remember the first time I ever ate peaches. It was in Ruthin Flower Show when I was about fifteen years old. Their taste took my breath away. Soon afterwards I came across an *englyn* by Saunders Lewis on the subject and I marvelled at the grafting of the sounds and the senses. The *englyn* also took my breath away.

It's a perfect unit of accumulated senses until a climax is reached where I feel I am drowning in the juice and the radiance. The 'velvet of summer' it says, and I can feel the skin of the peaches warm in my hand, reliving the feeling one gets on stroking the back of a piglet or a cat's ears. The words 'the luscious thrill of its taste' set one's teeth sweetly on edge, and delighting in the memory of the taste of the fruit I am forced to lose myself in the description of its form – full, round, smooth and shapely – a feast to the eyes like a crystal bowl or Gothic writing. The metaphor 'August blood' crowns it all. Blood which gives colour and life. August which has its own romance.

August is the Eisteddfod and the sounds of the Eisteddfod Field. The August of childhood when the corn was unloaded in abundance in the farmyard. The August of fruits, the buzz of flies and hot pavements. And August of the pregnant peaches and Ruthin Flower Show when four generations of the family met for their great annual chat.

Eirin Gwlanog

Melfed yr haf ar dafod – a phêr ias
Blas ei ffrwyth ar daflod;
Fferf a gwyrdd a phorffor gôd
Y daeth gwaed Awst i'th geudod.

Saunders Lewis

Siwan a Cherddi Eraill (Llyfrau Dryw, 1956)

Lord Crickhowell

I have chosen 'Friends Departed' by Henry Vaughan, the Silurist. Vaughan, the contemporary of Andrew Marvell and John Bunyan, came from a prominent Welsh family and is buried in a churchyard not very far from my home. The poem is about death, but it is also about hope. I read it at the memorial service to my father, Ralph Edwards. It deserves to be included in any Welsh anthology.

Friends Departed

They are all gone into the world of light!
   And I alone sit lingering here;
Their very memory is fair and bright,
   And my sad thoughts doth clear.

It glows and glitters in my cloudy breast
   Like stars upon some gloomy grove,
Or those faint beams in which this hill is dressed,
   After the sun's remove.

I see them walking in an air of glory,
   Whose light doth trample on my days:
My days, which are at best but dull and hoary,
   Mere glimmering and decays.

O holy Hope! and high Humility,
   High as the heavens above!
These are your walks, and you have showed them me,
   To kindle my cold love.

Dear beauteous Death! the jewel of the Just,
   Shining nowhere but in the dark;
What mysteries do lie beyond thy dust,
   Could man outlook that mark!

He that hath found some fledged bird's nest may know,
   At first sight, if the bird be flown;
But what fair well or grove he sings in now,
   That is to him unknown.

And yet, as angels in some brighter dreams
    Call to the soul, when man doth sleep;
So some strange thoughts transcend our wonted themes,
    And into glory peep.

If a star were confined into a tomb,
    Her captive flames must needs burn there;
But when the hand that locked her up gives room,
    She'll shine through all the sphere.

O Father of eternal life, and all
    Created glories under thee!
Resume thy spirit from this world of thrall
    Into true liberty.

Either disperse these mists, which blot and fill
    My perspective still as they pass,
Or else remove me hence unto that hill,
    Where I shall need no glass.

Henry Vaughan

The New Oxford Book of English Verse, 1250–1950, ed. Helen Gardner
(Oxford University Press, 1972)

Tony Curtis

I suppose that I am taking a risk in choosing one of my own poems, but it seems obvious that a poet should feel most strongly about a poem he himself has written.

Of course, some poems come to poets; other poems have to be chased by the poet: but for many years I have tried to avoid writing or chasing poems that are 'personal' and imagery that is 'private'. Such things will come if they need to. However, poetry should serve others' as well as the poet's interest. Each of my collections will be found to include a number of public or historical poems. Perhaps I am a frustrated historian; in any case the events and characters of the two world wars have been a consistent focus for much of my writing over the past decade. In 1995 Seren Books will publish my *War Voices: Selected War Poems 1970–95*. 'Soup' will be in that book and has appeared in two earlier collections, as well as being included in every reading which I have given since I wrote it in 1984.

'Soup' was written after a story of Elie Wiesel, who survived Auchswitz as a teenager. I have elaborated on what was a fairly brief mention of the Kapo's story-telling challenge. When human beings are at their extreme they need two things in order to survive: one of those things is soup (whatever you've got, boiled in water); the other thing is a sense of your identity and the identity of your people. The reader must decide at the end of my poem what has been gained and what lost by the boy's experience.

I hope that 'Soup' works both as a poem of remembrance and re-creation: I hope that it acts as an imaginative record of the darkest hours of this century in Europe. I hope too that it keeps alive our vigilance in the face of continuing cruelty around this flawed world.

Soup

One night our block leader set a competition:
two bowls of soup to the best teller of a tale.
That whole evening the hut filled with words –
tales from the old countries
of wolves and children
potions and love-sick herders
stupid woodsmen and crafty villagers.

Apple-blossom snowed from blue skies,
orphans discovered themselves royal.
Tales of greed and heroes and cunning survival,
soldiers of the Empires, the Church, the Reich.

And when they turned to me
I could not speak,
sunk in the horror of that place,
my throat a corridor of bones, my eyes
and nostrils clogged with self-pity.
'Speak,' they said, 'everyone has a story to tell.'
And so I closed my eyes and said:
I have no hunger for your bowls of soup, you see
I have just risen from the Shabbat meal –
my father has filled our glasses with wine,
bread has been broken, the maid has served fish.
Grandfather has sung, tears in his eyes, the old songs.
My mother holds her glass by the stem, lifts
it to her mouth, the red glow reflecting on her throat.
I go to her side and she kisses me for bed.
My grandfather's kiss is rough and soft like an apricot.
The sheets on my bed are crisp and flat
like the leaves of a book . . .

I carried my prizes back to my bunk: one bowl
I hid, the other I stirred
and smelt a long time, so long
that it filled the cauldron of my head,
drowning a family of memories.

Tony Curtis

Selected Poems 1970–1985 (Seren Books, 1985)

Cynog Dafis

Dwysfyfyrdod angerddol ar ormes, dioddefaint, daioni a grym a geir yn y gerdd ryfeddol hon o waith William Lewis y gwehydd o Langloffan, Sir Benfro. Wn i ddim sawl gwaith y'i cenais mewn cwrdd cymundeb, naill ai ar emyn-dôn Bach, 'Mannheim', neu'n well byth 'Via Crucis' E. T. Davies, a gafodd ei chyfansoddi, synnwn i ddim, ar gyfer y geiriau yma. Fe'i llwyddais i'w galw i gof yn gyfan yn y car ryw ddiwrnod a rhyfeddu at ei chyfoeth a'i dwyster.

Un lefel o ystyr yma yw'r eironi ingol yn yr ymosod cïaidd ar y perffaith gyfiawn, hardd a diniwed sydd yng nghymeriad yr Iesu. Mae yma ddealltwriaeth ar yr un pryd mai ymgiprys am rym sydd wrth ei wraidd, a'r symbolau pwerus o hynny yw'r gwaywffyn a'r chwip – yr olaf yn ymrithio fel aradr haearn yn arddu cwysau yng nghefn y dioddefydd. Mae'r poeri yn cwblhau'r darlun o arfogaeth gyfarwydd yr arteithiwr, ac fe ŵyr y darllennydd wrth gwrs mai dienyddiad ar y groes sydd i ddod.

Ond nid dyna'r cyfan. Nid meddaldod mo'r dioddefaint ond math arall o rym. Dyna'r argyhoeddiad sy'n ffrwydro i'r wyneb ym mhedair llinell ola'r gerdd. Wel, nid argyhoeddiad cweit, ond dyhead angerddol am i'r theori mai grym cariad sydd drechaf fod yn wir. Mae'r bardd yn gwybod pa mor galed y mae calon dyn yn gallu bod.

Yn ein hoes ni mae'r amheuaeth a'r dyhead yr un mor berthnasol a phoenus ag yr oedden nhw i'r gwehydd o Sir Benfro ddiwedd y ddeunawfed ganrif. Yn y car, wrth alw'r geiriau i gof, allwn i ddim peidio â chofio hefyd am Steve Biko.

~

This amazing poem written by William Lewis, the weaver from Llangloffan, Pembrokeshire, contains passionate, intense contemplations on oppression, suffering, goodness and strength. I don't know how many times I have sung it at Communion either to Bach's hymn tune, 'Mannheim', or better still to 'Via Crucis' by E. T. Davies, which was composed, I wouldn't be surprised, with these words in mind. I succeeded in remembering it all in the car one day and I was amazed at its richness and depth.

One level of meaning here is the agonizing irony in the brutal attack on perfect righteousness, beautiful and innocent, which is to be found in Jesus' character. There is at the same time an understanding that it is a scramble for power which is at its root, and the powerful symbols of this are the spear and the whip – the whip adopting the semblance of a metal plough, ploughing furrows in the back of the sufferer. The spitting completes the picture of the torturers' familiar weapons and the reader knows, of course, that execution on the cross is to come.

But that is not all. The suffering is not weakness but another form of strength. This is the conviction that explodes to the surface in the last four lines of the poem. Well, not quite conviction, but passionate desire that the theory concerning the superiority of the power of love may be true. The poet knows how hard man's heart can be.

In our age the doubt and the desire are just as relevant and painful as they were to the weaver from Pembrokeshire at the end of the eighteenth century. In the car whilst trying to remember the words, I couldn't help but remember Steve Biko as well.

Cof am y Cyfiawn Iesu

Cof am y cyfiawn Iesu,
   Y Person mwyaf hardd,
A'r noswaith drom anesmwyth
   Bu'n chwysu yn yr ardd;
A'i chwŷs yn ddafnau cochion
   Yn syrthio ar y llawr:
Bydd canu am ei gariad
   I dragwyddoldeb mawr.

Cof am y llu o filwyr
   Â'u gwayw-ffyn yn dod
I ddal yr Oen diniwed
   Na wnaethai gam erioed:
Gwrandewch y geiriau ddwedodd,
   (Pwy allsai ond Efe?)
'Gadewch i'r rhain fynd ymaith,
   Cymerwch Fi'n eu lle.'

Cof am yr wyneb siriol,
   Y poerwyd arno'n wir;
Cof am y cefen gwerthfawr,
   Lle'r arddwyd cŵysau hir;
O! annwyl Arglwydd Iesu,
   Boed grym dy gariad pur
Yn torri 'nghalon galed
   Wrth gofio am dy gur.

William Lewis

Llyfr Emynau y Methodistiaid Calfinaidd a Wesleaidd (1929)

Sir Goronwy Daniel

Yn ein byd cyfoes gosodir pwysau enfawr ar gystadlu: ar wneud yn well na neb arall yn yr ysgol a'r coleg, yn ein gwaith a'n chwaraeon a hyd yn oed yn ein horiau hamdden. Dyna'r ffordd i ennill yr holl fanteision sydd yn dod o gyrraedd y brig.

Mewn cyferbyniad mae'r bardd yn tynnu'n sylw at y rhai sydd yn gweld bod ganddynt ddyletswydd i fynd, nid i ble mae'r gwobrau gorau ar gael, ond i ble mae'r angen mwyaf am eu gwasanaeth. Dyna oedd dewis Islwyn iddo'i hun er yn deall yn dda y byddai'r tâl am ei ymdrechion yn iselderau'r byd yn ddim byd yn fwy na chydwybod da a llinell o olau efallai yn y ffurfafen a allai roi gobaith i eraill.

~

In our modern world enormous pressure is placed on competing, on doing better than anyone else in school or college, in our work and sports and even in our leisure time. This is the way of gaining all the advantages that result from reaching the top.

In contrast the poet draws attention to those who see that they have a duty to go, not to where the best prizes are to be had, but where there is the greatest need for their services. That was Islwyn's choice for himself although he well understood that the reward for his efforts in the depths of the world would be nothing more than a good conscience and maybe a ray of light in the firmament that could give hope to others.

Rhinwedd

Aed ereill i geisio anrhydedd a chlod, i'r lan ar uchelion y byd;
Gogoniant derchedig yn unig fo'n nod, a mawlfloedd y bobloedd
ynghyd;
Af innau i waered yn wylaidd fy ngwedd i fro dawel rhinwedd i fyw,
Ac yno cyfodaf fy mhabell mewn hedd dan gysgod cydwybod a Duw!
Os na chaf ogoniant daearol, caf fwy – fy nghymeradwyaeth fy hun,
Boddlondeb tufewnol, cydwybod ddi-glwy, bendithion melusach na
gwin.
Os na fydd ysplenydd afonydd o fawl yn llifo o'r ôl, bydd fy llwybr
Yn oleu gan burdeb, fel llinell o wawl 'r ol angel a groesoedd yr
wybr;

A phery y llinell pan dderfydd y byd, pan ballo disgleirdeb fy
ngwedd,
Fel miloedd o sêr yn tywynnu ynghyd yn danbaid goleua fy medd.

Hoff waith angylion, Rinwedd brid, yw dod ynghyd i'th noddi;
Wyt yn rhy werthfawr, rinwedd lân, i dân y farn dy doddi;
A *da* yw'r gwirioneddol *fawr*, a'r *da* yr awr ddiweddaf
Yn unig a goronir draw ar ddeheu law'r Goruchaf.
Y mae dy wobr ar ei thaith, os yw yn faith yn tario, –
Ei mawredd a'i bytholdeb sy yn peri y gohirio.

Mae perarogledd Rhinwedd, diau, 'n hyfryd
Wrth syllu ar ei delw yn afon bywyd.
Tu draw i holl linellau ei gelynion,
Tu hwnt i bechod ac i angeu creulon,
Mae llanw tragwyddoldeb yn llifeirio
Oll gyda hi, heb awel groes i'w lluddio.
Ond rhosyn plith y drain yw'r mwya 'i geinder,
A'r unwedd rhinwedd ar anialwch amser.
Arddunol ydyw yn ei myg unigedd,
A gwesgir allan ei *holl* beraroglledd.

O! pwy mor gryf, mor gadarn a'r rhinweddol;
Mae 'i wyneb, er mor hardd, o bres tragwyddol.
Cyfiawnder ydyw gwregys cryf ei lwynau,
Mae 'n graddol fagu nerth i gwrdd ag angau.
Fel eiddew am y dderwen, Rhinwedd union
A bleth am allu Duw ei breichiau gwynion.

Os isel yw ei bwthyn, wrth y ddôr
Mae claer warchodlu o angylion Iôr;
Symudiad eu sidanaidd esgyll sydd
Beroriaeth iddi wedi darfod dydd,
Peroriaeth y buasai Handel fawr
Yn tewi byth o'i chlywed ennyd awr.

Pan el i orffwys, oll yn ddedwydd flin,
Y mae rhyfeddol ddyfnder yn ei hun,
Fel dyfnder wybren o ddidyrfryn las,
Fel balmgwsg Efa cyn y codwm cas;
Fe allai cerub ddewis bod yn ddyn
Er cael mwynhau breuddwydion rhinwedd gun.

Os yw ei gwisg yn dlawd, hi gaiff ar frys
Ei newid oll am laeswych ŵn y llys;
Cyfoethog draill ei gynau gwynion fydd
Yn cuddio y cymylau'r olaf ddydd,
A Duw a'i harddel ger casgledig fyd
Fel aeres deg ei gyfoeth mawr i gyd.

Dedwyddyd pur yw marw iddo ef,
A newid poen am dirion hoen y nef.
Paham yr ofnai y dyfodol maith,
Pan nad oes yn ei hir ddaearol daith
Droadau gŵyr i beri iddo loes,
Wrth syllu 'n ol ar bererindod oes?
Mae marw cryf yn dilyn Rhinwedd fad
Trwy fythol ddeddf, fel ffrwyth yn dilyn had.

Oes o gyfiawnder, oes o ddweyd y gwir,
Ac oes heb athrod yn ei hystod hir,
Heb dorri 'i lw, heb newid byth mo'i air,
Heb farn usuriaeth yn melldigo 'i aur,
Oes lawn o gymhwynasau i'r tylawd,
Heb dderbyn enllib, heb niweidio 'i frawd –
Dos, ddedwydd ddyn! Cref yw dy galon di,
Colofnau rhinwedd a'i hategant hi.
Nid ofni, mwy, rhag unrhyw chwedl drwg,
Byth ni'th ysgogir er mor fawr y gwg.
Dos, ddedwydd ddyn! I ddyffryn angeu dos!
Nac ofna ddim, os tywyll yw y nos,
Y nos ddiweddaf yw am byth i ti,
O! mae un seren yn ei hentrych hi,
Sef gwên dy Dduw; chwaer-seren arall sydd
O fewn i'th enaid, sef cydwybod rydd.

Islwyn

Gwaith Barddonol Islwyn (Hughes a'i Fab, 1897)

Alan Davies

This work by Dylan Thomas is appropriate to anyone, anywhere, under any circumstances. Life brings hardship and happiness in some measure to everyone, regardless of their perceived position in society or personal security.

There are some people, however, who are noticeably less fortunate than others. They have not been blessed with a significant number of opportunities. Their chance of ensuring a measure of success is severely limited by their circumstances.

Whatever our position, we must be grateful for the fact that our good side outweighs our worst and help those who have not been able to grasp even the slimmest of opportunities to appreciate their strengths.

Under Milk Wood
(an extract)

Every morning when I awake,
Dear Lord a little prayer I make,
O please to keep thy lovely eye,
On all poor creatures born to die.

And every evening at sun-down,
I ask a blessing on the town,
For whether we last the night or no,
I'm sure is always touch and go.

We are not wholly bad or good,
Who live our lives under Milk Wood,
And thou, I know, will be the first,
To see our best side, not our worst.

O let us see another day,
Bless us all this night we pray,
And to the sun we all will bow,
And say, good-bye, but just for now.

Dylan Thomas

Under Milk Wood (Phoenix, 1992)

49

'Under Milk Wood'. Graphics by Paul Peter Piech.

Gilli Davies

I certainly have a favourite poem. In his book *A Calendar of Country Customs* Ralph Whitlock refers to Roy Palmer, author of *The Folklore of Warwickshire*, as being his source and the poem is simply called 'A Song Sung at Harvest Home Suppers'. Whatever its origin, I think it is very fine!

A Song Sung at Harvest Home Suppers

Let the wealthy and great
Live in splendour and state;
I envy them not, I declare it.
I eat my own lamb,
My chicken and ham,
I shear my own fleece, and I wear it.
I have lawns; I have bowers;
I have fruit; I have flowers;
The lark is my morning alarmer.
So, jolly boys, now,
Here's God speed the plough;
Long life and success to the farmer!

Roy Palmer

quoted in Ralph Whitlock, *A Calendar of Country Customs* (B. T. Batsford, 1978)

Lyn Davies

Fel pawb sy'n darllen barddoniaeth yn gyson, y mae gennyf nifer helaeth o 'hoff gerddi' gan lu o feirdd Ewropeaidd ac Americanaidd. Am ba bynnag reswm, 'rwy'n tueddu troi yn ôl at yr un math o gerddi, sef y rhai sy'n ymwneud â bywyd diwylliannol-ddiwydiannol Cymru yn y ganrif hon. Fel un a fagwyd yn y Sir Gâr wledig-ddiwydiannol y mae dicter a dwyster Gwenallt ynghyd â'r delweddau grymus a sensitif yng ngwaith Bryan Martin Davies a Dafydd Rowlands yn agos iawn at fy nghalon. Un o'r cerddi mwyaf o blith y rhai sy'n trafod de Cymru i'm meddwl i yw 'Y Dilyw 1939', Saunders Lewis. Cerdd sy'n datgan ing a gwewyr y bardd wrth iddo fyfyrio ar dynged Cymru ac Ewrop ar ddechrau'r Ail Ryfel Byd ydyw. Cerdd ddadleuol, a hefyd cerdd a gamddehonglwyd gan nifer o unigolion a ddylai fod wedi gwybod gwell yw 'Y Dilyw'. Ynddi ceir amlinelliad o syniadaeth gymdeithasol a gwleidyddol y bardd – syniadaeth sy'n para'n ddadleuol.

Fel llawer o gerddi 'mawr', cerdd sy'n cadw cyfrinachau ydyw (hyd yn oed yn yr oes honedig soffistigedig sydd ohoni). Yn sicr, ni ddylai'r eirfa a'r gyfeiriadaeth gyfoethog sydd ynddi beri trafferth i'r sawl a ddarllenodd (dyweder) *The Waste Land* T. S. Eliot (neu i'r sawl sy'n gyfarwydd â gwaith Yeats ac Ezra Pound). Y mae rhai o gyfeiriadau'r bardd yn ddigon cyfarwydd (megis yfed o Lethe, Apolo ac ati), eraill yn llai felly i gynulleidfaoedd heddiw, (er enghraifft, yr athronydd Bruening a brwydr Ebro yn ystod Rhyfel Cartref gwaedlyd Sbaen). Ynddi, llwyddodd y bardd i greu ymdeimlad grymus o'r cyfnod – yn yr un modd â'r cyfansoddwr Vaughan Williams yn ei Bedwerydd Simffoni neu Idris Davies (mewn modd cwbl wahanol) yn *Gwalia Deserta* (1938).

Ym Mhenygroes, y pentref lle'm magwyd, roedd 'impact' y cyfnod y mae Saunders Lewis yn delio mor ddeifiol ag ef, i'w deimlo gan lu o lowyr a daflwyd gyda'r glo diangen i'r tip i wynebu degawdau o segurdod a diawledigrwydd y dôl. Dengys 'Y Dilyw' nad mewn arian yn unig y mae mesur polisïau economaidd. Y mae ochr hagr, hyll a hallt i bolisïau o'r fath – 'Llysnafedd malwoden ar domen slag'. Tywysogion newydd y byd hwn oedd 'clercod y pegio'. Nhw oedd, ac yw, 'pendefigion y paith'. Ac yna, y cyfeiriad ysgubol at lyfr Genesis, 'Dilyw anobaith yw ein dylaith du' – a hynny ychydig amser yn unig cyn i genedl Goethe a 'genocide', Beethoven a'r Siambrau Nwy, Kant a'r 'jackboots' chwalu gobeithion yr hen a'r ifanc am genedlaethau i ddod.

Y mae i'r gerdd feirniadaeth gymdeithasol uniongyrchol. Y mae ynddi dosturi a dicter sy'n cymharu â'r mwyaf ysgytwol yng ngwaith Gwenallt (meddylier am y 'poer siliconaidd' yn Lewis a'r 'lili mor welw â'r nwy' yng ngwaith Gwenallt). Y mae ynddi hefyd y proffwydo patriachaidd a greodd drafferthion dehongli i rai – yr un proffwydo sydd yng Nghantawd Michael Tippett, *A Child of our Time*. Fel Tippett, fe welodd Lewis 'ulw simneiau' a'r 'geni ofer' yng nghanrif Auschwitz ac Aberfan. Ceir ynddi hefyd feirniadaeth gymdeithasol iasol, swrealaeth ac eironi ar raddfa eang. Taflodd y bardd ei sen ar fenthycwyr arian (y mae gwahaniaeth mawr rhwng ymosod ar usurwyr Iddewig ac ymosod ar Iddewiaeth ei hun).

Os ydyw'n torri'n nawddoglyd agos at yr asgwrn ar brydiau, y mae hefyd yn arddangos y ddealltwriaeth ddyfnaf o wir natur dyn: 'A thros y don daw sŵn tanciau'n crynhoi'. Nid cerdd cyfnod yn unig yw 'Y Dilyw 1939'. Y mae ynddi broffwydoliaethau sy'n fythol berthnasol – beth bynnag yw ein barn ni heddiw o gymeriad y sawl a'i cyfansoddodd.

~

Like everyone who reads poetry regularly, I have a large number of favourite poems by a host of European and American poets. For whatever reason, I tend to return to the same type of poems, namely those dealing with the cultural-industrial life of Wales in this century. As one who was brought up in rural-industrial Carmarthenshire, the anger and depth of Gwenallt together with the powerful and sensitive imagery to be found in the work of Bryan Martin Davies and Dafydd Rowlands are all close to my heart. One of the greatest poems of those which discusses south Wales is to my mind 'Y Dilyw 1939' by Saunders Lewis. It is a poem which renders the anguish and pain of the poet as he contemplates the fate of Wales and Europe at the outbreak of the Second World War. 'Y Dilyw' is a controversial poem and one that has been wrongly interpreted by a number of individuals who should have known better. It contains an outline of the political and social ideas of the poet – ideas that continue to be controversial.

·Like many 'great' poems, it is a poem which retains secrets (even in this supposedly sophisticated age). Indeed, its vocabulary and rich references should not prove difficult to those who have read *The Waste Land* by T. S. Eliot (or those who are familiar with the work of Yeats and Ezra Pound). Some of the poet's references are familiar enough (such as drinking from Lethe, Apollo and so forth), others less familiar to present-day audiences (for example, the philosopher Bruening and the Battle of Ebro during the bloody Spanish Civil

War). Within the poem the poet succeeded in creating a powerful sense of the period – in the same way as did the composer Vaughan Williams in his Fourth Symphony or Idris Davies (in a totally different manner) in *Gwalia Deserta* (1938).

In Penygroes, the village in which I was brought up, the impact of the period with which Saunders Lewis deals so scathingly was felt by a multitude of miners who were thrown with the unwanted coal onto the tip, to face decades of idleness and the evil of life on the dole. 'Y Dilyw' shows that economic policies cannot be measured in terms of money alone. There is an unpleasant, ugly and bitter side to such policies – 'Slime of a snail on a heap of slag'. The new princes of this world were the 'pegging clerks'. They were, and are, 'the gentry of this waste'. And then comes the sweeping reference to the book of Genesis – 'our black refuge is the deluge of despair' – and this was only a short time before the nation of Goethe and genocide, Beethoven and the gas chambers, Kant and the 'jackboots' destroyed the hopes of the young and old for generations to come.

The poem contains direct social criticism and pity and anger comparable with the most shocking of Gwenallt's works (consider the 'silicon spittle' in Lewis and Gwenallt's 'lily as pale as the gas'). It also contains the patriarchal prophesying which created problems of interpretation for some – the same prophesying which is to be found in Michael Tippett's cantata, *A Child of Our Time*. Like Tippett, Lewis saw 'the ash of chimneys', and the 'vain birth' in the century of Auschwitz and Aberfan. It also contains chilling social criticism, surrealism and irony on a wide scale. The poet rebukes money-lenders (there is a great difference between attacking Jewish usurers and attacking Judaism itself).

If it is patronizingly close to the bone at times, it also displays the deepest understanding of man's true nature: 'and from over the sea comes the sound of tanks gathering'. 'Y Dilyw' is not only a period poem. It contains prophesies which are forever relevant, whatever our opinion today may be of its composer.

Y Dilyw 1939

I

Mae'r tramwe'n dringo o Ferthyr i Ddowlais,
Llysnafedd malwoden ar domen slag;
Yma bu unwaith Gymru, ac yn awr

Adfeilion sinemâu a glaw ar dipiau di-dwf;
Caeodd y ponwyr eu drysau; clercod y pegio
Yw pendefigion y paith;
Llygrodd pob cnawd ei ffordd ar wyneb daear.

Unwedd fy mywyd innau, eilydd y penderfyniadau
Sy'n symud o bwyllgor i bwyllgor i godi'r hen wlad yn ei hôl;
Pa 'nd gwell fai sefyll ar y gongl yn Nhonypandy
Ac edrych i fyny'r cwm ac i lawr y cwm
Ar froc llongddrylliad dynion ar laid anobaith,
Dynion a thipiau'n sefyll, tomen un-diben â dyn.

Lle y bu llygaid mae llwch ac ni wyddom ein marw,
Claddodd ein mamau nyni'n ddifeddwl wrth roi inni laeth o
                                                    Lethe,
Ni allwn waedu megis y gwŷr a fu gynt,
A'n dwylo, byddent debyg i law petai arnynt fawd;
Dryllier ein traed gan godwm, ni wnawn ond ymgreinio i
                                                    glinig,
A chodi cap i goes bren a'r siwrans a phensiwn y Mond;
Iaith na thafodiaith ni fedrwn, na gwybod sarhad,
A'r campwaith a roisom i hanes yw seneddwyr ein gwlad.

                        II

Cododd y carthion o'r dociau gweigion
Dros y rhaffau sychion a rhwd y craeniau,
Cripiodd eu dylif proletaraidd
Yn seimllyd waraidd i'r tefyrn tatws,
Llusgodd yn waed o gylch traed y plismyn
A lledu'n llyn o boer siliconaidd
Drwy gymoedd diwyneb diwydiant y dôl.

Arllwysodd glaw ei nodwyddau dyfal
Ar gledrau meddal hen ddwylo'r lofa,
Tasgodd y cenllysg ar ledrau dwyfron
Mamau hesbion a'u crin fabanod,
Troid llaeth y fuwch yn ffyn ymbarelau
Lle camai'r llechau goesau llancesi;
Rhoed pensiwn yr hen i fechgynnos y dôl.

Er hynny fe gadwai'r lloer ei threiglo
A golchai Apolo ei wallt yn y gwlith
Megis pan ddaliai'r doeth ar eu hysbaid
Rhwng bryniau'r Sabiniaid ganrifoedd yn ôl;
Ond Sadwrn, Iau, ac oes aur y Baban,
Yn eu tro darfuan'; difethdod chwith
Ulw simneiau a'r geni ofer
A foddodd y sêr dan lysnafedd y dôl.

III

Ar y cychwyn, nid felly y gwelsom ni'r peth:
Tybiem nad oedd ond y trai a'r llanw gwaredol, yr ansefydlogi
darbodus
A fendithiai'n meistri fel rhan o'r ddeddf economaidd,
Y drefn wyddonol newydd a daflasai'r ddeddf naturiol
Fel Iau yn disodli Sadwrn, cynnydd dianterth bod.
A chredasom i'n meistri: rhoisom arnynt wisg offeiriadol,
Sbectol o gragen crwban a throwsus golff i bregethu,
I bregethu santeiddrwydd y swrplws di-waith ac ystwyth
ragluniaeth prisoedd;
Ac undydd mewn saith, rhag torri ar ddefod gwrtais,
Offrymem awr i ddewiniaeth dlos y cynfyd
Ac yn hen Bantheonau'r tadau fe ganem salm.

Yna, ar Olympos, yn Wall Street, mil naw cant naw ar hugain,
Wrth eu tasg anfeidrol wyddonol o lywio proffidau ffawd,
Penderfynodd y duwiau, a'u traed yn y carped Aubusson
A'u ffroenau Hebreig yn ystadegau'r chwarter,
Ddod y dydd i brinhau credyd drwy fydysawd aur.

Ni wyddai duwiau diwedda' daear
Iddynt wallio fflodiardau ola'r byd;
Ni welsant y gwŷr yn gorymdeithio,
Y dyrnau cau a'r breichiau brochus,
Rheng ar ôl rheng drwy ingoedd Fienna,
Byddar gynddaredd ymdderu Munich,
Na llusg draed na llesg drydar gorymdaith
Cwsgrodwyr di-waith a'u hartaith hurt.

Ond bu; bu gwae mamau yn ubain,
Sŵn dynion fel sŵn cŵn yn cwyno,
A myrdd fyrdd yn ymhyrddio'n ddihyder
I'r ffos di-sêr a'r gorffwys di-sôn.
Pwyll llywiawdwyr y gwledydd, pallodd,
Bu hau daint dreigiau ar erwau Ewrop,
Aeth Bruening ymaith o'u berw wyniau,
O grechwenau Bâle a'i hagr echwynwyr,
Rhuchion a rhython rhawt Genefa,
I'w fud hir ympryd a'i alltudiaeth.
A'r frau werinos, y demos dimai,
Epil drel milieist a'r *pool* pêl-droed,
Llanwodd ei bol â lluniau budrogion
Ac â phwdr usion y radio a'r wasg.

Ond duodd wybren tueddau Ebro,
Âi gwaed yn win i'n gwydiau newynog,
A rhewodd parlys ewyllys wall
Anabl gnafon Bâle a Genefa.
Gwelsom ein twyllo. Gwael siomiant ellyll
Yn madru'n diwedd oedd medr ein duwiau;
Cwympo a threisio campwaith rheswm
A'n delw ddihafal, dyn dihualau;
Crefydd ysblennydd meistri'r blaned,
Ffydd dyn mewn dyn, diffoddwyd hynny:
Nyni wynepglawr fawrion, – fesurwyr
        Y sêr a'r heuliau fry,
        Di-elw a fu'r daith,
        Ofer pob afiaith,
Dilyw anobaith yw ein dylaith du.

A thros y don daw sŵn tanciau'n crynhoi.

Saunders Lewis

Byd a Betws (Gwasg Aberystwyth, 1941)

Father Deiniol

Megis awdur y gerdd hon, gallaf finnau hefyd ddatgan o'm calon:

> Pan rodiwyf ddaear Ystrad Fflur
> O'm dolur ymdawelaf

ac yn wir, am ryw reswm, y mae'r dynfa i'r fangre gysegredig hon yn un gref iawn i mi, ac ni fethaf gyfle i ymweld â'r fro hynod, ac i weddïo yn yr Eglwys ger yr hen adfeilion.

Ac nid rhyfedd bod gweddi mor hawdd yno: mae'n siwr bod y mynaich hwythau wedi teimlo ynglŷn â'r lle, mai 'dyma borth y nefoedd', a'u bod, yn ystod eu canrifoedd o weddi a sagrafen beunyddiol, wedi agor llwybr gweddi uniongyrchol i'r nefoedd o'r 'porth' hwnnw – llwybr sydd yn dal yn llydan agored er dadfeilio'r adeiladau ac er ein hymbellhau o'r byd a'r oes a'r gymdeithas a greodd fynachlog Ystrad Fflur.

A hyn yw rhan o'r afael sydd gan Ystrad Fflur arnaf fi; nid yn unig rhamant y lle, ond y neges y mae pob carreg o'r 'adfeilion ffydd' yn ei datgan i'm henaid dro ar ôl tro – rhybudd amserol y gall Cymru hefyd droi'n 'adfail Ffydd'.

Ond os digwydd hynny, nid adfeilion rhamantus fydd ar ôl, ond eneidiau'n dadfeilio, a chenedl yn cael ei thrawmateiddio drachefn, fel y trawmateiddiwyd hi trwy gau'r mynachlogydd.

~

Like the writer of this poem I too can state from my heart that:

> On wandering the earth of Strata Florida
> from my grief I am soothed

and indeed, for some reason, the attraction of this sacred spot is a particularly strong one in my case. I never miss out on an opportunity to visit the remarkable area and pray in the church by the old ruins.

And it isn't surprising that praying is so easy there: surely the monks also felt that 'here was the gateway of heaven' and that they, during their centuries of prayer and daily sacrament, had opened a direct pathway of prayer to heaven from that 'gateway' – a path that is still wide open in spite of the ruined buildings and in spite of our being distanced from the world, age and society that created Strata Florida monastery.

This is part of the grip that Strata Florida has on me, not only the romance of the place, but the message that every stone of the 'ruins of faith' declares to my soul – time after time – a timely warning that Wales too can become one of 'faith's ruins'.

But if this occurs it won't be romantic ruins that remain, but souls crumbling and a nation traumatized once more, as it was by the closure of the monasteries.

Ystrad Fflur

Mae dail y coed yn Ystrad Fflur
    Yn murmur yn yr awel,
A deuddeng Abad yn y gro
    Yn huno yno'n dawel.

Ac yno dan yr ywen brudd
    Mae Dafydd bêr ei gywydd,
A llawer pennaeth llym ei gledd,
    Yn ango'r bedd tragywydd.

Er bod yr haf, pan ddêl ei oed,
    Yn deffro'r coed i ddeilio,
Ni ddeffry dyn, a gwaith ei law
    Sy'n distaw ymddadfeilio.

Ond er mai angof angau prudd
    Ar adfail ffydd a welaf,
Pan rodiwyf ddaear Ystrad Fflur
    O'm dolur ymdawelaf.

T. Gwynn Jones
Caniadau (Hughes a'i Fab, 1934)

Steve Eaves

Mae 'Caniad Solomon' yn un o'r dylanwadau llenyddol mwyaf arnaf. Ni allaf egluro'n fanwl iawn pam, na'i ddadansoddi'n feirniadol chwaith, oherwydd mae ei rythmau a'i ddelweddau yn ennyn ynof ymateb sy'n fwy *greddfol* nag ymenyddol. Ond byddaf yn troi'n ôl ato o hyd ac o hyd, ac erbyn hyn rwy'n teimlo ei fod yn rhan o'm gwead.

Weithiau bydd ambell linell neu ddelwedd yn dod i'm cof yn gwbl annisgwyl, a minnau yng nghanol rhyw sefyllfa-bob-dydd arferol. Ac yn sydyn reit mi fydd rhin arbennig y penillion hyn a sgrifennwyd ganrifoedd lawer yn ôl yn fyw iawn imi ac yn rhan o'm profiad i *rŵan*, ym mlynyddoedd olaf yr ugeinfed ganrif. Ac i mi, nid oes rhin na naws debyg: mae'n Ganiad llawn goleuni a lliw, a disgleirdeb y nwydau a'r synhwyrau. Mae'n frith o gyfeiriadau hudolus at beraroglau a pherlysiau, delweddau heulog, gwledig, a swyn enwau llefydd estron. Cenir clodydd drwyddo draw i harddwch y corff, a chlywir deisyfiad taer cariadon ar ei gilydd: 'Tyred gyda mi o Libanus, fy nyweddi . . .' Mae ceinder iaith yr hen argraffiad yn ategu'r swyn: 'gogleddwynt' a 'deheuwynt' yn lle 'gwynt y gogledd' a 'gwynt y de' y cyfieithiad newydd.

I mi, mae Caniad Solomon yn farddoniaeth hollol gyfareddol.

~

The Song of Solomon is one of the greatest literary influences upon me. I cannot explain in detail why, or analyse it critically either, because its rhythms and images kindle in me a response which is more *instinctive* than academic. But I turn back to it time and time again and by now I feel it is part of my composition.

Sometimes the odd line or image springs to mind totally unexpectedly whilst I am in the middle of an everyday situation. And suddenly the special essence of these verses which were written many centuries ago becomes very much alive to me and part of my experience *now* in the last few years of the twentieth century. And to me there is no similar essence or atmosphere: it is a song full of light and colour and the brilliance of the passions and the senses. It is full of magical references to fragrances and spices, sunny, rural images, and the magic of foreign place-names. Throughout the beauty of the body is praised and one hears the fervent pleading of lovers to each other: 'Come with me from Lebanon, my bride . . .' The elegance of the language of the old edition adds to the magic: 'gogleddwynt' (lit.

north wind) and 'deheuwynt' (lit. south wind) instead of 'gwynt y gogledd' (lit. the wind of the north) and 'gwynt y de' (lit. the wind of the south) of the new translation.

To me the Song of Solomon is totally enchanting poetry.

Caniad Solomon, pennod 4

7. Ti oll ydwyt deg, fy anwylyd; ac nid oes ynot frycheuyn.

8. Tyred gyda mi o Libanus, fy nyweddi, gyda mi o Libanus: edrych o ben Amana, o gopa Senir a Hermon, o lochesau y llewod, o fynyddoedd y llewpardiaid.

9. Dygaist fy nghalon, fy chwaer a'm dyweddi; dygaist fy nghalon ag un o'th lygaid, ag un gadwyn wrth dy wddf.

10. Mor deg yw dy gariad, fy chwaer, a'm dyweddi! pa faint gwell yw dy gariad na gwin, ac arogl dy olew na'r holl beraroglau!

11. Dy wefusau, fy nyweddi, sydd yn diferu fel dil mêl: y mae mêl a llaeth dan dy dafod, ac arogl dy wisgoedd fel arogl Libanus.

12. Gardd gaeëdig yw fy chwaer, a'm dyweddi: ffynnon gloëdig, ffynnon seliedig yw.

13. Dy blanhigion sydd berllan o bomgranadau, a ffrwyth peraidd, camffir, a nardus;

14. Ie, nardus a saffrwn, calamus a sinamon, a phob pren thus, myrr, ac aloes, ynghyd â phob rhagorol berlysiau:

15. Ffynnon y gerddi, ffynnon y dyfroedd byw, a ffrydiau o Libanus.

16. Deffro di, ogleddwynt, a thyred, ddeheuwynt, chwyth ar fy ngardd, fel y gwasgarer ei pheraroglau: deued fy anwylyd i'w ardd, a bwytaed ei ffrwyth peraidd ei hun.

Translated by William Morgan

Y Beibl, 1588

Hywel Teifi Edwards

Er pan ddarllenais hi gyntaf y mae'r gerdd hon wedi ennill lle diogel ymhlith y cerddi y byddaf yn troi atynt pan fydd creulondeb dyn at gyd-ddyn yn bygwth fy llethu. Y mae'r crwt a ganai'r piano gyda'r tyst hyfrytaf y gwn amdano i'n hawydd oesol i ail-greu yn sgil pob ffrwydriad o'r drwg sydd ynom. Yn ymdrech y pianydd bach anafus, amherffaith i ddod o hyd i felodïau Handel ynghanol dicter y barics, gwelaf a chlywaf wirionedd i'w drysori. Ni fynnwn ildio i ddiefligrwydd. Mae crwtyn J. Gwyn Griffiths ymhob un ohonom. Waeth pa mor aflêr ein doniau gallant greu 'dwndwr y dadeni' wedi pob chwalfa, gallant watwar pob cais i droi'r byd yn adfeilion.

~

Ever since I first read it, this poem has earned itself a secure place amongst the poems that I turn to when man's cruelty towards his fellow men threatens to overwhelm me. The boy playing the piano is one of the best examples that I know of our age-old desire to re-create following every explosion of the wickedness inside of us. In the effort of the young, disabled, amateur pianist to play the melodies of Handel in the midst of the bitterness of the barracks, I see and hear a truth to be treasured. We don't wish to yield to fiendishness. J. Gwyn Griffiths's little boy is in all of us. However ragged our talents they can create the 'din of regeneration' after every upset, they can mock every attempt to destroy the world.

I'r Crwt a Ganai'r Piano

(yng ngwersyll y ffoaduriaid o Latfia a Lithwania ac Esthonia yn Lübeck, yr Almaen, yn ôl tystiolaeth y Parchedig Walter Bottom)

Mae'n uffern ar y ddaear yr ochr hon i'r bedd
wrth weld yr Arglwydd Satan yn bennaf yn y wledd.
Yma, mewn barics hen, lle'r heidiwyd torf
i'r gorlan lwyd, ddiobaith, cenaist ti i deyrnas Nef.
O cân, Feseia bychan yr Ewrop newydd!

Ceir ugain teulu'n gecrus mewn un neuadd,
diffeithwch durfing heb Ganaan dros ei orwel.
Tywyll eu llygaid gan hiraeth am henwlad;
mae'r trysor yno, ni bydd arall mwy.
Ond cenaist ti.
O cân, aderyn unadeiniog gwanwyn newydd!

Crochan y cenhedloedd chwâl yw hwn; lle hawdd
i gablu a chasáu, cyn dysgu caru dim.
Gorchfygaist ti'r amgylchfyd,
trewaist y piano a oedd fud
â chanig flêr, gyfewin.

Gwyn fyd na chlywid hi
tros Ewrop ddu, ei Dwyrain a'i Gorllewin.
O cân, ddysgwr bach dygn yr ysgol newydd!

Yn awr gyfyngaf dy Gaersalem sarn
ti brynaist faes, yn ernes am a fydd,
heb hidio'r sgrechian croch a'r rhegi hir
na'r muriau gwag a'r lloriau llwm.
Mynnaist ail-greu toredig ddarn o Handel,
mynych dy ddiscord a'th ailgynnig
a'th gywiro dyfal; ond ymlaen â hi . . .
O cân, watwarwr bach y bywyd adfeiliedig,
daw dwndwr y dadeni o'th biano di.

J. Gwyn Griffiths

Blodeugerdd o Farddoniaeth Gymraeg yr Ugeinfed Ganrif,
eds. Gwynn ap Gwilym and Alan Llwyd (Gwasg Gomer/Barddas, 1987)

Menna Elfyn

Dyma'r gerdd sydd yn dod yn ôl ataf o hyd ac o hyd; mae'n hudol, yn ysbrydol, ac yn mynegi rhyw ddirgelwch a oedd yn gynhaliaeth i ferch ddeunaw oed. Ei dysgu ar gof, a'i hadrodd imi fy hun ar adegau tywyll. Bu'n gyfaill ar hyd y blynyddoedd. Gall cerddi olygu gwahanol bethau i wahanol bobl ond i mi gyfeillion ydyn nhw y gallwch chi droi atyn nhw am gyngor i geisio dod i ddeall y byd yn well.

Soned orffenedig yw hi ac eto dyw hi ddim wedi ei gorffen a dyna'i rhagoriaeth. Y mae'n ddiamser, yn gallu perthyn i'r hen a'r ifanc, i'r hyderus a'r swil. I rai efallai disgrifiad yw o'r bydysawd yn ei ogoniant yn gwnued i berson deimlo'n fach ond i mi y mae'n mynegi gallu person i godi i fyd uwchlaw natur a mater ac yn rhoi iddi'r nerth i fod yn gyfrifol am ei thynged ei hun. Mae'r gair teml hefyd yn air sy'n llawn o gyfriniaeth a hud ac roedd hynny'n gweddu i ferch y chwedegau oedd yn ffoli arni.

~

Here is the poem that comes back to me time and time again; it is magical, spiritual and expresses a certain mystery that was sustenance to an eighteen-year-old girl. I learnt it by heart and recited it to myself when times were bleak. It has been a friend over the years. Poems can mean different things to different people but to me they are friends you can turn to for advice to try and gain a better understanding of the world.

It is a completed sonnet and yet it isn't finished and that is its excellence. It is timeless, able to belong to the young and the old, to the confident and the shy. To some maybe it is a description of the universe in its glory making a person feel small, but to me it expresses a person's ability to rise to a world above nature and matter, giving her the strength to be responsible for her own fate. The word temple is also a word full of mysticism and magic and that was fitting for a girl of the sixties captivated by it.

Dinas Noddfa

Pan yrr y Sêr eu cryndod drwy dy waed
  Gan siglo dy gredoau megis dail;
Pan brofo'r Nos y pridd o'r hwn y'th wnaed
  A'i hofn yn chwilio'th sylwedd hyd i'th sail;
Neu pan wrandewi rigwm trist y Môr
  Sy'n dweud yn dywyll ei lesmeiriol gŵyn
A'r Gwynt sy'n mynd a dyfod heibio'th ddôr
  Yn gryg drwy'r coedydd, ac yn floesg drwy'r brwyn;
Dilyn y doeth, a chyfod iti gaer
  Lle ceffi noddfa rhag eu gormes gref,
Yn arglwydd dy ddiddymdra, ac yn saer
  Dy nef dy hun. Neu ynteu dilyn ef
Pan adeilado deml, nid o waith llaw,
Goruwch dirgelwch Natur a thu draw.

R. Williams Parry

Yr Haf a Cherddi Eraill (Gwasg y Bala, 1924)

Islwyn Ffowc Elis

Y Ddaear heb Ddyn: dyna fyddai paradwys. Roedd y dyn cyntefig yn ddigon diniwed, yn hela'i fwyd ac yn gwarchod ei rai bach fel yr anifeiliaid eraill. Ond wedi miliwn o flynyddoedd ar y ddaear mae wedi tyfu mor wybodus ac mor bwerus fel y gall lygru'r blaned sy'n gartref iddo ac ymlid ei gyd-greaduriaid gwannach o fod. Yn naturiol – neu'n annaturiol – mae'r ychydig yn fwy llwyddiannus na'r lliaws. A chymaint yw gwanc yr ychydig am gyfoeth a phŵer nes bod miliynau yn Asia ac Affrica heb fwyd a miloedd yng Nghymru heb gartref.

Cododd bardd y soned hon yn gynnar iawn un bore, a gwelodd greaduriaid y maes a'r coed yn chwarae'n ddi-ofn yn absenoldeb dyn. Da, meddai ef, fyddai i'r haul beidio â chodi, a chadw dynion yn eu gwelyau i gysgu, ac yn y man i farw, nes carthu'r byd o'u holion ffiaidd hwy.

Ar wahân i'r dicter cyfiawn sy ynddi, rwy'n caru'r gerdd hon am fod iddi ffurf a miwsig – weithiau'n felys, weithiau'n gras – rhinweddau a aeth ar goll o gymaint o 'farddoniaeth' heddiw. Y cwbl a wnaeth R. Williams Parry oedd cymryd y soned Shakespearaidd a dim ond llacio ychydig ar ei mydr i'w gwneud yn 'soned laes'. Roedd hynny'n ddigon o ryddid iddo ef.

~

Earth without Man: that would be paradise. Primeval man was innocent enough, hunting his food and minding his young like other animals. But after a million years on the earth he has grown so knowledgeable and so powerful that he can corrupt the planet that's home to him and drive his weaker fellow creatures to extinction. Naturally – or unnaturally – the minority is more successful than the multitude. And the greed of the minority for wealth and power is so great that millions in Africa and Asia are without food and thousands in Wales without a home.

The writer of this sonnet arose very early one morning, and saw the creatures of the field and wood playing without fear in the absence of man. It would be good, he said, if the sun didn't rise, and kept men sleeping in their beds, leading to eventual death, until the world was purged of their loathsome remains.

Apart from the justifiable anger that it contains, I love this sonnet because it has form and music – sometimes sweet, sometimes harsh – virtues that are missing from so much of today's 'poetry'. All that

'Rhyfeddodau'r Wawr'. Graphics by Anthony Evans.

R. Williams Parry did was to take the Shakespearian sonnet and slacken its metre somewhat to make it a 'loose sonnet'. That was enough freedom for him.

Rhyfeddodau'r Wawr

Rhyfedd fu camu'n ddirybudd i'r wawrddydd hardd
   A chyrraedd sydyn baradwys heb groesi Iorddonen;
Clywed mynyddlais y gwcw yng nghoed yr ardd,
   A gweld yr ysguthan yn llithro i'r gwlydd o'r onnen;
Rhyfedd fu gweled y draenog ar lawnt y paun
   A chael y cwningod yn deintio led cae o'u twnelau,
Y lefran ddilety'n ddibryder ar ganol y waun,
   Y garan anhygoel yn amlwg yn nŵr y sianelau.
Rhyfeddach fyth, O haul sy'r tu arall i'r garn,
   Fai it aros lle'r wyt a chadw Dyn yn ei deiau,
Nes dyfod trosolion y glaswellt a'u chwalu'n sarn
   Rhag dyfod drachefn amserddoeth fwg ei simneiau;
Ei wared o'i wae, a'r ddaear o'i wedd a'i sawyr,
Cyn ail-harneisio dy feirch i siwrneiau'r awyr.

R. Williams Parry

Cerddi'r Gaeaf (Gwasg Gee, 1952)

Gwynfor Evans

Mynega'r emyn mawr hwn galon yr efengyl Gristnogol gyda grymuster cynhyrfus. Roedd ei awdur, Gwilym Hiraethog, yn un o Gymry mwyaf y ganrif ddiwethaf. Ei unig addysg ffurfiol oedd ychydig aeafau mewn ysgol fach Seisnigaidd. Pan briododd yn ddwy ar hugain oed roedd yn dal i fod yn was fferm. Ond cyn pen cenhedlaeth roedd bri arno fel llenor a newyddiadurwr, darlithydd, a gwleidydd a phregethwr o ddylanwad cenedlaethol. Ymgorfforai'r gorau mewn Ymneilltuaeth Gristnogol, a mynega'r emyn hanfod y ffydd a'i cynhaliai.

~

This great hymn expresses the heart of the Christian gospel with exciting strength. Its author, Gwilym Hiraethog, was one of the greatest Welshmen of the last century. His only formal education was a few winters in a small anglicized school. When he married at twenty-two he was still a farm labourer. But within a generation he was famous as an author, journalist, lecturer, politician and preacher of national significance. He embodied the best in Christian Nonconformity, and this hymn expresses the essence of the faith that sustained him.

Dyma Gariad fel y Moroedd

Dyma gariad fel y moroedd,
  Tosturiaethau fel y lli:
T'wysog bywyd pur yn marw,
  Marw i brynu'n bywyd ni:
Pwy all beidio â chofio amdano?
  Pwy all beidio â thraethu'i glod?
Dyma gariad nad â'n angof
  Tra fo nefoedd wen yn bod.

Ar Galfaria yr ymrwygodd
  Holl ffynhonnau'r dyfnder mawr;
Torrodd holl argaeau'r nefoedd
  Oedd yn gyfain hyd yn awr;
Gras a chariad megis dilyw
  Yn ymdywallt yma 'nghyd,
A chyfiawnder pur a heddwch
  Yn cusanu euog fyd.

Gwilym Hiraethog

Gweithiau Barddonol Gwilym Hiraethog (1855)

J. Wynford Evans

Choosing a single favourite poem is invidious – the need each favourite fills is different, according to the mood. Thinking it over, the two themes most common to my favourites seem to be the passage of time, and joy in love.

All use words exquisitely, from Alun Lewis,

> Softly the civilised centuries fall
> Paper on paper, Peter on Paul.

to Robert Herrick,

> Gather ye rosebuds while ye may,
> Old time is still a'flying.

In the end, I have selected a poem with a long perspective and continuity, expressed in wonderful calm – Gray's 'Elegy Written in a Country Churchyard'.

('Elegy Written in a Country Churchyard' was also chosen by Lord Callaghan and appears on page 21)

Meredydd Evans

Roedd R. Williams Parry ac R. Silyn Roberts yn gyfeillion agos ac os bu cerdd ddilys a diffuant erioed, dyma hi. Cyfyd hon o ddyfn-deroedd adnabyddiaeth dau a ymserchai yng nghwmni ei gilydd. Mae'n gerdd wirioneddol ddynol. Rhyfeddaf yn ogystal at ei rhinweddau llenyddol: ei throsiadau, grym yr ieithwedd a symledd ei mesur gwerinol. Dyma fardd sy'n medru ein cyfareddu â'r cyfarwydd.

Eithr y mae i'r gerdd hefyd gysylltiadau cynnes, personol â chyfnodau plentyndod a llencyndod yn fy hanes. Bu Silyn yn weinidog ym Methel, Tanygrisiau, o 1905 hyd 1913 a gadawodd ei ôl yn ddiamheuol ar ardal Stiniog yn gyffredinol. Y canlyniad oedd i mi gael fy magu yn sŵn ei enw ac ansawdd ei gyfraniad, yn arbennig, i addysg oedolion yn y cylch. Roedd hefyd yn Sosialydd hollol agored ei broffes ac nid peth cyffredin oedd hynny yn hanes un o weinidogion Yr Hen Gorff! Diamau fod y syniadau hyn amdano yn fyw yn fy meddwl pan syllwn, fel y gwnawn yn aml, ar ddarlun ohono ar un o furiau Festri Fawr Bethel.

Yna, pan euthum i Fangor yn 1941, ces gyfle i adnabod ei briod, Mary Silyn Roberts, a fu'n gynnes ei chroeso imi ar ei haelwyd droeon am y rheswm syml fy mod yn un o 'hogia Tangrisia'. Rhyfedd fel y gall darn o dir glymu pobl ynghyd. Gwir na chwrddais i â Silyn erioed ond cyffyrddodd â mi yn sicr trwy ddarlun ym Methel a chwmnïaeth gwraig nobl ym Mangor.

~

R. Williams Parry and R. Silyn Roberts were close friends and if there was ever a genuine and sincere poem, then this is it. This rises from the depth of acquaintance of two who cherished each other's company. It's a truly human poem. I marvel also at its literary virtues: its metaphors, the force of the diction and the simplicity of its folk metre. Here is a poet who is able to enchant us with the familiar.

But this poem also holds warm, personal connections with periods of my childhood and youth. Silyn was the minister of Bethel, Tanygrisiau, from 1905 to 1913 and without a doubt he left his mark on the Blaenau Ffestiniog area in general. As a result I was brought up to the sound of his name and the renown of his contribution, especially to adult education in the area. He was also an openly committed Socialist, something rare in a Presbyterian minister!

Without a doubt these thoughts about him were alive in my mind when I stared, as I frequently did, at a picture of him on one of the walls in the vestry at Bethel.

Then, when I went to Bangor in 1941, I had the opportunity to get to know his wife, Mary Silyn Roberts, who welcomed me warmly to her home many times, for the simple reason that I was one of the 'Lads of Tangrisia'. It's amazing how a piece of land can bind people together. It's true that I never met Silyn but he touched me for sure through a picture in Bethel and the company of a fine woman in Bangor.

Yn Angladd Silyn

Mor ddedwydd ydyw'r 'deryn gwyllt
  Heddiw a hyllt yr awel;
Yfory, pan fo'i dranc gerllaw,
  Fe gilia draw i'w argel;
A neb ni wêl na lle na dull
  Ei farw tywyll, tawel.

Tithau, a garai grwydro'r rhos
  Pan losgai'r nos ei lleuad, –
Yr awr o'r dydd pan gasgl y byw
  I roddi'r gwyw dan gaead,
Daethost lle gwêl y neb a fyn
  Ddyffryn dy ddarostyngiad.

O na bai marw'n ddechrau taith
  Trosodd i'r paith diwethaf,
Lle ciliai'r teithiwr tua'r ffin
  Fel pererin araf,
Cyn codi ar y gorwel draw
  Ei law mewn ffarwel olaf.

R. Williams Parry

Cerddi'r Gaeaf (Gwasg Gee, 1952)

Val Feld

I rarely have time to read poetry these days but I have dug out some poems that were given to me by a homeless woman many years ago in the early days when we were still Welsh Housing Aid. I can't remember the exact date but I would imagine that it must have been 1983, although our involvement with her and her husband spanned over very many years.

Theirs was a desperately sad story of how very ordinary people can become trapped in a cycle of homelessness, where they become dependent on the goodwill or otherwise of people who often have their own interests and their own profit at heart. I hope they have found a way of living a normal life after all that happened to them, but I wonder.

My favourite poem is 'Family of Three on the Dole'.

FAMILY OF THREE ON THE DOLE

RENT IS PAID
ISANT THAT GOOD
£52 POUNDS LEFT
FOR CLOTHES AND FOOD

WAIT A MUNIUT
SOMEONE AT THE DOOR
COAL MAN MY DEAR
£14 KNOW MORE.

THEN THE ELECTRIC
PAID ON THE BOOK
£7.30 A FORTNIGHT
IS ALL THAT THEY TOOK

THEN THE
MILK AND THE BREAD
ONLY A FEW POUNDS MORE
THATS THE FINISH
OFF THOSE AT THE DOOR

NOW WE GET DOWN
TO BYING THE FOOD
£30 IS LEFT
ISANT THAT GOOD

BUT WHAT OF
THE WASHING
I QUITE FORGOT
YOU NEED POWDER BLEACH
NOT A LOT

£25 POUNDS LEFT
ITS DWINDLING AWAY
DEVIDED IN THREE
LEAVES £1 ODD EACH A DAY

BUT WHAT OFF
THE CLOSTHES
TROUSERS DRESSES OR SHOES
IF YOU SPEND OUT ON THES
NOTHING THEN LEFT FOR
         FOOD.

Trudy Jeffreys

Paul Ferris

This was the first poem that came into my head when I thought about choosing one, which is as good a reason as any when making arbitrary choices. Betjeman is a good travel companion. His sub-urban scene-setting is always masterly, but the second half of the poem, where he mourns an obliterated past, is what I read it for, quoting 'silent under soot and stone' to myself when stuck in a traffic jam at the Northolt traffic lights. Betjeman sometimes sounds as if he is satirizing the very nostalgia he indulges in. Here, the note of regret is pure and unashamed.

Middlesex

Gaily into Ruislip Gardens
    Runs the red electric train,
With a thousand Ta's and Pardon's
    Daintily alights Elaine;
Hurries down the concrete station
With a frown of concentration,
Out into the outskirt's edges
Where a few surviving hedges
Keep alive our lost Elysium – rural Middlesex again.

Well cut Windsmoor flapping lightly,
    Jacqmar scarf of mauve and green
Hiding hair which, Friday nightly,
    Delicately drowns in Drene;
Fair Elaine the bobby-soxer,
Fresh-complexioned with Innoxa,
Gains the garden – father's hobby –
Hangs her Windsmoor in the lobby,
Settles down to sandwich supper and the television screen.

Gentle Brent, I used to know you
    Wandering Wembley-wards at will,
Now what change your waters show you
    In the meadowlands you fill!

Recollect the elm-trees misty
And the footpaths climbing twisty
Under cedar-shaded palings,
Low laburnum-leaned-on railings,
Out of Northolt on and upward to the heights of Harrow hill.

Parish of enormous hayfields
  Perivale stood all alone,
And from Greenford scent of mayfields
  Most enticingly was blown
Over market gardens tidy,
Taverns for the *bona fide*,
Cockney anglers, cockney shooters,
Murray Poshes, Lupin Pooters
Long in Kensal Green and Highgate silent under
                                        soot and stone.

John Betjeman

Collected Poems (John Murray, 1962, 2nd edn.)

Peter Finch

Cobbing's work has always fascinated me. When we toured Wales together in the seventies I became aware that beyond the seemingly simple sound text of 'Wan, do, tree' lay something else that recalled the magical counting of witches and the way that numbers form the basis of all languages. We can say 'yes' and 'no' in a few tongues other than our own and usually we can count a little as well. Cobbing is the champion of the sound performance, of course. His poem, roared, spluttered and chanted, goes far beyond any possible visual representation. The locals of west Wales, hearing this in the village halls, took it in their stride. Only the dogs were put out. I did my own:

> even
> dye
> tree
> pedal car
> limp
> quake
> scythe
> who is
> now
> egg
> even egg
> dyed egg

but really I owe it all to Bob Cobbing.

> **wan**
> **do**
> **tree**
> **fear**
> **fife**
> **seeks**
> **siphon**
> **eat**
> **neighing**
> **den**
> **elephan'**
> **twirl**

Bob Cobbing

Kurrirrurriri (Writers' Forum, 1977)

Paul Flynn

This is a favourite poem. It is by R. D. Laing.

When read in a lowland Scots accent it conversationally, simply and directly describes the contract that we play out throughout our lives from youth to age.

Before Death

Now all our guests have come and gone away
And you and I can hold each other close.
No need for haste as we await the day
The night falls into. No need suppose
We've failed to find what we had lost before
We caught the gleam in one another's eyes
Which signalled hope returned, to teach us more
Than seemed our crumpled hearts could realise.
The ghosts of youth are weary of the stage.
There's no one left to offer us a fight.
No sermons we must sit through at our age.
No passing fancies shrouding our delight.
Sweetheart, our love is true, but can't outlast
Our ruined raddled flesh. O hold me fast.

I cannot say that I'm the man that I
Once was. He slaved away to set me free.
He left a nice soft bed on which to lie
To whom he'd be when he had reached eighty
He did the sowing. I reap what was sown.
He picked and pressed the grapes. I drink the wine.
I still am paying interest on his loan.
I am the legacee of his design.
The baton now is in the hands of age,
Not youth. The future still presents its trial.
Whatever is the writing on the final page
I'm what's come out of all those years' denial.

I ask myself if he would be happy
If he could know he's turned out to be me.

R. D. Laing

Matters of Life and Death (Charisma, 1978)

'He's turned out to be me', from 'Before Death'. Graphics by Keith Bayliss.

Ken Follet

I love this poem because it looks at a familiar, even mundane scene and makes us realize how very peculiar ordinary life is.

The Whitsun Weddings

That Whitsun, I was late getting away:
    Not till about
One-twenty on the sunlit Saturday
Did my three-quarters-empty train pull out,
All windows down, all cushions hot, all sense
Of being in a hurry gone. We ran
Behind the backs of houses, crossed a street
Of blinding windscreens, smelt the fish-dock; thence
The river's level drifting breadth began,
Where sky and Lincolnshire and water meet.

All afternoon, through the tall heat that slept
    For miles inland,
A slow and stopping curve southwards we kept.
Wide farms went by, short-shadowed cattle, and
Canals with floatings of industrial froth;
A hothouse flashed uniquely: hedges dipped
And rose: and now and then a smell of grass
Displaced the reek of buttoned carriage-cloth
Until the next town, new and nondescript,
Approached with acres of dismantled cars.

At first, I didn't notice what a noise
    The weddings made
Each station that we stopped at: sun destroys
The interest of what's happening in the shade,
And down the long cool platforms whoops and skirls
I took for porters larking with the mails,
And went on reading. Once we started, though,
We passed them, grinning and pomaded, girls
In parodies of fashion, heels and veils,
All posed irresolutely, watching us go,

As if out on the end of an event
   Waving goodbye
To something that survived it. Struck, I leant
More promptly out next time, more curiously,
And saw it all again in different terms:
The fathers with broad belts under their suits
And seamy foreheads; mothers loud and fat;
An uncle shouting smut; and then the perms,
The nylon gloves and jewellery-substitutes,
The lemons, mauves, and olive-ochres that

Marked off the girls unreally from the rest.
   Yes, from cafés
And banquet-halls up yards, and bunting-dressed
Coach-party annexes, the wedding-days
Were coming to an end. All down the line
Fresh couples climbed aboard: the rest stood round;
The last confetti and advice were thrown,
And, as we moved, each face seemed to define
Just what it saw departing: children frowned
At something dull; fathers had never known

Success so huge and wholly farcical;
   The women shared
The secret like a happy funeral;
While girls, gripping their handbags tighter, stared
At a religious wounding. Free at last,
And loaded with the sum of all they saw,
We hurried towards London, shuffling gouts of steam.
Now fields were building-plots, and poplars cast
Long shadows over major roads, and for
Some fifty minutes, that in time would seem

Just long enough to settle hats and say
   I nearly died
A dozen marriages got under way.
They watched the landscape, sitting side by side
– An Odeon went past, a cooling tower,
And someone running up to bowl – and none
Thought of the others they would never meet
Or how their lives would all contain this hour.
I thought of London spread out in the sun,
Its postal districts packed like squares of wheat:

There we were aimed. And as we raced across
    Bright knots of rail
Past standing Pullmans, walls of blackened moss
Came close, and it was nearly done, this frail
Travelling coincidence; and what it held
Stood ready to be loosed with all the power
That being changed can give. We slowed again,
And as the tightened brakes took hold, there swelled
A sense of falling, like an arrow-shower
Sent out of sight, somewhere becoming rain.

Philip Larkin

Collected Poems (Faber & Faber, 1988)

Michael Foot

Idris Davies was a great poet of Wales and his works have given me enormous pleasure and I had this one up on the wall of my office in the House of Commons for many years.

The Sacred Road

They walked this road in seasons past
When all the skies were overcast,
They breathed defiance as they went
Along these troubled hills of Gwent

They talked of justice as they strode
Along this crooked mountain road,
And dared the little lords of Hell
So that the future should be well.

Because they did not count the cost
But battled on when all seemed lost,
This empty ragged road shall be
Always a sacred road to me.

Idris Davies

Collected Poems of Idris Davies (Gwasg Gomer, 1972)

Karl Francis

In his many poems R. S. Thomas explores the journeys of Jesus Christ in our living today. 'I still believe he comes stealthily as of old ... taken on trust like flowers in the dark country.' To believe in the belonging of Christ is the difficulty, I suppose, for many believers in the spirit, who do not believe in the Church. In another poem similarly entitled 'The Coming', which is perhaps a better, clearer poem, Thomas writes of Christ seeing the cross and telling God 'I'll go there'. A man who sees this journey; Jesus takes up his cross, embraces all the obstacles heading to Calvary and then offers us the choice of becoming flowers in dark places.

My father was a communist who admired Christ but did not believe in his deity; he did not believe in the virgin birth and did not believe in the resurrection of the body. My father did not go to the chapel and if he did occasionally, for his children's sake, he listened in awe to the brilliant oratory of our minister whom he knew would be drunk in the streets on Monday night. My father was as good and gentle and brave as any of the disciples. I as a Christian – I was baptized at the age of fifty-one – do not believe in the Heaven that excludes good men and women whatever their political beliefs. I believe R. S. Thomas is saying much the same in his great poetry. He touches mankind with his work and in my opinion is the wisest of those poets writing in the English language throughout the world.

What then do my father, R. S. Thomas, Jesus Christ and his father have to do with the Land of My Fathers. I must say everything. We, the Welsh, have lost our spiritual path. Our denial of the Holy Spirit helps imprison us. Once we were teachers to the world. And in the arrogance of our self-fulfilled materialism we have become an ignorant nation led by bigotry. Leaderless. Class-driven. White. Male.

Daily, we tell lies about our language and our history. We have become victims of our own self-deception. There was a brilliant moment in the miners' strike in 1984 when the Welsh Congress was formed, when it looked as if Plaid, Labour, the Women's Movement, the Liberals, Christians and Communists would bury their differences. It lasted two weeks. Ten years later we are offered a new assembly. A little talking-shop. Second to Scotland; Wales is not a country. R. S. Thomas tells us it is our responsibility to change this. Small countries talk peace unto nations. It is not enough to read R. S. Thomas. To agree with him is not to believe. To follow him would not be his way, but to follow Jesus? If R. S. Thomas has taught me one lesson outside poetry, it is that being Welsh is of no interest to Christ. Being Welsh is Being. At heart Wales remains *Yr Hen Wlad*; but Being Human is the Heart.

Coming

To be crucified
again? To be made friends
with for his jeans and beard?
Gods are not put to death

any more. Their lot now
is with the ignored.
I think he still comes
stealthily as of old,

invisible as a mutation,
an echo of what the light
said, when nobody
attended; an impression

of eyes, quicker than
to be caught looking, but taken
on trust like flowers in the
dark country towards which we go.

R. S. Thomas

Experimenting with an Amen (Macmillan, 1986)

Raymond Garlick

All my adult life, both personal and professional, has been concerned with poetry, so it would be easier to choose a dozen favourite poems rather than just one. All twelve would probably be Anglo-Welsh poems, and I suspect half of them would be by one of the finest English-language poets writing anywhere at the present time, R. S. Thomas.

I was probably the first person to see the poem I have in fact chosen, which was submitted for publication in *Dock Leaves* and appeared there in the summer of 1954. I still remember the feeling of eager anticipation on picking up the long envelope with the familiar handwriting from the doormat, opening it, and reading 'On Hearing a Welshman Speak'. It is a quintessentially Anglo-Welsh poem, celebrating in one of the languages of Wales the life of the other. For the poet the sound of Welsh being spoken evokes the whole history of its speakers, back through Goronwy Owen to William Morgan, Glyn Dŵr, Dafydd ap Gwilym and beyond – to those earlier centuries when the invaders were not always successful.

On Hearing a Welshman Speak

And as he speaks time turns,
The swift years revolve
Backwards. There Goronwy comes
Again to his own shore.
Now in a mountain parish
The words leave the Book
To swarm in the honeyed mind
Of Morgan. Glyn Dŵr stands
And sees the flames fall back
Like waves from the charred timbers
Before taking his place
Behind the harp's slack bars
From which the singer called him.
Look at this resinous church,
As the long prayers are wound
Once more on the priest's tongue,

Dafydd reproves his eyes'
Impetuous falconry
About the kneeling girl.
Stones to the walls fly back,
The gay manors are full
Of music; the poets return
To feed at the royal tables.
Who dreams of failure now
That the oak woods are loud
With the last hurrying feet
Seeking the English plain?

R. S. Thomas

Poetry For Supper (Hart-Davis, 1958)

Huw Garmon

Mae 'Hon' (T. H. Parry Williams) yn gerdd am hen thema, ond un sy'n berthnasol i bob cenhedlaeth o Gymry. Mae 'dyletswydd', 'cyfrifoldeb' a'r 'Gymraeg' yn feini trymion a'r ymwybyddiaeth o'r pethau hyn yn gallu bod yn llyffethair i'r creadigol. Nid yw bob amser yn hawdd delio â nhw, yn enwedig wrth fod yna gymaint o borfeydd brasach yn agored i'r Cymro Cymraeg. I mi, mae cerdd 'Creu Cyswllt' Gerwyn Wiliams yn fersiwn mwy newydd, llai ystrydebol na 'Hon' (efallai dim ond am ei bod yn llai cyfarwydd). Rwy'n credu fod ganddi fwy o apêl at Gymry fy nghenhedlaeth i.

Mae apêl personol arall iddi hefyd gan ei bod yn adlais mwy llythrennol, daearyddol o'r man y cefais fy magu, sef ym Mhenmynydd, Ynys Môn, ar gefnen o dir sy'n edrych allan ar fynyddoedd Gwynedd, yr holl ffordd o'r Gogarth i Lŷn. 'Pengorwelion' ydi'r enw lleol ar y man.

Fe dreuliais ddwy flynedd yn Llundain, ac yno 'roeddwn i'n teimlo cymysgedd o ryddhad oddi wrth ormes y 'mynyddoedd' ac eto rhyw hiraeth am gynefin. Mewn ffordd, 'roedd cael bod yn rhan o fawredd gwahanol yr Eingl-Sacsoniaid gwyn yn ddihangfa rhag cyfrifoldeb, ac roedd canolbwyntio ar y presennol cymaint yn haws mewn byd oedd wedi ei greu gan ddyn yn hytrach na chael fy atgoffa'n barhaol o wychder tirweddol fy mro. Doedd edrych allan ar floc o fflatiau ddim yn cymhlethu bywyd ac roedd eu bodolaeth nhw'n fwy defnyddiol i ateb problemau bob dydd na'r 'Wyddfa a'i chriw'.

Wedi dychwelyd adra mae'r 'mynyddoedd' yr un mor rhyfeddol orthrymus ag erioed, ond mae'r olygfa wedi'i goleuo bellach gan oren yr A55.

~

'Hon' (T. H. Parry Williams) is a poem on an old theme, but one which is relevant to every generation of Welsh people. 'Duty', 'responsibility' and the 'Welsh language' are heavy burdens and an awareness of these can fetter the creative. It isn't always easy to deal with them, especially as there are so many richer pastures open to a Welsh-speaking Welsh person. To me, Gerwyn Wiliams's poem 'Creu Cyswllt' is a newer, less stereotyped version than 'Hon' (maybe only because it is less familiar). I believe it has greater appeal for Welsh people of my generation.

It also has another personal appeal as a more literal, geographic echo of the place in which I was brought up, namely Penmynydd, Anglesey, on a ridge of land which looks out on the mountains of Gwynedd, the whole way from Gogarth to the Llŷn Peninsula. 'Pengorwelion' is the local name for the spot.

I spent two years in London and there I felt a mixture of freedom from the oppression of the 'mountains' and yet a certain homesickness for the familiar. In a way, being able to be a part of the different grandeur of the white Anglo-Saxons was an escape from responsibility and concentrating on the present was so much easier in a world created by man rather than being continually reminded of the splendour of the landscape of my homeland. Looking out on a block of flats didn't complicate life and their existence was more useful to answer everyday problems than 'Snowdon and her crew'.

Having returned home the 'mountains' are as wonderfully oppressive as ever, but the view is now lit up by the orange of the A55.

Creu Cyswllt

'Dyma'r mynyddoedd.
Ni fedr ond un iaith eu codi'.
Llygadwn. Rhyfeddwn.
Mi fyddai'n braf
gallu cymryd hyn,
pob gronyn ohono,
yn ganiataol.
Mi fyddai'n ddihangfa
gallu smocio a photio
hyd foethusrwydd hysbysebiadol anghofrwydd
gan wfftio at y goleuni beichus
a lapio'r tywyllwch amdanom yn dynn.
Ond dim ond inni graffu
mae yng nghilfachau'r mynyddoedd
bosteri gwleidyddol a lliwiau plaid
sy'n cydio yn ein cof
a'n caethiwo.

Mor annelwig yw'r ffiniau
rhwng ein presennol plastig
a'n gorffennol euraid,
rhwng y concrid a'r tir,
ac fe ddryswyd ein hemosiynau'n lân
rhwng ein gorfoledd a'n gwae.
Mor annelwig yw ein ffiniau
nes crebachu'n ystrydebau.

Ac eto,
llusgwn i ganol
strim-stram-strellach ein heddiw,
greiriau anymarferol ein cynhysgaeth
a cheisiwn greu cyswllt â'r dydd.
Creu cyswllt –
neu ollwng gafael.

Gerwyn Wiliams

Colli Cyswllt (Eisteddfod Genedlaethol Urdd Gobaith Cymru,
Yr Wyddgrug, 1984)

Beti George

Fues i erioed yn aelod parhaol o'r gymdeithas yna. Dwy i ddim yn siarad yr un iaith â nhw. Ond, jiw, dwy'n teimlo'n ofnadw o agos atyn nhw. A theimlo'r cynhesrwydd yn amdo amdanaf. Y 'shwt mae' a'r wên a'r croeso i blentyn o'r wled. Gwyn carlwm y starch dillad y gwely plu a'r gobenny' . . . Yr hwter yn y bore, a'r bwcedi gwastraff glo yn ymlusgo ar hyd gwifrau yn yr awyr y tu fas i'r ffenest llofft. 'Na, peidiwch cau'r cyrtens!' Pice ar y mân, y taffish peppermint, fish a chips o siop am ddeg y nos – a'r gole ar y stryd. Yr hufen iâ – eiscrim – cynta. Chwydu – hwtu – dros bobman wrth y bys stop . . . S'dim ots, rodd e'n ffein! Wel, wel, croten Tom a Sarah o'r wled. Atgofion melys plentyndod ar wyliau haf yn Nantymoel a Blaengarw lle, yn wahanol i gartre yn Sir Aberteifi, ro'n nhw'n credu mewn sbwylo plant.

Mae 'Y Llen', pryddest Dyfnallt Morgan, yn cael ei chynnwys yn netholiad y prifeirdd Alan Llwyd a Gwynn ap Gwilym o farddoniaeth Gymraeg yr ugeinfed ganrif. Diolch am eu gweledigaeth. Trof ati'n aml.

Trwyddi gwelaf wytnwch a chadernid cymdeithas ynysig ac hunan-gynhaliol y Cymoedd. Cymdeithas na chafodd ac nad yw yn cael ei nabod yn iawn gan weddill Cymru:

S'dim sens bod 'annar y byd ddim yn gwpod
Shwt ma 'annar arall y byd yn byw.

Digiaf wrth yr esgeulustod ohoni. Hi a wnaeth Brydain yn Fawr. Hi a ddefnyddiwyd i gyfoethogi'r lleiafrif, ac i chwyddo coffrau banc Lloegr. Ar awr caledi a chyni, mae'n cael ei hanwybyddu. Collodd ei defnyddioldeb.

Ymgollaf yn swyn y Wenhwyseg oedd yn arfer dawnsio ar wefusau'r colier a'i wraig – ond nid ar wefusau eu plant. Roedd yn rhaid i'r groten fech o'r wled gael ei galw o flaen sêt fawr y capel i ganu neu adrodd adnod neu ddwy i brofi i'r deg neu ddwsin o addolwyr fod yr hen iaith yn dal yn fyw. Dyw'r colier a'i wraig ddim yn bod bellach. A dyw'r Gwm'reg ddim yn dawnsio ar wefusau'r wynebau uwchben byrddau sglodion meicro'r ffatri o Siapan.

Wyt ti'n gwpod
Fel ma cyrtens yr 'Ippodrome yn cau . . . yn ddistaw bach . . .
Ar ddiwadd y perfformans?

Wel falna mae 'co!
Wi'n gweld llai o'r 'en scenery bob tro . . .'

Ond mae'r Gymraeg wedi dechrau dawnsio ar wefusau plant plant y colier, ac

Hei, gewn ni gwrdd yn y matsh dy' Satwrn . . .
. . . Os byddwn ni byw.

~

I was never a permanent member of that community. I don't speak the same language as them. But, God I feel so close to them. I feel the warmth like a shroud around me. The 'how's things' and the smile and the welcome to a child from the country. The stoat-whiteness of the starched sheets and pillow of the featherbed. The hooter in the morning and the slag buckets crawling along wires in the sky outside the bedroom window. 'No, don't shut the curtains!' Welsh cakes, peppermint sweets, shop fish and chips at ten o'clock at night – and the street lights. The first ice cream. Throwing up everywhere by the bus stop . . . No matter, it was good! Well, well, Tom and Sarah's little girl from the country. Sweet memories of childhood summer holidays in Nantymoel and Blaengarw where, unlike home in Cardiganshire, they believed in spoiling children.

Dyfnallt Morgan's 'pryddest', 'Y Llen' is included in Alan Llwyd and Gwyn ap Gwilym's selection of twentieth-century Welsh poetry. I am grateful for their vision. I often turn to it.

Through it I see the toughness and strength of the self-supporting, insular community of the Valleys. A community that wasn't and isn't properly understood by the rest of Wales.

No sense that 'alf the world doesn' know
'ow the other 'alf lives.

I am angered by the way this community is neglected. It made Britain Great. It was used to make a minority rich and to swell the coffers of English banks. At a time of hardship and adversity it is ignored. It has lost its usefulness.

I lose myself in the magic of the local dialect which used to be so much a part of the speech of the miner and his wife – but not of their children. The little girl from the country had to be called in front of the chapel elders to sing or recite a verse or two from the Bible to prove to the dozen or so worshippers that the language of heaven was still alive. The miner and his wife no longer exist. And no Welsh is to be heard amongst the workers in the Japanese microchip factory.

> You know
> 'ow the curtains at the 'Ippodrome close . . . slowly . . .
> At the end of the performance?
> Well it's like that down there!
> I sees less of the old scenery everytime . . .

But the Welsh language has begun to dance on the lips of the miner's grandchildren and

> Hey, we'll meet in the match on Saturday
> . . . If we're alive.

Y Llen
(detholiad/an extract)

> Allwn i byth pito mynd
> I anglodd yr 'en foi.
> Buws a'n biwr iawn i fi flynydda 'nôl
> Pan es i'n grwtyn ato fa yn y talcan glo
> A buas i'n wilia lot sha fa . . .
> O'dd lot co?
> Be' ti'n wilia, 'chan –
> Preifet yw 'i 'eddi 'ta nw, 'ed!
> Am un-ar-ddeg 'to'dd neb
> Wrth gât y fynwant ond 'êrs,
> Dou gar a fi.
> . . .
> Ond wotsho'r plant o'n i,
> A meddwl!
> 'Na le'r o'dd Glatys a Susie,
> A'u gwrwod gwrddon' nw yn yr A.T.S. –
> A reini weti c'el gwaith ar y Tradin' Estate 'nawr;

A Isaac a'i wraig –
Merch o Ireland a fe weti troi'n Gathlic gyta 'i . . .
A dim un o'onyn' nw'n diall Cwmr'eg.
Ond wi'n canmol nw am g'el anglodd Cwmr'eg iddo fa,
A o'n nw weti catw'r 'en foi'n itha' teidi 'yd y diwadd 'ed.
(I galon a 'eth yn ddiswmwth).
Do, do, nison' nw i d'letsw'dd reit i wala; weti'r cyfan
Dim ond ta'cu o'dd a iddyn' nw, a peth arall,
O'dd a m'es o'u byd nw'n deg.
Wyt titha a finna'n gwpod rwpath am 'yn,
Wath dyw'n plant ni ddim yn wilia'r 'en iaith, otyn' nw?

Dyfnallt Morgan

Y Llen a Myfyrdodau Eraill (Gwasg Gee, 1967)

Tanni Grey

(Tanni's mother replied on her behalf as Tanni was competing at the World Championships in Berlin)

When I was seven, I was sent this book by my aunt. It was much used with many pages being coloured or written on, they in turn became loose and had to be stuck back with what we now term 'sellotape'! When our eldest daughter was old enough to read she was given the book, but it was Tanni who took to it with enthusiasm. When she was about seven she was told that everyone in the class must find and learn a poem. This book which had been lost was eventually located and the poem was duly chosen and learnt by heart! Since then Tanni has had to learn many pieces for her exams in secondary school and university but none have had the same appeal as the very first rhyme.

As soon as Tanni had your letter she had no hesitation in finding the book which had been misplaced again. I am sure she would say that it brings back memories of her junior school, the friends she made and of a headmaster who accepted her completely and gave her the opportunity to take part in 'normal education' (as opposed to special schools) and this is something for which she has always been grateful.

A Week's Food

Milk is nice for Monday,
Milk begins with M;
Treacle Tarts for Tuesday,
I'm rather fond of them;
Walnuts do for Wednesday;
Thursday, Toast and Tea;
Friday Figs; and Saturday Soup;
And Sundays –
　　　　Wait and See!

E. C. Brereton

A Little Book of Rhymes New and Old, collected and illustrated by C. M. Barker
(Blackie & Son Ltd.)

'Thursday, Toast and Tea', from 'A Week's Food'. Graphics by Sue Hunt.

R. Geraint Gruffydd

Fe ganwyd y gerdd hon ym Mhowys tua chanol y nawfed ganrif gan fardd dienw a oedd yn cyfansoddi cylch o englynion am Heledd, tywysoges o Bowys ddwy ganrif ynghynt yr oedd ei brawd Cynddylan wedi'i ladd gan y Saeson a'i diroedd wedi'u hanrheithio. Rhan o diroedd Cynddylan oedd y Dref-wen, ac fe hoffaf y gerdd am dri rheswm yn bennaf:

1. Er mor syml ei mesurau – dau englyn milwr a thri englyn byr crwca – fe berthyn iddi fiwsig hudolus iawn.
2. Y mae ei delweddaeth – y lluniau y mae'n eu tynnu – yn eithriadol o rymus. Rhennid y gymdeithas Geltaidd yn dri dosbarth: yr offeiriaid, y milwyr a'r llafurwyr tir. Yn y gerdd y mae ymdrech y llafurwyr i beri i'r tir ddwyn ffrwyth yn cael ei difetha gan weithgarwch y milwyr. Cyferbynnir gwaed a gwellt, llawenydd yr adar prae a diflaniad y bobl, tarian ddrylliog wedi brwydr ac ychain yn gorffwys neu'n aredig.
3. Y mae'n dweud gwir am fywyd. Bygythir yr elfennau ffrwythlon yn barhaus gan elfennau dinistriol. Fe all fod yn arwyddocaol nad oes sôn yn y gerdd am drydydd dosbarth y gymdeithas Geltaidd, sef yr offeiriaid.

~

This poem was sung in Powys by an unknown poet in the mid-ninth century as part of a series of *englynion* about Heledd, a princess of Powys two centuries previously, whose brother Cynddylan had been killed by the English and his lands plundered. Y Dref-wen was part of his land and there are three main reasons why I like the poem:

1. In spite of the simplicity of its metre – two examples of the *englyn milwr* and three of the *englyn byr crwca* – its music is most magical.
2. Its imagery – the pictures it creates – is exceptionally powerful. Celtic society was divided into three classes: the priests, the soldiers and the agricultural labourers. In this poem the efforts of the agricultural labourers to make the land productive are destroyed by the soldiers. Blood and grass are contrasted, the joy of the birds of prey and the disappearance of the people, a broken shield after battle and oxen resting or ploughing.

3. It states a truth about life. The fruitful elements are continually threatened by the destructive elements. It may be significant that there is no mention in the poem of the third class in Celtic society, namely the priests.

Y Dref-Wen

Y Dref-wen ym mron y coed –
Ysef ei hefras erioed:
Ar wyneb ei gwellt ei gwaed.

Y Dref-wen yn ei thymyr –
Ei hefras ei glas fyfyr:
Ei gwaed o dan draed ei gwŷr.

Y Dref-wen yn ei dyffrynt –
Llawen y byddair wrth gyfamrudd cad.
Ei gwerin neur dderynt.

Y Dref-wen rhwng Tren a Throdwydd –
Oedd gnodach ysgwyd don yn dyfod o gad
Nogyd ych i echwydd.

Y Dref-wen rhwng Tren a Thrafal –
Oedd gnodach ei gwaed ar wyneb ei gwellt
Nog eredig brynar.

* efras: arfer
myfyr: beddrod
byddair: aderyn prae
cyfamrudd: cythrwfl
neur dderynt: y maent wedi darfod amdanynt
gnodach: mwy arferol
ysgwyd don: tarian ddrylliog
nogyd: nag
echwydd: gorffwys canol dydd
brynar: tir wedi'i adael heb ei droi am gyfnod

Anon.

Jenny Rowland, *The Story of Heledd* (Gwasg Gregynog, 1994)

Peter Hain

I am not particularly poetry-orientated but a short poem-like extract that has special meaning to me is John Donne's 'No Man is an Island'.

My parents had a particularly traumatic three years before we left South Africa at the beginning of 1966, both having been banned during that period, with friends detained, a friend executed, raids and harassment by the Special Branch, etc. I was a teenager at the time, more interested in soccer, cricket, rugby and motor-racing than politics, but was obviously very involved in what was happening and ended up reading our friend's funeral service when the police prevented my father from doing so.

John Donne's words seemed to me then to epitomize why people like my parents took the stand that they did, and since then has served for me as a pointer to the fundamental interdependence of people and the reason why we should all make every effort to assist those less fortunate than ourselves.

No man is an *Island*, entire of it self; every man is a piece of the *Continent*, a part of the *main*; if a *clod* be washed away by the *sea*, *Europe* is the less, as well as if a *promontory* were, as well as if a *manor* of thy *friends* or of *thine own* were; any man's *death* diminishes *me*, because I am involved in *Mankind*; And therefore never send to know for whom the *bell* tolls; It tolls for *thee*.

John Donne

Meditation XVII, 1631

Arfon Haines Davies

Pe baech yn gofyn i mi ddewis hoff ffilm neu hoff gân, does dim dwywaith y byddai fy newis i heddiw yn wahanol iawn i fy newis i yfory neu hyd yn oed ddoe; ond gyda barddoniaeth dim ond un ateb sydd – 'Eifionydd' gan R. Williams Parry.

Clywais y gerdd yma gynta pan yn ddisgybl yn Ysgol Gymraeg Alexander Road, Aberystwyth. Mi roeddwn yn hoff iawn o 'Tylluanod', 'Clychau'r Gog' a'r 'Llwynog' ond, i mi, roedd 'Eifionydd' wastad yn ffefryn.

Mae pob pennill yn creu darlun byw ac yn llawn disgrifiadau lliwgar; ac erbyn y diwedd mae rhywun yn ysu i ddianc gyda R. Williams Parry o'r dyffryn diwydiannol i lonyddwch a heddwch y Lôn Goed.

Er cymaint mae'r gerdd yn ei olygu i mi, mae'n eironig mewn ffordd mai dim ond rhyw ddwy flynedd yn ôl y cerddais ar hyd y Lôn Goed am y tro cynta. Sylweddolais yn syth fod yno ryw 'lonydd gorffenedig' yn perthyn iddi, bron y buaswn yn dweud fy mod wedi cael y teimlad fy mod mewn rhyw le arallfydol.

Ychydig flynyddoedd yn ôl cefais anrheg annisgwyl iawn – copi o 'Eifionydd' yn llawysgrifen R. Williams Parry. I mi, dyna un o'r trysorau mwya gwerthfawr gallai unrhyw un ei gael: ei hoff gerdd yn llawysgrifen ei hoff fardd. 'Eifionydd' gan R. Williams Parry ydy'r trysor hwnnw i mi.

~

If you were to ask me to choose my favourite film or song, without a doubt my choice today would be very different from my choice tomorrow or even yesterday; but with poetry only one answer is possible – 'Eifionydd' by R. Williams Parry.

I heard this poem first whilst a pupil in the Welsh school in Alexandra Road, Aberystwyth. I was very fond of 'Tylluanod', 'Clychau'r Gog' and 'Y Llwynog', but 'Eifionydd' was always a favourite.

Every verse creates a vivid picture and is full of colourful descriptions; and by the end one is longing to escape with R. Williams Parry from the industrial valley to the stillness and peace of the Lôn Goed.

In spite of how much the poem means to me it is ironic in a way that it was only about two years ago that I walked along the Lôn Goed for the first time. I realized at once that it possessed a certain 'perfect stillness'; I could almost say that I felt I was in another world.

A few years ago I received a most unexpected gift – a copy of 'Eifionydd' in R. William Parry's handwriting. To me that is one of the most valuable treasures anyone could possibly have: one's favourite poem handwritten by one's favourite poet. In my case 'Eifionydd' by R. Williams Parry is that treasure.

Eifionydd

O olwg hagrwch Cynnydd
   Ar wyneb trist y Gwaith
Mae bro rhwng môr a mynydd
   Heb arni staen na chraith,
Ond lle bu'r arad' ar y ffridd
Yn rhwygo'r gwanwyn pêr o'r pridd.

Draw o ymryson ynfyd
   Chwerw'r newyddfyd blin,
Mae yno flas y cynfyd
   Yn aros fel hen win.
Hen, hen yw murmur llawer man
Sydd rhwng dwy afon yn Rhos Lan.

A llonydd gorffenedig
   Yw llonydd y Lôn Goed,
O fwa'i tho plethedig
   I'w glaslawr dan fy nhroed.
I lan na thref nid arwain ddim,
Ond hynny nid yw ofid im.

O! mwyn yw cyrraedd canol
   Y tawel gwmwd hwn,
O'm dyffryn diwydiannol
   A dull y byd a wn;
A rhodio'i heddwch wrthyf f'hun
Neu gydag enaid hoff, cytûn.

R. Williams Parry

Cerddi'r Gaeaf (Gwasg Gee, 1952)

Patrick Hannan

I've never met anyone more meticulous about his work than John Ormond. Like the craftsmen about whom he writes in this poem, he would chisel and polish and then stand back for a time to consider what adjustment or improvement might be needed for perspective of meaning. He brought this fierce concentration to his work as a film-maker as well as to his poetry and prose, which is one explanation of the reason why, when he died in 1990, people regretted that, despite his achievements, his output in both images and words had not been even greater.

I have chosen this poem to remember a friend, and this one in particular to remember someone who did not think that humour had no place in art.

Cathedral Builders

They climbed on sketchy ladders towards God,
With winch and pulley hoisted hewn rock into heaven,
Inhabited sky with hammers, defied gravity,
Deified stone, took up God's house to meet Him,

And came down to their suppers and small beer;
Every night slept, lay with their smelly wives,
Quarrelled and cuffed the children, lied,
Spat, sang, were happy or unhappy,

And every day took to the ladders again;
Impeded the rights of way of another summer's
Swallows, grew greyer, shakier, became less inclined
To fix a neighbour's roof of a fine evening,

Saw naves sprout arches, clerestories soar,
Cursed the loud fancy glaziers for their luck,
Somehow escaped the plague, got rheumatism,
Decided it was time to give it up,

To leave the spire to others; stood in the crowd
Well back from the vestments at the consecration,
Envied the fat bishop his warm boots,
Cocked up a squint eye and said, 'I bloody did that.'

John Ormond

Requiem and Celebration (Christopher Davies, 1969)

David Hanson

One of my favourite poems is 'In Flanders Fields' by John McCrae. I find the poem a poignant and lasting memorial to the futility of war, especially poignant as John McCrae himself died at the end of the First World War, as a result of wounds.

My grandfather fought in the First World War and I can well recall as a young boy his telling me in stark terms of the horror of that conflict.

Whilst I am not a pacifist and can see the merits of a just conflict I can always touch base with this poem to remind me that wars happen when politicians fail.

In Flanders Fields

In Flanders fields the poppies blow
Between the crosses, row on row
    That mark our place; and in the sky
    The larks, still bravely singing, fly
Scarce heard amid the guns below.

We are the Dead. Short days ago
We lived, felt dawn, saw sunset glow,
    Loved and were loved, and now we lie
        In Flanders fields.

Take up our quarrel with the foe:
To you from failing hands we throw
    The torch; be yours to hold it high.
    If ye break faith with us who die
We shall not sleep, though poppies grow
        In Flanders fields.

John McCrae

'In Flanders Fields'. Graphics by Paul Peter Piech.

Lord Hooson

Mae gen i lawer iawn o hoff gerddi yn Gymraeg ond 'rwyf wedi dewis yr un isod oherwydd fod perthynas imi wedi ei hysgrifennu ac mi ddysgais ei hadrodd pan oeddwn yn ifanc iawn. 'Roeddwn yn byw, tra'n hogyn, mewn llecyn ble 'roedd nifer o gennin pedr ac 'rwy'n byw yn awr yn Llanidloes mewn lle sydd â digonedd ohonynt.

~

I have got many favourite poems in Welsh but I have chosen the one below because a relative of mine wrote it and I learnt to recite it when I was very young. As a young boy I lived in a spot where there were a number of daffodils and I now live in Llanidloes in a place where there are many.

Daffodil

Fe'th welais di ar lawnt y plas,
　　A gwyntoedd Mawrth yn oer eu min;
Ar feysydd llwyd a gweirglodd las,
　　Ac awel Ebrill fel y gwin;
Ni welwyd un erioed mor llon,
　　Â'th fantell werdd a'th euraid rudd,
Yn dawnsio yn y gwynt a'r glaw
　　I bibau pêr rhyw gerddor cudd.

Fe'th welais di mewn llestr pridd
　　Ar ffawydd fwrdd gwerinwr tlawd;
Mewn ffiol ddrud o risial pur
　　Yn neuadd wych y da ei ffawd;
Ond ofer yno bob rhyw gerdd;
　　Ni ddawnsit mwy; ac ar dy rudd
'Roedd hiraeth am y gwynt a'r glaw,
　　A phibau pêr y cerddor cudd.

I. D. Hooson

Cerddi a Baledi (Gwasg Gee, 1956)

106

The following is not my favourite English poem but I think it's a very striking one. I made a note of it during the 1939–45 war. I believe the poet was a Scottish communist but I know nothing at all about him; it was probably occasioned by the enormous loss of life on the Russian Front – on both sides – in the 1943–5 period. I know I should have chosen a more cheerful poem but I have done so for my Welsh choice.

The Private

His task is done
whether the battle's lost or won

His was a harder way than those that merely pray.
And easier than
That of the thinking man.
He moved with his herd in pride
Against another herd, and died.

Singer

Lord Howe

'A' favourite poem, said the bidding letter – not 'the'. No need, therefore, to remain faithful to any earlier choice. So I have picked John Betjeman's 'Myfanwy'. For I enjoy Betjeman and I love the name.

Quite apart from being the title of Joseph Parry's evocative Welsh song, the word's derivation has its own charm. Some Welsh romantics regard it as the equivalent of the (originally) Scottish 'Arabella'. Others, perhaps more accurately, trace it to two Welsh words: 'Banwy' for 'woman' and 'my', described as an archaic prefix 'denoting reverent affection and endearment'.

Betjeman has transformed it into a quintessentially English poem, which evokes a string of nostalgic, post-adolescent memories and secret thoughts. Hopefully for others as well as myself?

Myfanwy

Kind o'er the *kinderbank* leans my Myfanwy.
　White o'er the play-pen the sheen of her dress,
Fresh from the bathroom and soft in the nursery
　Soap-scented fingers I long to caress.

Were you a prefect and head of your dormit'ry?
　Were you a hockey girl, tennis or gym?
Who was your favourite? Who had a crush on you?
　Which were the baths where they taught you to swim?

Smooth down the Avenue glitters the bicycle,
　Black-stockinged legs under navy-blue serge,
Home and Colonial, Star, International,
　Balancing bicycle leant on the verge.

Trace me your wheel-tracks, you fortunate bicycle,
　Out of the shopping and into the dark,
Back down the Avenue, back to the pottingshed,
　Back to the house on the fringe of the park.

Golden the lights on the locks of Myfanwy,
  Golden the light on the book on her knee,
Finger-marked pages of Rackham's Hans Anderson,
  Time for the children to come down to tea.

Oh! Fuller's angel-cake, Robertson's marmalade,
  Liberty lampshade, come, shine on us all,
My! what a spread for the friends of Myfanwy,
  Some in the alcove and some in the hall.

Then what sardines in the half-lighted passages!
  Locking of fingers in long hide-and-seek.
You will protect me, my silken Myfanwy,
  Ringleader, tom-boy, and chum to the weak.

John Betjeman

Collected Poems (John Murray, 1958)

Kim Howells

Among my favourite poetry is this passage from the last poem in William Wordsworth's *Lyrical Ballads*, 'Lines composed a few miles above Tintern Abbey'.

Published in 1798, in the midst of one of the most turbulent periods in European history, it intrigues and inspires me because it addresses the significance and the meaning of the search for refuge and strength in wild and open places. Only in such places have I been able to measure the changes, the gains and losses, which have accrued in my own life. Wordsworth describes such an experience with extraordinary clarity in blank verse which has a majesty as profound as the great peaks and forests from which he drew such strength, but he uses language which escapes the narrow bounds of any established political or religious codes. I draw reassurance and a sense of physical well-being from this poem of the same order and intensity as that which I have drawn from the touch of sun-warmed granites and sandstones high on the wild precipices above our clouded valleys and plains.

Lines Composed a Few Miles above Tintern Abbey
(an extract)

> For I have learned
> To look on nature, not as in the hour
> Of thoughtless youth; but hearing oftentimes
> The still, sad music of humanity,
> Not harsh nor grating, though of ample power
> To chasten and subdue. And I have felt
> A presence that disturbs me with the joy
> Of elevated thoughts; a sense sublime
> Of something far more deeply interfused,
> Whose dwelling is the light of setting suns,
> And the round ocean, and the living air,
> And the blue sky, and in the mind of man,
> A motion and a spirit, that impels
> All thinking things, all objects of all thought,
> And rolls through all things.

William Wordsworth

Lyrical Ballads (1798)

Emyr Humphreys

Dywed nodyn Syr Thomas Parry ar ddiwedd *Blodeugerdd Rhydychen o Farddoniaeth Gymraeg* mai hen fesur traethodl a ddefnyddiwyd gan Dafydd ap Gwilym sy'n cynnal y gerdd swynol hon. Rhyfedd o beth oedd cyfoeth y corff o farddas gan feirdd anhysbys a ddaeth i'r golwg yn llawysgrifau'r unfed ganrif ar bymtheg. Tra oedd beirdd y tywysogion yn cymhlethu cerdd dafod er mwyn diogelu eu statws, mynnai cenedlaethau o feirdd llai uchelgeisiol ganu yn eu ffordd eu hunain am y gwych a'r gwael ym mywyd beunyddiol y werin bobl. Prin bod enghraifft well o ddwyster ffyddlondeb merch ifanc at ei chariad mewn llenyddiaeth na'r gerdd hon. Nid oes gwell enghraifft chwaith o deithi naturiol yr iaith lafar at farddoniaeth pan mae hi'n cael llonydd megis i ddatblygu yn ei thir ei hun.

~

Sir Thomas Parry's note in *The Oxford Book of Welsh Verse* states that this charming poem is based on the *traethodl* metre as used by Dafydd ap Gwilym. The wealth of poetry by unknown poets that has been found in sixteenth-century manuscripts is amazing. Whilst the poets of the princes were complicating poetic art in order to secure their status, generations of less ambitious poets insisted on singing in their own particular way about the great and not so great aspects of everyday life of ordinary folk. There is scarcely a better example in literature than this poem of the intensity of a young girl's faithfulness to her lover. There is no better example either of the natural poetic qualities of the spoken language when it is given peace as it were to develop in its own right.

Crys y Mab

Fal yr oeddwn yn golchi
Dan ben pont Aberteifi,
A golchffon aur yn fy llaw,
A chrys fy nghariad danaw,
Fo ddoeth ata' ŵr ar farch
Ysgwydd lydan, buan, balch,
Ac a ofynnodd im a werthwn
Grys y mab mwya' a garwn.

Ac a ddoedais i na werthwn
Er canpunt nac er canpwn,
Nac er lloned y ddwy fron
O fyllt a defed gwynion,
Nac er lloned dau goetge
O ychen dan eu hieue,
Na er lloned Llanddewi
O lysiau wedi sengi.
Faldyna'r modd y cadwn
Grys y mab mwya' a garwn.

Anon.

The Oxford Book of Welsh Verse, ed. Thomas Parry
(Oxford University Press, 1962)

Languages should resound with the music of their poets. Words like
tenant and lease and rent are the staple diet of any Housing Act: they
occur in newspaper adverts from one end of the English-speaking
world to the other. When a poet like George Herbert takes hold of
them they become working parts of a miraculous machine that can
provide us with a visionary understanding of the human condition.
In my youth it always seemed to me that the Welsh connections of
Donne, Herbert and Vaughan somehow could supply keys to a
deeper understanding of their mysterious powers. As in this poem
they had a capacity to see through the light of common day and
discern another reality. I longed to detect in their work a
continuation of the imaginative dexterity of the late medieval
aristocratic Welsh poets who practised their art in the same
landscape. Surely they shared the same taste for extravagant conceits
and those poetic cadenzas known as *dyfalu*. More soberly I came to
realize that these are qualities shared by many poets in many
languages. All the same it still makes me cross to see arrogant
scholarly notes describe the Herberts as a Norman family on the
Welsh border, and Vaughan and his twin as characteristic products
of Jesus College, Oxford.

Redemption

Having been tenant long to a rich Lord,
Not thriving, I resolved to be bold,
And make a suit unto him, to afford
A new small-rented lease, and cancell th'old.

In heaven at his manor I him sought:
They told me there, that he was lately gone
About some land, which he had dearly bought
Long since on earth, to take possession.

I straight return'd, and knowing his great birth,
Sought him accordingly in great resorts,
In cities, theatres, gardens, parks, and courts:
At length I heard a ragged noise and mirth
Of thieves and murderers: there I him espied,
Who straight, *Your suit is granted*, said, & died.

George Herbert

From *The Temple*, 1633, *The Works of George Herbert* (Clarendon Press, 1941)

John Humphrys

My favourite poem: there are many, but since yours is a Welsh publication, I have to choose 'Fern Hill' by Dylan Thomas.

Like all good poems, it must be read aloud, or perhaps I should say 'sung aloud', because that is the effect of reading the best of Thomas. The poem evokes pure joy, tinged with the deepest melancholy: the careless pleasures of youth and the knowledge that they will come to an end. The best way to visit Fern Hill is in the imagination. With Thomas to paint the pictures, you don't need to make the journey.

Fern Hill

Now as I was young and easy under the apple boughs
About the lilting house and happy as the grass was green,
   The night above the dingle starry,
     Time let me hail and climb
   Golden in the heydays of his eyes,
And honoured among wagons I was prince of the apple towns
And once below a time I lordly had the trees and leaves
     Trail with daisies and barley
   Down the rivers of the windfall light.

And I was green and carefree, famous among the barns
About the happy yard and singing as the farm was home,
   In the sun that is young once only,
     Time let me play and be
   Golden in the mercy of his means,
And green and golden I was huntsman and herdsman, the calves
Sang to my horn, the foxes on the hill barked clear and cold,
     And the sabbath rang slowly
   In the pebbles of the holy streams.

All the sun long it was running, it was lovely, the hay
Fields high as the house, the tunes from the chimneys, it was air
    And playing, lovely and watery
     And fire green as grass.

And nightly under the simple stars
As I rode to sleep the owls were bearing the farm away,
All the moon long I heard, blessed among stables, the nightjars
    Flying with the ricks, and the horses
        Flashing into the dark.

And then to awake, and the farm, like a wanderer white
With the dew, come back, the cock on his shoulder: it was all
    Shining, it was Adam and maiden,
        The sky gathered again
    And the sun grew round that very day.
So it must have been after the birth of the simple light
In the first, spinning place, the spellbound horses walking warm
    Out of the whinnying green stable
        On to the fields of praise.

And honoured among foxes and pheasants by the gay house
Under the new made clouds and happy as the heart was long,
    In the sun born over and over,
        I ran my heedless ways,
    My wishes raced through the house high hay
And nothing I cared, at my sky blue trades, that time allows
In all his tuneful turning so few and such morning songs
    Before the children green and golden
        Follow him out of grace,

Nothing I cared, in the lamb white days, that time would take me
Up to the swallow thronged loft by the shadow of my hand,
    In the moon that is always rising,
        Nor that riding to sleep
    I should hear him fly with the high fields
And wake to the farm forever fled from the childless land.
Oh as I was young and easy in the mercy of his means,
        Time held me green and dying
    Though I sang in my chains like the sea.

Dylan Thomas

Collected Poems, 1934–1952 (Dent, 1952)

Dafydd Hywel

Mae'r gerdd hon yn dweud y cwbwl imi am fy nghenedlaetholdeb ac fy nheimlad am y wlad a'i phobol. Yn amal dwy yn bersonol yn digalonni ynglŷn â difaterwch y bobol sy'n trigo yn y wlad fechan hon, ond ar ddiwedd y dydd nid bai Cymru fo hynny.

Pam o pam nad ŷn ni fel pobol yn parchu ein hetifeddiaeth? Hanner siawns mae llawer o'n cyd-Gymry yn clochdar am bwysigrwydd ac enwogrwydd y wlad dros Glawdd Offa, er fod ein hanes ni yn llawer mwy diddorol.

Ond fel mae'r gerdd yn gorffen, fedrai un ddilorni Cymru faint a fynnai ond – 'Duw a'm gwaredo, ni allaf ddianc rhag HON'.

~

This poem says everything to me about my nationalism and my feeling for the country and her people. Often I am personally disheartened by the indifference of the people who live in this small country, but at the end of the day that isn't Wales's fault.

Why, oh why don't we as a people respect our inheritance? Given half a chance many of our fellow Welsh people boast about the importance and fame of the country the other side of Offa's Dyke, although our history is a lot more interesting.

But as the poem ends, one could abuse Wales as much as one would wish to but – 'God deliver me, I cannot escape from THIS'.

('Hon' was also chosen by Harold Carter and appears on page 31)

Sir Geoffrey Inkin

This ageless piece of writing indicates that political correctness is not a new phenomenon!

London, 1802

Milton! thou shouldst be living at this hour:
England hath need of thee: she is a fen
Of stagnant waters: altar, sword, and pen,
Fireside, the heroic wealth of hall and bower,
Have forfeited their ancient English dower
Of inward happiness. We are selfish men;
O raise us up, return to us again,
And give us manners, virtue, freedom, power!
Thy soul was like a Star, and dwelt apart;
Thou hadst a voice whose sound was like the sea:
Pure as the naked heavens, majestic, free.
So didst thou travel on life's common way,
In cheerful godliness; and yet by heart
The lowliest duties on herself did lay.

William Wordsworth

Poetical Works, ed. T. Hutchinson (Oxford University Press, 1905)

While this seems like a good recipe for an interesting life and very incorrect!

First Fig

My candle burns at both ends;
It will not last the night;
But ah, my foes, and oh, my friends –
It gives a lovely light!

Edna St Vincent Millay

Collected Poems, ed. Norma Millay (Harper Brothers, New York, 1920)

Nigel Jenkins

It is, of course, impossible: one has too many 'favourite poems' to be able to settle comfortably on just one. But here is *a* favourite, with a few words attempting to explain my enthusiasm for it.

If, as a young poet, you write in Welsh your culture may oblige you with the services of an 'athro barddol' (bardic teacher); but if you flop into this world with English as the first language that greets your ears, you're out there largely on your own. When I started trying to write poetry at the age of sixteen I had everything to learn and no one to teach me, apart from the two Dylans (disastrous influences) and the pop lyricists. My education really began when I discovered Penguin's series of modern poets in translation, and Federico García Lorca (1898–1936) in particular.

This poem, from the most famous book in the whole of Spanish literature, is Lorca at his wonder-working best. He was both a hugely popular people's poet and as restlessly modern an artist as it was possible to be, without spinning off into the lonely wardrobes of hermetic incomprehensibility.

Lorca loved the sensuous, dignified, persecuted gypsy culture of his native Andalusia. The gypsies, as he re-imagines them in his poetry, represent not only 'the fire, blood and alphabet of Andalusian and universal truth' but the essence of his own artistic and sexual personality. Against them stand the forces of repression and death, embodied above all by the paramilitary Civil Guard.

The luscious, dangerous electricities that surge through this non-imagist, non-touristic poem recreate, in the foreshortened narrative of an hour's intense pleasure, the complex tensions of an entire society.

'La Casada Infiel' has been translated into English by dozens of poets, but no one, I think, has done a better job than Swansea's own Malcolm Parr.

The Unfaithful Wife

And I took her down to the river,
thinking she was a virgin
but she had a husband.

118

All this took place on St James's night,
and almost as if it had to.
The streetlamps had gone out,
and the crickets were blazing fire.
When we reached the street corner
I touched her sleeping breasts,
and suddenly they opened up for me
like sprays of hyacinth.
The starch in her petticoat
rustled in my ears
like a piece of silk
torn by ten knives.
The silver light gone from their branches,
the trees loom larger,
and a horizon of dogs
barks far from the river.

We passed the blackberry bushes,
the rushes and the hawthorn.
Under her mane of thick hair
I made a hollow in the sand.
I took off my tie.
She took off her dress.
I took off my belt and revolver.
She took off her four petticoats.
Neither tuberoses nor seashells
have such delicate skin,
nor do mirrors by moonlight
shine with such brilliance.
Her thighs escaped me
like fish surprised,
half-filled with fire
half-filled with cold.
That night I ran
the best of roads,
riding a filly of mother-of-pearl
without reins or stirrups.
As a man I have no wish
to repeat the things she said to me.
The light of understanding
makes me most discreet.
I took her, stained with kisses and sand,

away from the river,
the sword blades of the iris
waging war with the air.

I behaved like the man I am.
Like a true gipsy,
I gave her a big sewing basket
of straw-coloured satin as a present.
And I didn't want to fall in love
because she had a husband
although she told me she was a virgin
when I took her down to the river.

Federico García Lorca

'La Casada Infiel', *Romancero Gitano (Gypsy Ballads)*,
translated by Malcolm Parr, *Serious Games* (Swansea Poetry Workshop, 1992)

'The Unfaithful Wife'. Graphics by William Brown.

Peter Johnson

My choice is the work of John Betjeman.

The English set poets of schooldays appealed little. Milton was fine, Blake too, good muscular stuff. But Wordsworth and the gang, no thanks. By the sixth form I was firmly in the twentieth-century camp. I read and enjoyed from Edward Thomas to Dylan Thomas, T. S. Eliot to D. J. Enright.

When I was a boy we would take our summer holidays in Slough, one of the great centres of Welsh migration in the thirties and there I came upon John Betjeman. His famous 1937 poem called 'Slough' seemed to be known by everyone. Not surprising. Few towns can have suffered so much at the hands of a literary adversary.

> Come friendly bombs, and fall on Slough,
> It isn't fit for humans now . . .

brilliantly caught Betjeman's thoughts on the outcome of the alliance between the needs of modern manufacturing and the solutions of modern architecture.

Forty years later, the maestro turned from the barren buildings of the age to the empty people who inhabited the offices. 'Executive' is a hatchet job, executed in meticulous rhyme and with accuracy. You *know* this man, don't you?

Executive

I am a young executive. No cuffs than mine are cleaner;
I have a Slimline briefcase and I use the firm's Cortina.
In every roadside hostelry from here to Burgess Hill
The *maitres d'hotel* all know me well and let me sign the bill.

You ask me what it is I do. Well actually, you know,
I'm partly a liaison man and partly P.R.O.
Essentially I integrate the current export drive
And basically I'm viable from ten o'clock till five.

For vital off-the-record work – that's talking transport-wise –
I've a scarlet Aston Martin – and does she go? She flies!
Pedestrians and dogs and cats – we mark them down for slaughter.
I also own a speed-boat which has never touched the water.

She's built of fibre-glass of course. I call her 'Mandy-Jane.'
After a bird I used to know – No soda, please, just plain –
And how did I acquire her? Well to tell you about that
And to put you in the picture I must wear my other hat.

I do some mild developing. The sort of place I need
Is a quiet country market town that's rather run to seed
A luncheon and a drink or two, a little *savoir faire* –
I fix the Planning Officer, the Town Clerk and the Mayor.

And if some preservationist attempts to interfere
A 'dangerous structure' notice from the Borough Engineer
Will settle any buildings that are standing in our way –
The modern style, sir, with respect, has really come to stay.

John Betjeman

A Nip in the Air (John Murray, 1974)

Alwyn Rice Jones

This is a gem of a poem about the way 'power' has been both a destructive and a constructive element in history. In these words, skilfully put together in the form of a parable by the priest–poet R. S. Thomas, we discover that these elements of power continually work in ourselves.

The physical power of the Pharaohs once broke the backs and the personalities of the people who were slaves to the system. The arguments of philosophers in Delphi provided answers to problems – thus manipulating people's process of thinking and acting.

But the Judaean experience was rather different – Jesus was the Son of God. The Gospel – The Good News – was a person. People have been invited ever since to respond to this Gospel.

Leonardo da Vinci possessed the truth and psychological approach of the Gospel and this was enshrined in the 'loving' smile on his Madonna. But, the poet asks, is this a reflection of what goes on – or does not go on – in our modern machine-driven age?

The *five* pictures of this poem can also be applied to the situation faced by Shelter Cymru. Shelter is a movement contending against power in the physical sense as well as the power of rational or logical thinking – both seeking to manipulate people. However, when the ill-devised plans of governments and landlordism are placed against the values of the Gospel and the concern for the loving care of persons in society, then we are facing an entirely different humane and Christian situation.

Power

Under the Pharaohs it was power;
backs broke under the stones
for galleries where the mice play.

At Delphi the power shifted
to the mind that gave uncomfortable
answers to its own questions.

In Judaea it was the beginning
of an ability to play blind
for tall stakes at the foot of the cross.

Leonardo possessed it,
but the price to be paid
was that the smile of his Madonna

was a reflection of the smile
on the countenance of the machine
he was in adultery with.

R. S. Thomas

Counterpoint (Bloodaxe Books, 1990)

Barry Jones

Favourite is too strong a word. But R. S. Thomas's works are informative for parliamentarians. It is a bitter poem – a perfectly presented, nicely balanced literary missile. A guerrilla's shot from the hillside as it were.

It is topical. Caernarvon Castle is to be 'privatized'. The Royals are very topical too. He has fired off a fusillade at the Welsh Establishment. Perhaps the Citizen's Charter has led to cleaner streets?!

He takes a poke at the clergy yet he is a priest himself. I heard him in September, interviewed on Radio 4. Such a cultured, quiet, refined voice for a rebel. Such bitter, cynical, brilliant, nasty poems.

I am not even a closet Nationalist. But it seems to me that Wales will have an Assembly, an embryonic parliament, before the end of the century. He has encouraged protests to put it mildly. The next century might see some of his objectives realized.

I believe his reputation as a poet will grow. He reminds me of Courbet, the nineteenth-century French painter: an uncompromising customer! The Literary City would say, 'Buy his Shares'.

To Pay for His Keep

So this was on the way
to a throne! He looked round
at the perspiring ranks
of ageing respectables:
police, tradesmen, councillors,
rigid with imagined
loyalty; and beyond them at
the town with its mean streets and
pavements filthy with
dog shit.
        The castle was
huge. All that dead weight
of the past, that overloading
of the law's mounting
equipment! A few medals

would do now. He permitted
himself a small smile,
sipping at it in the mind's
coolness.
      And never noticed,
because of the dust raised
by the prayers of the fagged
clergy, that far hill
in the sun with the long line
of its trees climbing
it like a procession
of young people, young as himself.

R. S. Thomas

What is a Welshman? (Christopher Davies, 1974)

Bobi Jones

Hoff gerdd? Rhaid mai 'Mair Fadlen' gan Saunders Lewis ydyw.

Gellid dadlau ynghylch cerdd 'fwyaf' y byd i gyd. Byddwn yn barod ddigon i droi i Michelangelo Buonarroti i fodloni fy marn ar hynny. Yn wir, pe'm holid ynghylch cerdd 'fwyaf' y Gymraeg, teimlwn yn weddol fodlon mai 'Marwnad Llywelyn ap Gruffudd' gan Ruffudd ab yr Ynad Coch yn y drydedd ganrif ar ddeg fyddai f'ateb. Ond nid am 'fawredd' y gofynnwyd, ond hoffter personol.

Rhaid mai cerdd Gymraeg fydd yr ateb felly. A ninnau yng Nghymru yn syllu i lawr llwnc difancoll diwylliannol unigolyddol a'n hunaniaeth yn wynebu tranc terfynol neu adfywiad rhyfeddol – ac yn hyn o beth yn cyfrannu yn ddramatig ac yn drawmatig mewn argyfwng rhyngwladol na ŵyr y gwledydd gorfawr ddim amdano. Rhaid i'm dewis lefaru mewn iaith o ganol hyn. Ni wna ond y Gymraeg y tro. Ac am yr un rheswm rhaid iddi darddu o amgylchfyd gweddol gyfoes er bod marwnad Gruffudd ab yr Ynad Coch yn od o berthnasol heddiw.

O ran deallusrwydd a dychymyg dramatig, o ran synwyrusrwydd ffurfiol, mae hon yn gerdd sy'n fy modloni'n llwyr. Dywed rywbeth o bwys am bobl, am eu dimensiwn corfforol a'u dimensiwn ysbrydol, am eu hanghenion daearol a thragwyddol mewn rhythmau manwl ac iaith ddofn ac ysgytwol. Mae'r 'naturiol' yma ynghyd â'r 'goruwchnaturiol' wedi'u cyflwyno mewn ieithwedd emosiynol a synhwyrus oedolyn, sy'n gamp gelfyddydol a phersonol gwbl anghyffredin.

~

Favourite poem? It has to be 'Mair Fadlen' by Saunders Lewis.

One can argue about the greatest poem in the world. I would be quite prepared to turn to Michelangelo Buonarroti to satisfy my opinion in that respect. Indeed, if I was asked about the greatest poem in Welsh I'm quite sure my answer would be 'Marwnad Llywelyn ap Gruffudd' by Gruffudd ab yr Ynad Coch in the thirteenth century. But I wasn't asked about 'greatness' but personal choice.

The answer has to be a Welsh poem therefore. And us in Wales staring down the gullet of cultural, individualistic perdition and our identity facing a final death or amazing revival – and in this contributing dramatically and traumatically in an international crisis the superpowers know nothing of. My choice must speak in a language from the heart of this. Only Welsh will do. And for the same reason it must spring from a relatively modern surrounding although Gruffudd ab yr Ynad Coch's elegy is oddly relevant today.

From the point of view of intelligence, dramatic imagination and formal sensuousness this is a poem which satisfies me completely. It says something of worth about people, about their physical and spiritual dimensions, about their earthly and eternal needs in detailed rhythms and deep, shocking language. The 'natural' is here together with the 'supernatural' presented in the emotional and sensuous literary style of an adult, which is a most unusual artistic and personal achievement.

Mair Fadlen

'Na chyffwrdd â mi'

Am wragedd ni all neb wybod. Y mae rhai,
Fel hon, y mae eu poen yn fedd clo;
Cleddir eu poen ynddynt, nid oes ffo
Rhagddo nac esgor arno. Nid oes drai
Na llanw ar eu poen, môr marw heb
Symud ar ei ddyfnder. Pwy – a oes neb –
A dreigla'r maen oddi ar y bedd dro?

Gwelwch y llwch ar y llwybr yn llusgo'n gloff;
Na, gedwch iddi, Mair sy'n mynd tua'i hedd,
Dyfnder yn galw ar ddyfnder, bedd ar fedd,
Celain yn tynnu at gelain yn y bore anhoff;
Tridiau bu hon mewn beddrod, mewn byd a ddibennwyd
Yn y ddiasbad brynhawn, y gair Gorffennwyd,
Y waedd a ddiwaedodd ei chalon fel blaen cledd.

Gorffennwyd, Gorffennwyd. Syrthiodd Mair o'r bryn
I geudod y Pasg olaf, i bwll byd
Nad oedd ond bedd, a'i anadl mewn bedd mud,
Syrthiodd Mair i'r tranc difancoll, syn,
Byd heb Grist byw, Sabath dychrynllyd y cread,
Pydew'r canmil canrifoedd a'u dilead,
Gorweddodd Mair ym meddrod y cread cryn.

Yng nghafn nos y synhwyrau, ym mhair y mwg;
Gwynnodd y gwallt mawr a sychasai ei draed,
Gwywodd holl flodau atgo' ond y gawod waed;
Cwmwl ar gwmwl yn ei lapio, a'u sawr drwg
Yn golsyn yn ei chorn gwddf, ac yn difa'i threm
Nes diffodd Duw â'u hofnadwyaeth lem,
Yn y cyd-farw, yn y cyd-gladdu dan wg.

Gwelwch hi, Niobe'r Crist, yn tynnu tua'r fron
Graig ei phoen i'w chanlyn o'r Pasg plwm
Drwy'r pylgain du, drwy'r gwlith oer, drwy'r llwch trwm,
I'r man y mae maen trymach na'i chalon don;
Afrwydd ymlwybra'r traed afrosgo dros ddraen
A thrafferth dagrau'n dyblu'r niwl o'i blaen,
A'i dwylo'n ymestyn tuag ato mewn hiraeth llwm.

Un moeth sy'n aros iddi dan y nef,
Un anwes ffarwel, mwynder atgofus, un
Cnawdolrwydd olaf, trist-ddiddanus, cun,
Cael wylo eto dros ei esgeiriau Ef,
Eneinio'r traed a golchi'r briwiau hallt,
Cusanu'r fferau a'u sychu eto â'i gwallt,
Cael cyffwrdd â Thi, Rabboni, O Fab y Dyn.

Tosturiwn wrthi. Ni thosturiodd Ef.
Goruwch tosturi yw'r cariad eirias, pur,
Sy'n haearneiddio'r sant drwy gur ar gur,
Sy'n erlid y cnawd i'w gaer yn yr enaid, a'i dref
Yn yr ysbryd nefol, a'i ffau yn y santeiddiolaf,
Sy'n llosgi a lladd a llarpio hyd y sgarmes olaf,
Nes noethi a chofleidio'i sglyfaeth â'i grafanc ddur.

Bychan a wyddai hi, chwe dydd cyn y Pasg,
Wrth dywallt y nard gwlyb gwerthfawr arno'n bwn,
Mai'n wir 'i'm claddedigaeth y cadwodd hi hwn';
Ni thybiodd hi fawr, a chued ei glod i'w thasg,
Na chyffyrddai hi eto fyth, fyth â'i draed na'i ddwylo;
Câi Thomas roi llaw yn ei ystlys; ond hi, er ei hwylo,
Mwyach dan drueni'r Bara y dôi iddi'r cnawd twn.

Dacw hi yn yr ardd ar glais y wawr;
Gwthia'i golygon tua'r ogof; rhed,
Rhed at ei gweddill gwynfyd. Och, a gred,
A gred hi i'w llygaid? Fod y maen ar lawr,
A'r bedd yn wag, y bedd yn fud a moel;
Yr hedydd cynta'n codi dros y foel
A nyth ei chalon hithau'n wag a siêd.

Mor unsain â cholomen yw ei chŵyn,
Fel Orphews am Ewridicê'n galaru
Saif rhwng y rhos a chrio heb alaru
'Maent wedi dwyn fy Arglwydd, wedi ei ddwyn',
Wrth ddisgybl ac wrth angel yr un llef
'Ac ni wn i ple y dodasant ef',
Ac wrth y garddwr yr un ymlefaru.

Hurtiwyd hi. Drylliwyd hi. Ymsuddodd yn ei gwae.
Mae'r deall yn chwil a'r rheswm ar chwâl, oni
Ddelo a'i cipia hi allan o'r cnawd i'w choroni –
Yn sydyn fel eryr o'r Alpau'n disgyn tua'i brae –
A'r cariad sy'n symud y sêr, y grym sy'n Air
I gyfodi a bywhau: 'a dywedodd Ef wrthi, Mair,
Hithau a droes a dywedodd wrtho, Rabboni'.

Saunders Lewis

Siwan a Cherddi Eraill (Llyfrau Dryw, 1956)

Derwyn Morris Jones

Cyfieithiad Saesneg rhagorol, yn dwyn yr enw 'Gravitas', a'm cyflwynodd gyntaf i'r gerdd gyffrous hon. Ymserchais ynddi ar unwaith. Ar y pryd yr oeddwn yn paratoi pregeth Gŵyl Ddewi i'w thraddodi, o bobman yn y byd, yn yr Eglwys Annibynnol Gymraeg yn Efrog Newydd! Yr oedd dau o'm hoff feirdd, Waldo a Gwenallt, eisoes wedi dod i'r adwy wrth i mi fyfyrio uwchben fy nhestun, sef geiriau'r Apostol Paul, 'Efe a wnaeth o un gwaed bob cenedl o ddynion.'

'Beth yw adnabod?' hola Waldo, gan ateb, 'Cael un gwraidd dan y canghennau'. Canfod er pob gwahaniaeth sydd rhyngom fel pobl – gwahaniaethau sy'n rhan o fwriad Crëwr daionus – ein hundod creiddiol, a llawenhau yn y naill beth a'r llall.

A dyma ddarganfod cerdd hyfryd Pennar Davies yn adrodd am ddigwyddiad syml y bu'n rhan ohono ar y Kingsway yn Abertawe wrth gerdded yno gyda'i fab Owain un diwrnod. 'Amnaïd ddireidus' y nawmlwydd ar lanc croenfrown, a'i wên yntau yn 'ateb hael a llawn i'r cyfarchiad hwyliog'. Peth bach yn wir rhwng dau, ond gwêl Pennar ynddo arwydd o'n gobaith yn hyn o fyd, a chyflawni bwriad ein creu.

Rwy'n dianc o'r swyddfa yn Tŷ John Penri, Abertawe, yn fynych ar yr awr ginio, a rhoi tro heibio Ffordd y Brenin sydd yn ymyl, a'r gerdd hon yn aml yn cadw cwmni i mi. Ond bûm hefyd yn ystod fy ymweliad ag Efrog Newydd yn Harlem, lle dywedwyd wrthyf ei bod yn rhy beryglus i ŵr diarth ddod mâs o'r car, heb sôn am gwrdd â llygaid rhywun a'i gyfarch.

Pa mor wir bynnag ysywaeth yw hynny, mentro ymuno yn y cyfarch llawen y sonia Pennar amdano yw ffordd gobaith a gorfoledd yng nghreadigaeth Duw.

~

An excellent English translation, entitled 'Gravitas', was my first introduction to this exciting poem. I fell in love with it at once. At the time I was preparing a St David's Day sermon to be delivered at, of all places, the Independent Welsh Church in New York! Two of my favourite poets, Waldo and Gwenallt, had already come to my aid as I pondered upon my text, namely the words of the Apostle Paul, 'He who from one blood made every nation of man.'

'What is knowing?' asks Waldo, his answer being, 'Having one root under the branches'. Discovering in spite of all the differences between us as people – differences which are part of the intention of a bountiful Creator – our central unity, and rejoicing in the one and the other.

And then I discovered Pennar Davies's beautiful poem recalling a simple happening he was part of as he walked along the Kingsway in Swansea one day with his son Owain. 'The playful nod' of the nine-year-old to the coloured boy, whose smile was 'a full and generous response to the happy greeting'. A small thing between two indeed, but Pennar saw in it a sign of our hope in this world and the fulfilment of the intention of our creation.

I often escape from the office in Tŷ John Penri, Swansea, in the lunch hour and go for a walk on the nearby Kingsway with this poem as my companion. But during my visit to New York I was also in Harlem where I was told it was too dangerous for a stranger to get out of the car, let alone catching someone's eye and greeting him.

However true that sadly may be, attempting to join in the happy greeting that Pennar mentioned is the way of hope and joy in God's creation.

Disgyrchiant

Bu gofod hael ac amser cyfrwys ac ynni siriol
a goleuni – ie, y goleuni sy'n llwyddo
i deithio'n gyson tua chwe miliwn miliwn
o filltiroedd y flwyddyn – yn cydfwriadu
i lunio
heddiw yn Ffordd y Brenin yn Abertawe
ymdaro wrth fodd eu calonnau.

Heddiw yn y stryd brysur a thrystiog
rhoddodd Owain naw mlwydd amnaïd ddireidus
lawn o gyfeillgarwch didelerau
ar lanc croenfrown, llygatchwim, wyneblwys,
main ac ystwyth o gorff,
llanc o'r India neu o Bacistan.
Wedi ennyd o betruster syn fe ddaeth ei wên,
yn ateb hael a llawn i'r cyfarchiad hwyliog.
Am eiliad lwythog unwyd
y lliwiau a'r cyfandiroedd.

Dadlennwyd y disgyrchiant cyntafanedig
a fyn dynnu ymwybod at ymwybod,
asbri at asbri, corff at gorff.
Llifodd o lygaid y naill i lygaid y llall
yr hyfrydwch sanctaidd.
Llamai rhyngddynt y trydan gorfoleddus
sydd yn datgan
mai un ac amryw yw ein dynoldeb,
mai arbennig a chyffredin yw pob enaid byw.

Onid yn y cyfarch hwn
yn nisgyrchiad yr ysbryd,
y mae ein gobaith?
Onid i ddadlennu'r disgyrchiant yma
y rhoddwyd y bachgennyn yn y canol?
Onid dyma pam y dywedwyd wrthym
am dderbyn y deyrnas fel dyn bach?
Onid y ffolineb ffieiddiaf
yw bod ofnau ac eiddigeddau
a gormes ein haeddfedrwydd
yn ein carcharu ni
rhag cydnabod ein gilydd
mor smala ac mor rhywiog?

Wrth ragweld y cyfarch hwn
y cydganodd sêr y bore.
I gael ymuno yn y cyfarch hwn
y llafuriodd Ewclid Lwys
a Galileo Sant
a Newton Wyn ac Einstein Fendigaid.

Pennar Davies

Llef: Casgliad o Gerddi (Cyhoeddiadau Barddas, 1987)

Gwyn Jones

I have never been someone who conforms for the sake of it. Life is too short always to take the 'easy route' and to keep doing the same old things that others have already done. There is much more fun and excitement in exploring new pastures and finding new ways of doing things.

Each time I'm tempted towards that 'easy route' this wonderful poem makes me think again.

So far it's been good advice.

The Road Not Taken

Two roads diverged in a yellow wood,
And sorry I could not travel both
And be one traveller, long I stood
And looked down one as far as I could
To where it bent in the undergrowth;

Then took the other, as just as fair,
And having perhaps the better claim,
Because it was grassy and wanted wear;
Though as for that the passing there
Had worn them really about the same,

And both that morning equally lay
In leaves no step had trodden black.
Oh, I kept the first for another day!
Yet knowing how way leads on to way,
I doubted if I should ever come back.

I shall be telling this with a sigh
Somewhere ages and ages hence:
Two roads diverged in a wood, and I –
I took the one less travelled by,
And that has made all the difference.

Robert Frost

Complete Poems of Robert Frost (Jonathan Cape, 1951)

Harri Pritchard Jones

Fy newis ydy 'I'r Lleidr Da' gan Saunders Lewis. Y rheswm dros ei dewis hi ydy ei bod yn gyfuniad mor ddiddorol a chyffrous o'r ysbrydol a'r materol a'r cnawdol; yn eu priodi mewn paradocsau sy'n llawn tyndra creadigol. Yn priodi ieithwedd dyner a dyrchafol efo geiriau a disgrifiadau cignoeth o arw a ffiaidd; yn mynegi mor wallgof ydy ffydd, chwedl Kierkegaard, yn union fel y mae syrthio mewn cariad. Yr un pryd, drwy'r dryswch a'r budreddi a'r ing fe ddatgelir anferthedd y cariad hwnnw ac urddas Duw a dyn.

Cerdd fawr iawn yn fy meddwl bach i.

~

My choice is 'I'r Lleidr Da' by Saunders Lewis. The reason for choosing it is that it is such an interesting and exciting combination of the spiritual, the material and the physical; marrying them in paradoxes which are full of creative tension. Marrying tender and elevating diction with painfully harsh and hateful words and descriptions; expressing the madness of faith, to quote Kierkegaard, just as is falling in love. At the same time through the confusion, the filth and the anguish the enormity of that love is revealed and the dignity of God and man.

An enormous poem in my little mind.

I'r Lleidr Da

Ni welaist ti Ef ar fynydd y Gweddnewid
  Na'r nos yn cerdded y lli;
Ni welaist erioed gelanedd yn gwrido pan drewid
  Elor a bedd gan ei gri.

Ar awr ei gignoethi a'i faw y gwelaist ti Ef,
  Dan chwip a than ddrain,
A'i hoelio'n sach o esgyrn tu allan i'r dref
  Ar bolyn, fel bwgan brain.

Ni chlywaist ti lunio'r damhegion fel Parthenon iaith,
  Na'i dôn wrth sôn am ei Dad,
Cyfrinion yr oruwch ystafell ni chlywaist chwaith,
  Na'r weddi cyn Cedron a'r brad.

Mewn ysbleddach torf o sadyddion yn gloddest ar wae,
   A'u sgrech, udo, rheg a chri,
Y clywaist ti ddolef ddofn tor calon eu prae,
   'Paham y'm gadewaist i?'

Tithau ynghrog ar ei ddeau; ar ei chwith, dy frawd;
   Yn gwingo fel llyffaint bling,
Chweinllyd ladronach a daflwyd yn osgordd i'w wawd,
   Gwŷr llys i goeg frenin mewn ing.

O feistr cwrteisi a moes, pwy oleuodd i ti
   Dy ran yn y parodi garw?
'Arglwydd, pan ddelych i'th deyrnas, cofia fi,'–
   Y deyrnas a drechwyd drwy farw.

Rex Judaeorum; ti gyntaf a welodd y coeg
   Gabledd yn oracl byw,
Ti gyntaf a gredodd i'r Lladin, Hebraeg a Groeg,
   Fod crocbren yn orsedd Duw.

O leidr a ddug Baradwys oddi ar hoelion stanc,
   Flaenor bonedd y nef,
Gweddïa fel y rhodder i ninnau cyn awr ein tranc
   Ei ganfod a'i brofi Ef.

Saunders Lewis

Byd a Betws (Gwasg Aberystwyth, 1941)

Ieuan Wyn Jones

Dyma gopi o'm hoff gerdd, sef 'Yr Afon' – detholiad o bryddest Caradog Prichard 'Y Briodas'.

~

Here is a copy of my favourite poem, namely 'Yr Afon' – an extract from Caradog Prichard's *pryddest* 'Y Briodas'.

Yr Afon

Pan glywais Wyry'r marian
    Yn seinio gynta'r gair,
Nid oedd ond milltir arian,
    O'm llwybyr yn y gwair;
'Tyrd, tyrd', meddai hi, 'mae 'ngwyrthiau'n stôr
O Dy'n y Maes i donnau môr'.

O filmil llygaid gleision
    Dôi'i gwahodd uwch fy mhen;
Hedydd a chog oedd gweision
    Huotla'r Wyry wen;
Ond pan gyrhaeddais Bont y Tŵr
Rhoes bun ei darlun yn y dŵr.

Dyfnach oedd glas ei llygaid
    Na'r glas rhwng dail y coed,
A syllai â'i holl enaid
    I fyny yn ôl fy nhroed,
Ac yn fy mlaen yr euthum i
A mynd â'r darlun hefo mi.

Ac O! mae'r gwyrthiau olaf
    Yn awr yn dod i'm rhan;
Yn ofer mwy yr holaf
    Am gwmni fy nwy lan,
A syllu'r wyf trwy'r llygaid glas
O donnau môr ar Dy'n y Maes.

Caradog Prichard

Cerddi: Y Casgliad Cyflawn (Christopher Davies, 1979)

John Elfed Jones

Wedi hir bendroni, y gerdd sy'n golygu cymaint imi, ac un rwy'n hynod hoff ohoni, yw cerdd a sgrifennodd Euryn Ogwen i mi ar fy ymddeoliad o fod yn Gadeirydd Bwrdd yr Iaith Gymraeg yn 1993.

Y rheswm am y dewis? Yn ystod fy mywyd cefais y fraint o fod yn rhan o nifer helaeth o gyrff a sefydliadau, pob un yn ei wahanol ffordd yn cyfrannu at ddiwylliant ein gwlad ac er budd y gymdeithas sydd ohoni yng Nghymru. Er profi siom sawl tro, cefais bleser digymysg o fod yn rhan o'r llu fudiadau sy'n gwneud cymaint dros Gymru: yr Urdd, yr Eisteddfod, Prifysgol Cymru, Coleg Harlech, y Llyfrgell Genedlaethol – mae'r rhestr yn faith, a'r gwaith a wnaed ac a wneir yn glodwiw.

Ac yna ffurfiwyd Bwrdd yr Iaith i gynghori'r Llywodraeth ar yr hyn y dylesid ei wneud i hybu'r iaith. 'Roedd disgwyliadau'r Cymry Cymraeg yn uchel – yn oruchel, ac yn amhosib i'w cyflawni o fewn y gyfundrefn wleidyddol sy'n bodoli ym Mhrydain.

Penderfynodd Bwrdd yr Iaith amcanu at yr hyn y tybient oedd yn ymarferol bosib – ac 'roedd 'na lawer yn barnu nad oedd hi'n bosib i'r Bwrdd ddylanwadu ar y Llywodraeth i ddwyn Mesur Iaith newydd gerbron y Senedd – ond fe aed ati i ymladd y frwydr holl bwysig honno.

Cyfnod diflas, yn bersonol, oedd y pum mlynedd o 1988 hyd at 1993. 'Roedd 'na foddhad, wrth gwrs, wrth i strategaeth y Bwrdd Iaith ddechrau argyhoeddi y Llywodraeth fod angen ystyried Deddf Iaith newydd – ond roedd na ddiflastod hefyd yn yr ymgecru di-ddiwedd sy'n rhan o'n natur ni fel Cymry.

'Roedd y boen yn fwy na'r pleser yn aml iawn – ac 'roedd ffieidd-dra personol nifer o Gymry Cymraeg yn gadael craith. Cafwyd cwpled i'r iaith ar raglen radio *Talwrn y Beirdd* a oedd yn datgan yn gryno ac yn union sut y teimlwn yn ystod y cyfnod hwnnw:

> Mae poen yn ei chwmpeini
> A siom yn ei hymgom hi.

Pan benderfynais ymddeol o Gadeiryddiaeth y Bwrdd Iaith wedi sicrhau Deddf Iaith newydd – cyflwynodd fy nghyd-aelodau y gerdd yma gan Euryn Ogwen imi. Mae'n ymgorffori yn berffaith sut y teimlwn, a pham na allaf fyth roi'r gorau i weithio dros yr iaith yn fy ffordd fach fy hun.

~

After much thought, the poem that means so much to me, and one that I'm extremely fond of, is a poem that Euryn Ogwen wrote for me on my retirement as Chairman of the Welsh Language Board in 1993.

The reason for the choice? During my life I have had the honour of being part of a large number of bodies and movements, every one in its different way contributing to the culture of our country and to the benefit of society in Wales. In spite of experiencing disappointment on many occasions, I had the undivided pleasure of being associated with numerous movements which do so much for Wales: the Welsh League of Youth, the Eisteddfod, the University of Wales, Harlech College, the National Library – the list is a long one, and the work completed, together with that in progress, is most commendable.

And then the Welsh Language Board was formed to advise the Government on what should be done to promote the language. The expectations of Welsh speakers in Wales were high – too high – and impossible to accomplish within the political framework that exists in Britain.

The Language Board decided to aim at that which was practically possible – and many were of the opinion that it was not possible for the Board to influence the Government to bring a new Language Bill before Parliament – but one set forth to fight that vital battle.

On a personal level the five years from 1988 to 1993 were a miserable period. There was satisfaction, of course, as the Language Board's strategy began to convince the Government of the need to consider a new Language Act – but there was also disgust in the endless squabbling which is part of our Welsh nature.

Frequently the pain was greater than the pleasure – and the personal hatred of many Welsh speakers left its scar. There was a couplet about the language on the radio programme *Talwrn y Beirdd* which stated concisely and totally how I felt during that period:

> There is pain in her company
> and disappointment in her conversation.

When I decided to retire from the Chairmanship of the Language Board, having ensured a new Language Act, my fellow members presented me with this poem by Euryn Ogwen. It embodies perfectly how I felt and why I can never stop working for the language in my own little way.

I J.E.J.

Pan fyddi'n troi at lan rhyw afon dawel,
neu rwyfo'r cwch cyn lluchio'r lein i'r dŵr,
pan glywi sŵn ei chwynfan ar yr awel
a'r dail yn troi a bygwth storm, rwy'n siwr
y byddi dithau'n diawlio'i phresenoldeb –
dyheu am beidio'i chario ar dy gefn.
Ni'th ad yn llonydd byth. Hyd dragwyddoldeb
mi fydd yn hongian arnat – dyna'r drefn.

Ond wedi bachu'r 'sgodyn a'r ymrafael,
wrth dynnu'r anwadalwch byw i'r lan,
mi deimli bwysau'r lludded yn dy adael
a balchder buddugoliaeth fydd dy ran.

Nyddwyd edau'n hanfod mewn oes o'r blaen
i weu y rhwyd sy'n gallu dal y straen.

Euryn Ogwen

R. Brinley Jones

Pan dderbyniais wahoddiad i fod yn Bennaeth Coleg Llanymddyfri a minnau ar y pryd yn Gyfarwyddwr Gwasg Prifysgol Cymru yng Nghaerdydd, roeddwn mewn tipyn o benbleth. Roedd yn rhaid pwyso a mesur y manteision a'r anfanteision o symud o ferw byw reit ynghanol prifddinas Cymru, gyda'r theatr a'r opera a'r llyfrgell a'r siopau, i ganol y wlad. Gwyddwn am draddodiad gwiw a diddorol Coleg Llanymddyfri a'i hanes yn estyn yn ôl i gyfnod chwyldroadau mawr y bedwaredd ganrif ar bymtheg: bu'r athrawon ifainc disglair yno yn trafod y maniffesto Comiwnyddol oedd newydd ei gyfansoddi. Gwyddwn ychydig am ogoniant y wlad o gwmpas Llanymddyfri – ond yn fwy na dim enwau William Williams Pantycelyn, y Pêr Ganiedydd, a Rhys Prichard, yr Hen Ficer, y ddau a fu'n anadlu awelon y Tywi ac a orffwysai hefyd yn ei sŵn – dyna beth a olygai'r dref i mi. Yn wir i grwt bach a fagwyd yn ardal y cymoedd glo, bu cannwyll y ficer a her yr emynydd yn cyhoeddi arbenigrwydd y dref hyfryd honno a orweddai ynghanol y dyfroedd – y Tywi, y Brân, y Gwydderig a'r Bawddwr.

Bellach pwysais lawer ar brofiad a chyngor y Ficer Prichard a aned yn y dref yn 1579 ac a fu farw yno yn 1644. Yr unig egwyl oddi yno oedd ei arhosiad yng Ngholeg Iesu, Rhydychen – lle bûm innau'n fyfyriwr ganrifoedd wedyn. Ymdrechodd Rhys Prichard yn deg i argyhoeddi ei gyd-ddynion am efengyl iachawdwriaeth a cheisiodd gynnig patrwm o safon bywyd. Roedd iechyd cymdeithas yn bwysig iddo. Roedd gofal ei blwyfolion ac yn wir ei gyd-Gymry yn ysgogiad i gyfansoddi'r gwersi ar gân – a hynny mewn iaith seml, ddealladwy a adnabyddir bellach fel *Cannwyll y Cymry*.

Dewisais y penillion hyn – drosiad o'r ganfed salm – fel datganiad o'm diolch innau ac er mwyn cofio'r cymwynaswr Rhys Prichard, Ficer Llanymddyfri, a gynigiodd ymgeledd i'w gyd-ddynion a hynny am genedlaethau. Mae'r dewis yn fy atgoffa hefyd am dafodiaith bert Llanymddyfri, dref a fu mor annwyl gennyf ac a fu mor garedig i mi a'm teulu. Bydd y 'gannwyll' yn dal i'm goleuo pan fydd y ffordd yn dywyll ac yn llithrig.

~

On receiving an invitation to become Principal of Llandovery College whilst Director of the University of Wales Press in Cardiff, my mind was in a quandary. One had to weigh up the advantages and disadvantages of moving from the bustle of life in the heart of

Wales's capital with its theatre, opera, library and shops to the middle of the countryside. I knew of the interesting and worthy tradition of Llandovery College with its history stretching back to the great revolutionary period of the last century: the young talented teachers there discussed the Communist Manifesto which had recently been published. I knew something of the splendour of the countryside around Llandovery, but more than anything the names of William Williams Pantycelyn, 'Y Pêr Ganiedydd', and Rhys Prichard, 'Yr Hen Ficer', both of whom breathed the breezes of the Tywi and rested in its sound – that's what the town meant to me. Indeed to a small boy brought up in the industrial valleys, the candle of the vicar and the challenge of the hymnist proclaimed the distinctiveness of that beautiful town, which nestled in the midst of the waters of the Tywi, the Brân, the Gwydderig and the Bawddwr.

I also leaned heavily on the experience and advice of Vicar Prichard who was born in the town in 1579 and who died there in 1644. His only time away from there was spent in Jesus College, Oxford – where I too was a student centuries later. Rhys Prichard endeavoured to convince his fellow men of the gospel of salvation and tried to offer a set of standards to live by. Society's health was important to him. The care of his parishioners and indeed his fellow Welshmen moved him to compose the lessons in verse – and that in simple, understandable language which is now known as *Cannwyll y Cymry*.

I chose these verses – a metaphor of the 100th Psalm – as a declaration of my thanks and in order to remember the benefactor, Rhys Prichard, the Vicar of Llandovery, who offered succour to his fellow men for generations to come. The choice reminds me also of the beautiful Llandovery dialect, a town that's been so dear to me and so kind to me and my family. The 'candle' will continue to enlighten me when the road is dark and slippery.

Psalm 100

Dewch holl dylwythe'r ddaiar,
Dewch bawb a llawen lafar:
Cenwch glod a chalon rwydd,
I Dduw, ein Harglwydd hygar.

Dewch fawr a bach drachefen,
Dewch bawb sy'n troedo'r ddairen,
Dewch addolwch Dduw yn *llon,   * llawen
Bob rhai a chalon lawen.

Gwybyddwch hyn yn siccir,
Mae'r Arglwydd grassol, geirwir,
Y sydd Frenin nef a llawr,
Ac *Emprwr mawr yr holl dir.   * pennaeth

Gwybyddwch nad chwi'ch hunain
Ach gwnaeth o'r pridd mor gywrain:
Ei waith ef ych o'r llwch a'r llaid,
Ei blant a'i ddefaid bychain.

O Dewch iw byrth gan hynny,
Dan ddiolch a than ganu,
Fach a mawr ar fore a hwyr,
Yn *brudd iw lwyr foliannu.   * o ddifrif

O Dewch iw Demel sanctaidd,
Yn drefnus, ac yn gruaidd,
I glodforu enw Duw,
Cans hyfryd yw a gweddaidd.

Daionus a thosturiol,
Yw'r Arglwydd wrth ei bobol:
O oes i oes y peri Air,
Dros fyth fe gair yn rassol.

Rhys Prichard

Canwyll y Cymru, 1681

R. Gerallt Jones

Er i mi ymhoffi'n fawr yng ngwaith sawl bardd, Robert Williams Parry yw'r un sy'n ddifeth yn llwyddo i yrru ias i lawr fy nghefn. Ac o holl gerddi Williams Parry, er i mi gydnabod yn barod iawn iddo gyfansoddi sawl cerdd rymusach a sawl cerdd bwysicach, yr un sy'n seinio amlaf yn fy mhen yw'r ail o'r ddwy soned, 'Gadael Tir'. Credaf fod dau reswm am hyn, a'r ddau'n gysylltiol.

Fel llanc, nid oeddwn yn llenyddol iawn fy niddordebau; roeddwn yn fwy hoff o lawer o griced a phêl-droed. Ond bu raid i mi dreulio peth amser yn llonydd un haf ar ôl damwain ar feic, a dyna pryd y darganfyddais farddoniaeth, am y tro cyntaf y tu allan i ystafell ddosbarth, a meddwi ar hud geiriau. Y bardd a achosodd hyn oedd Williams Parry, a'r gerdd gyntaf i gyd i mi erioed ffoli arni oedd ail soned 'Gadael Tir'. Ar ôl taro arni yn yr ardd ar brynhawn o haf yn Llŷn oesoedd yn ôl, i mi o hyd, sigl a swae a miwsig trist y soned hon, yn ogystal ag agnosticiaeth iach a chwbl ddaearol ei neges, yw craidd a chalon barddoniaeth.

~

Although I am very fond of the work of a number of poets, Robert Williams Parry is the one without doubt who excites me most. Out of all of Williams Parry's poems, although I freely admit he composed many that are more powerful and more important, the one that comes most frequently to mind is the second of the two sonnets, 'Gadael Tir'. I believe there are two reasons for this, and the two are connected.

As a boy, I wasn't particularly literary-orientated; I far preferred cricket and football. But I was forced to rest for some time one summer after an accident on a bicycle, and that is when I discovered poetry for the first time outside the classroom, and became drunk on the magic of words. The poet responsible for this was Williams Parry and the first poem I became infatuated with was the second sonnet 'Gadael Tir'. Since I discovered it whilst in the garden one summer afternoon in Llŷn a long time ago, it is the rhythm and sad music of this sonnet, together with the healthy and totally earthly agnosticism of its message, that is still for me the root and the heart of poetry.

Gadael Tir
2

Pan ddelo'r dydd im roddi cyfrif fry
   O'm goruchwyliaeth ar y ddaear lawr,
A dyfod hyd y fan lle clywir rhu
   Y môr ar benrhyn tragwyddoldeb mawr;
A llwyr gyffesu llawer llwybyr cam
   Mewn mynych grwydro ffôl a wybu'm traed,
A phledio'r dydd y'm gwnaed o lwch a fflam,
   O gnawd a natur, ac o gig a gwaed;
Odid na ddyry'r Gŵr a garai'r ffridd
   Ac erwau'r unigeddau wedi nos,
I un na wybu gariad ond at bridd,
   Ryw uffern lonydd, leddf, ar ryw bell ros,
Lle chwyth atgofus dangnefeddus wynt
Hen gerddi gwesty'r ddaear garodd gynt.

R. Williams Parry

Yr Haf a Cherddi Eraill (Gwasg y Bala, 1924)

Terry Jones

I suppose I'd pick 'Do Not Go Gentle Into That Good Night' by Dylan Thomas – because of its rage, its sense of tragedy and the elusive-allusive quality of the verse.

Do Not Go Gentle Into That Good Night

Do not go gentle into that good night,
Old age should burn and rave at close of day;
Rage, rage against the dying of the light.

Though wise men at their end know dark is right,
Because their words had forked no lightening they
Do not go gentle into that good night.

Good men, the last wave by, crying how bright
Their frail deeds might have danced in a green bay,
Rage, rage against the dying of the light.

Wild men who caught and sang the sun in flight,
And learn, too late, they grieved it on its way,
Do not go gentle into that good night.

Grave men, near death, who see with blinding sight
Blind eyes could blaze like meteors and be gay,
Rage, rage against the dying of the light.

And you, my father, there on the sad height,
Curse, bless, me now with your fierce tears, I pray.
Do not go gentle into that good night.
Rage, rage against the dying of the light.

Dylan Thomas

Collected Poems, 1934–1952 (Dent, 1952)

146

Phyllis Kinney

Ymhell cyn i mi siarad Cymraeg, roeddwn i'n canu caneuon gwerin Cymru, gan fwynhau'r alawon ond ynganu'r geiriau fel perot heb eu deall nhw. Y geiriau Cymraeg cyntaf i gyffwrdd fy nghalon oedd geiriau 'Hiraeth'. Yn y gerdd hon mae symlrwydd yn cuddio celfyddyd – nodwedd i'w chael mewn mwy nag un hen bennill. Mae sawl pennill yn gallu sefyll ar ei ben ei hun, ac weithiau mae'n bosib llunio cân gyfan trwy gyfuno tri neu bedwar pennill unigol, ond mae penillion 'Hiraeth' yn ffurfio dilyniant bythgofiadwy ar eu pen eu hun. Un peth arall: cofiwch fod y rhain yn cael eu galw yn benillion telyn. Mae'r gerdd 'Hiraeth' i'w chael ar ei gorau pan genir hi gan ddatgeiniad ac efallai mai'r ffaith i mi ei chlywed yn cael ei chanu am y tro cyntaf gan Meredydd Evans sy'n cyfrif, yn rhannol o leiaf, am yr effaith arna' i.

~

Long before I spoke Welsh, I sang Welsh folk songs, enjoying the tunes but pronouncing the words like a parrot without understanding them. The first Welsh words to touch my heart were the words of 'Hiraeth'. In this poem simplicity hides art – a characteristic of more than one folk verse. Many verses are able to stand on their own and sometimes it is possible to form a complete song by combining three or four individual verses. But the verses of 'Hiraeth' form an unforgettable sequence on their own. One other thing: remember that these are called *penillion telyn* (verses for harp accompaniment). The poem 'Hiraeth' is at its best when sung and maybe the fact that I heard it sung for the first time by Meredydd Evans accounts, partly at least, for the effect it has on me.

Hiraeth

Dwedwch, fawrion o wybodaeth,
O ba beth y gwnaethpwyd hiraeth;
A pha ddefnydd a roed ynddo
Na ddarfyddo wrth ei wisgo?

Derfydd aur a derfydd arian,
Derfydd melfed, derfydd sidan;
Derfydd pob dilledyn helaeth,
Eto er hyn ni dderfydd hiraeth.

Hiraeth mawr a hiraeth creulon,
Hiraeth sydd yn torri 'nghalon,
Pan fwy' dryma'r nos yn cysgu
Fe ddaw hiraeth ac a'm deffry.

Hiraeth, hiraeth, cilia, cilia,
Paid â phwyso mor drwm arna';
Nesa dipyn at yr erchwyn,
Gad i mi gael cysgu gronyn.

Anon.

Hen Benillion, ed. T. H. Parry Williams (Gwasg Gomer, 1956)

Glenys Kinnock

This poem still moves me, and it ensured that when I first read it, at the age of fourteen, I would never have any illusions about the nature of war. Its powerful imagery and painful reminder of our mortality have a timeless quality and transcend any description of the poem as simply 'a war poem'.

Strange Meeting

It seemed that out of battle I escaped
Down some profound dull tunnel, long since scooped
Through granites which titanic wars had groined.
Yet also there encumbered sleepers groaned,
Too fast in thought or death to be bestirred.
Then, as I probed them, one sprang up, and stared
With piteous recognition in fixed eyes,
Lifting distressful hands as if to bless.
And by his smile I knew that sullen hall,
By his dead smile I knew we stood in Hell.
With a thousand pains that vision's face was grained;
Yet no blood reached there from the upper ground,
And no guns thumped, or down the flues made moan.
'Strange friend,' I said, 'here is no cause to mourn.'
'None,' said the other, 'save the undone years,
The hopelessness. Whatever hope is yours,
Was my life also; I went hunting wild
After the wildest beauty in the world,
Which lies not calm in eyes, or braided hair,
But mocks the steady running of the hour,
And if it grieves, grieves richlier than here.
For by my glee might many men have laughed,
And of my weeping something had been left,
Which must die now. I mean the truth untold,
The pity of war, the pity war distilled.
Now men will go content with what we spoiled,
Or, discontent, boil bloody, and be spilled.
They will be swift with swiftness of the tigress,

149

None will break ranks, though nations trek from progress.
Courage was mine, and I had mystery,
Wisdom was mine, and I had mastery;
To miss the march of this retreating world
Into vain citadels that are not walled.
Then, when much blood had clogged their chariot-wheels
I would go up and wash them from sweet wells,
Even with truths that lie too deep for taint.
I would have poured my spirit without stint
But not through wounds; not on the cess of war.
Foreheads of men have bled where no wounds were.
I am the enemy you killed, my friend.
I knew you in this dark; for so you frowned
Yesterday through me as you jabbed and killed.
I parried; but my hands were loath and cold.
Let us sleep now . . .'

Wilfred Owen

The Poems of Wilfred Owen, ed. Jon Stallworthy (Chatto and Windus, 1990)

'Strange Meeting'. Graphics by Paul Peter Piech.

Neil Kinnock

This is Idris Davies with one of his best mixtures of the angry and the lyrical.

Most of all, by acknowledging Wales to be the Land of Mams, Idris at least gives a passing salute to the unsung heroines.

It's a pity that he didn't go further. The strengths, sacrifices, patience, selflessness, wisdom, endurance, imagination, creativity and magical ability to make food appear, clothes last, money stretch and families thrive are all qualities of poverty-trapped Mothers which could be praised to the poetic skies without a hint of bathos. There are fragments of tribute elsewhere in Idris Davies's work, of course. Mrs Evans, Olwen, Maggie Fach and the nameless soothing lover on the moorland in 'The Angry Summer' are all admired women. But, having hit the truth with 'Land of My Mothers', Idris could have done full justice. Perhaps he did, and its been lost. Who knows?

Land of My Mothers

Land of my mothers, how shall my brothers praise you?
With timbrels or rattles or tins?
With fire.
How shall we praise you on the banks of the rhymneying waters,
On the smoky shores and the glittering shores of Glamorgan,
On wet mornings in the bare fields behind the Newport docks,
On fine evenings when lovers walk by Bedwellty Church,
When the cuckoo calls to miners coming home to Rhymney
                                                    Bridge,
When the wild rose defies the Industrial Revolution
And when the dear old drunken lady sings of Jesus and a little
                                                    shilling.

Come down, O girls of song, to the bank of the coal canal
At twilight, at twilight
When mongrels fight
And long rats bite
Under the shadows of pit-head light,
And dance, you daughters of Gwenllian,
Dance in the dust in the lust of delight.

And you who have prayed in golden pastures
And oiled the wheels of the Western Tradition
And trod where bards have danced to church,
Pay a penny for this fragment of a burning torch.
It will never go out.

It will gather unto itself all the fires
That blaze between the heavens above and the earth beneath
Until the flame shall frighten each mud-hearted hypocrite
And scatter the beetles fattened on the cream of corruption,
The beetles that riddle the ramparts of Man.

Pay a penny for my singing torch,
O my sisters, my brothers of the land of my mothers,
The land of our fathers, our troubles, our dreams,
The land of Llewellyn and Shoni bach Shinkin,
The land of sermons that pebble the streams,
The land of the englyn and Crawshay's old engine,
The land that is sometimes as proud as she seems.

And the sons of the mountains and sons of the valleys
O lift up your hearts, and then
Lift up your feet.

Idris Davies

Collected Poems of Idris Davies (Gwasg Gomer, 1972)

'Garmon, Garmon'. Graphics by Cen Williams

Elfyn Llwyd

Fy hoff gerdd yw yr araith sydd yn cychwyn: 'Garmon, Garmon,/ Gwinllan a roddwyd yw Cymru fy ngwlad' gan Saunders Lewis allan o'i ddrama *Buchedd Garmon*. Y rheswm am hyn yw fod y geiriau yma yn syml, yn apelgar ofnadwy ac yn crisialu llawer o'r hyn rwyf yn deimlo dros fy ngwlad.

~

My favourite poem is the speech which begins: 'Garmon Garmon,/Gwinllan a roddwyd yw Cymru fy ngwlad' by Saunders Lewis, to be found in his drama *Buchedd Garmon*. The reason for this is that these words are simple, extremely appealing and crystallize a great deal of what I feel for my country.

> Garmon, Garmon,
> Gwinllan a roddwyd i'm gofal yw Cymru fy ngwlad,
> I'w thraddodi i'm plant
> Ac i blant fy mhlant
> Yn dreftadaeth dragwyddol;
> Ac wele'r moch yn rhuthro arni i'w maeddu,
> Minnau yn awr, galwaf ar fy nghyfeillion,
> Cyffredin ac ysgolhaig,
> Deuwch ataf i'r adwy,
> Sefwch gyda mi yn y bwlch,
> Fel y cadwer i'r oesoedd a ddêl y glendid a fu.

Saunders Lewis

Buchedd Garmon (Gwasg Aberystwyth, 1937)

Lionel Madden

This sad and subtle poem was written by Philip Larkin in 1954, when he was thirty-two, and was published in the following year in *The Less Deceived*, the volume of poems that established his reputation. It is a poem which has always spoken to me personally. Not surprisingly, it appeals to me because it is the work of a professional librarian – and there have not been many poets in our ranks! Larkin spent his whole career as a librarian and during the 1960s both my wife and I were members of his staff in Hull University Library.

I find the opening stanza a haunting evocation of the position of the person who is, by choice or accident, rootless. To find oneself with no place to which one belongs and no person to whom one is irrevocably attached seems to me a very sad condition. Yet many people do pass through life without enjoying any close attachment to either a person or a place; while others, as the second stanza reminds us, find that long-term reality does not measure up to their dreams.

This poem deserves to be read aloud. I admire its memorability, its tight construction, its skilful choice of vocabulary and the reminder of Larkin's unmistakable tone of voice.

Places, Loved Ones

No, I have never found
The place where I could say
This is my proper ground,
Here I shall stay;
Nor met that special one
Who has an instant claim
On everything I own
Down to my name;

To find such seems to prove
You want no choice in where
To build, or whom to love;
You ask them to bear
You off irrevocably,
So that it's not your fault
Should the town turn dreary,
The girl a dolt.

Yet, having missed them, you're
Bound, none the less, to act
As if what you settled for
Mashed you, in fact;
And wiser to keep away
From thinking you still might trace
Uncalled-for to this day
Your person, your place.

Philip Larkin

The Less Deceived (The Marvell Press, 1955)

George Melly

Ted Hughes, while not in my view in the same class as Auden or Eliot, is a fine twentieth-century poet. His limitation is a narrowness of vision; so much of his work seems to describe the evisceration of one creature by another; but this same Darwinian pessimism can produce poems of extraordinary intensity.

'Pike' is a case in point. One of its strengths is that Hughes doesn't write as if he *were* a pike; a device which sometimes may justify the accusation of knowing anthropomorphism. Here he describes this killing machine objectively and then, towards the conclusion of the poem, projects our prehistoric fears of nature, of great predators, of dark still waters. I must admit, however, that, as a passionate angler, 'Pike' may have prejudiced my judgement, but not I would say to an absurd degree.

It's beautifully built. It starts with baby pike, lively but not endearing, 'killers from the egg'. It moves on to describe three of these kept in an aquarium who, although well-fed, cannibalize each other until only one is left 'with a sag belly and the grin it was born with'. Hughes then recalls two jack (young) pike, over two feet long, he once found dead in the reeds, 'One jammed past its gills down the other's gullet'.

Yet these images, while exact and far from reassuring, are only the prelude to the last four verses.

The setting is a pond, 'fifty yards across' and 'as deep as England'. It is believed to hold pike 'too immense to stir', and young Hughes fishes for them by night 'with the hair frozen on my head'.

While not a poem I choose to recite to myself casting in the dark for sea-trout, it remains a favourite. I love panic induced by words. The conclusion of 'Pike' is, for me, as terrifying as Coleridge's 'fearful fiend' dogging the footsteps of the solitary traveller on the lonely road.

> . . . the dream
> Darkness beneath night's darkness had freed,
> That rose slowly towards me, watching.

Pike

Pike, three inches long, perfect
Pike in all parts, green tigering the gold.
Killers from the egg: the malevolent aged grin.
They dance on the surface among the flies.

Or move, stunned by their own grandeur,
Over a bed of emerald, silhouette
Of submarine delicacy and horror.
A hundred feet long in their world.

In ponds, under the heat-struck lily pads –
Gloom of their stillness:
Logged on last year's black leaves, watching upwards.
Or hung in an amber cavern of weeds

The jaws' hooked clamp and fangs
Not to be changed at this date;
A life subdued to its instrument;
The gills kneading quietly, and the pectorals.

Three we kept behind glass,
Jungled in weed: three inches, four,
And four and a half: fed fry to them –
Suddenly there were two. Finally one

With a sag belly and the grin it was born with.
And indeed they spare nobody.
Two, six pounds each, over two feet long,
High and dry and dead in the willow-herb –

One jammed past its gills down the other's gullet:
The outside eye stared: as a vice locks –
The same iron in this eye
Though its film shrank in death.

A pond I fished, fifty yards across,
Whose lilies and muscular tench
Had outlasted every visible stone
Of the monastery that planted them –

159

'Pike'. Graphics by Adrian Paul Metcalfe.

Stilled legendary depth:
It was as deep as England. It held
Pike too immense to stir, so immense and old
That past nightfall I dared not cast

But silently cast and fished
With my hair frozen on my head
For what might move, for what eye might move.
The still splashes on the dark pond,

Owls hushing the floating woods
Frail on my ear against the dream
Darkness beneath night's darkness had freed,
That rose slowly towards me, watching.

Ted Hughes

Lupercal (Faber & Faber, 1970)

161

Robert Minhinnick

Although I had some earlier knowledge of Coleridge's poetry –
chiefly 'The Rime of the Ancient Mariner' – I only discovered 'Frost
at Midnight' after buying an ancient copy of the Landsdown Poets
edition of his work in Galloway & Morgan in Aberystwyth in 1971.

On the flyleaf there is a faint dedication dated May 1880, and then
ten unsigned pages by the Landsdown editor, a over-heated treatise
on 'the genius of Coleridge, even in its wildest abberrations'.

In a volume that contained all of the more famous work, it was the
'meditative' pieces to which I returned, chiefly 'This lime tree bower
my prison' and 'Frost at Midnight', both ignored in the introduction.
The latter, composed in February 1798, I knew immediately to be an
extraordinary poem, a depiction of a trance or period of profound
mental stillness in which the writer's powers of observation and
description are at their height.

From the magnificent first line to the conclusion of the last verse
paragraph, the poem has a sense of completeness rare in Coleridge.
It was a work that hugely influenced Wordsworth, and in its
attention to small detail, anticipates the later great outpourings of
English 'nature' poetry. Yet it is sobering to note that 'Frost at
Midnight', as with much else of Coleridge's best writing, languished
largely unseen for several years after composition.

Frost at Midnight

The frost performs its secret ministry,
Unhelped by any wind. The owlet's cry
Came loud – and hark, again! loud as before.
The inmates of my cottage, all at rest,
Have left me to that solitude, which suits
Abstruser musings: save that at my side
My cradled infant slumbers peacefully.
'Tis calm indeed! so calm, that it disturbs
And vexes meditation with its strange
And extreme silentness. Sea, hill, and wood,
This populous village! Sea, and hill, and wood,
With all the numberless goings on of life,
Inaudible as dreams! the thin blue flame

'Frost at Midnight'. Graphics by Adrian Paul Metcalfe.

Lies on my low-burnt fire, and quivers not;
Only that film, which fluttered on the grate,
Still flutters there, the sole unquiet thing.
Methinks, its motion in this hush of nature
Gives its dim sympathies with me who live,
Making it a companionable form,
Whose puny flaps and freaks the idling Spirit
By its own moods interprets, everywhere
Echo or mirror seeking of itself,
And makes a toy of Thought.

                    But O! how oft,
How oft, at school, with most believing mind,
Presageful, have I gazed upon the bars,
To watch that fluttering stranger! and as oft,
With unclosed lids, already had I dreamt
Of my sweet birth-place, and the old church-tower,
Whose bells, the poor man's only music, rang
From morn to evening, all the hot Fair-day,
So sweetly, that they stirred and haunted me
With a wild pleasure, falling on mine ear
Most like articulate sounds of things to come!
So gazed I, till the soothing things I dreamt
Lulled me to sleep, and sleep prolonged my dreams!
And so I brooded all the following morn,
Awed by the stern preceptor's face, mine eye
Fixed with mock study on my swimming book:
Save if the door half opened, and I snatched
A hasty glance, and still my heart leaped up,
For still I hoped to see the stranger's face,
Townsman, or aunt, or sister more beloved,
My play-mate when we both were clothed alike!

  Dear Babe, that sleepest cradled by my side,
Whose gentle breathings, heard in this deep calm,
Fill up the interspersed vacancies
And momentary pauses of the thought!
My babe so beautiful! it thrills my heart
With tender gladness, thus to look at thee,
And think that thou shalt learn far other lore
And in far other scenes! For I was reared
In the great city, pent 'mid cloisters dim,

And saw nought lovely but the sky and stars.
But thou, my babe! shalt wander like a breeze
By lakes and sandy shores, beneath the crags
Of ancient mountain, and beneath the clouds,
Which image in their bulk both lakes and shores
And mountain crags: so shalt thou see and hear
The lovely shapes and sounds intelligible
Of that eternal language, which thy God
Utters, who from eternity doth teach
Himself in all, and all things in himself.
Great universal Teacher! he shall mould
Thy spirit, and by giving make it ask.

   Therefore all seasons shall be sweet to thee,
Whether the summer clothe the general earth
With greenness, or the redbreast sit and sing
Betwixt the tufts of snow on the bare branch
Of mossy apple-tree, while the night thatch
Smokes in the sun-thaw; whether the eve-drops fall
Heard only in the trances of the blast,
Or if the secret ministry of frost
Shall hang them up in silent icicles,
Quietly shining to the quiet Moon.

Samuel Taylor Coleridge

Coleridge's Poetical Works, ed. Ernest Hartley Coleridge
(Oxford University Press, 1988)

Owen Money

My favourite poem is 'Cargoes' by John Masefield. I learnt this at school and remain fond of it.

Cargoes

QUINQUIREME of Nineveh from distant Ophir
Rowing home to haven in sunny Palestine,
With a cargo of ivory,
And apes and peacocks,
Sandalwood, cedarwood, and sweet white wine.

Stately Spanish galleon coming from the Isthmus,
Dipping through the Tropics by the palm-green shores,
With a cargo of diamonds,
Emeralds, amethysts,
Topazes, and cinnamon, and gold moidores.

Dirty British coaster with a salt-caked smoke stack
Butting through the Channel in the mad March days,
With a cargo of Tyne coal,
Road-rail, pig-lead,
Firewood, iron-ware, and cheap tin trays.

John Masefield

The Collected Poems of John Masefield (Heinemann, 1923)

Rupert Moon

My favourite poem was written by Wordsworth during the French Revolution. The reason I chose this is that it typifies my outlook on life. I try and live life for today and make the most of the opportunities that come my way. It is foolish to look back and view what might have been, as you only have one chance of living your life – unfortunately there are no action replays!

French Revolution
As It Appeared to Enthusiasts at its Commencement

Oh! pleasant exercise of hope and joy!
For mighty were the auxiliars which then stood
Upon our side, we who were strong in love!
Bliss was it in that dawn to be alive,
But to be young was very heaven! – Oh! times,
In which the meagre, stale, forbidding ways
Of custom, law, and statute, took at once
The attraction of a country in romance!
When Reason seemed the most to assert her rights,
When most intent on making of herself
A prime Enchantress – to assist the work
Which then was going forward in her name!
Not favoured spots alone, but the whole earth,
The beauty wore of promise, that which sets
(As at some moment might not be unfelt
Among the bowers of paradise itself)
The budding rose above the rose full blown.
What temper at the prospect did not wake
To happiness unthought of? The inert
Were roused, and lively natures rapt away!
They who had fed their childhood upon dreams,
The playfellows of fancy, who had made
All powers of swiftness, subtilty, and strength
Their ministers, – who in lordly wise had stirred
Among the grandest objects of the sense,
And dealt with whatsoever they found there

As if they had within some lurking right
To wield it; – they, too, who, of gentle mood,
Had watched all gentle motions, and to these
Had fitted their own thoughts, schemers more mild,
And in the region of their peaceful selves; –
Now was it that both found, the meek and lofty
Did both find, helpers to their heart's desire,
And stuff at hand, plastic as they could wish;
Were called upon to exercise their skill,
Not in Utopia, subterranean fields,
Or some secreted island, Heaven knows where!
But in the very world, which is the world
Of all of us, – the place where in the end
We find our happiness, or not at all!

William Wordsworth

Poetical Works, ed. T. Hutchinson (Oxford University Press, 1905)

Eluned Morgan

As a vicar's daughter, brought up in a highly politicized working-class environment, I often thought there to be an inextricable link between religion and Socialism. But when the biblical slanging match between politicians got under way back in 1988 I had to reassess this link.

This poem reflects the disgust that many people felt at the time, as Thatcher entered a new realm of political debate which had been avoided until this point. Christian Socialism was a concept which I understood, but the use of the phrase 'Charity begins at home' as a justification for the promotion of individualism and self-interest appalled me. Politicians from both sides of the chamber jumped onto the theological bandwagon quoting contradictory verses as a justification for their own political philosophy. While the debating continued the real victims with the 'raggle taggle bellies' were silent and ignored.

The tongue-in-cheek tone, the subtle swipes at the government, and the cheeky use of the word 'preying' takes a justifiable dig at politicians. The poem, I feel, develops on the concentrated theme, and demands the full attention of the reader, leading to the second verse which takes the debate into the realms of ridicule. The monetary expressions used while discussing a spiritual theme grate on the ear, leaving the reader to wonder if there are any no-go areas for this Thatcherite philosophy.

Charity Begins at Home

Not content with the lives of betrayal
lionizing their peers
licking wounds,
M.P.'s now it seems,
covet the business of
spiritual illumination.
Throwing open the doors
of secret assembly
they spill forth,
thumping manifestoes,
and make a corporate bid for the C of E.
Preying from pulpits
erected by temporary beneficiaries

of government employment schemes,
they confer holy virtue
on hedonist piety,
and legitimise self-interest
with the words of Paul.
Hollow-tongued sophists
braying,
mask the real emptiness of raggle taggle bellies:–
their voice is seldom heard.

I wonder what the One God
Above-it-all-God,
The Man-God thinks of it all?
He should be appalled.
Or is he off somewhere perhaps?
fishing,
creating new worlds
leaving the denationalised corporation
to manage affairs
and to answer questions from shareholders.

Nic Blandford

Mihangel Morgan

Dywedwyd am yr 'Hen Benillion' eu bod yn 'gerddi mawr ar raddfa fechan'. Mae'r enghraifft hon, gan fardd anhysbys, yn gampwaith – os oes ystyr i'r gair hwnnw o gwbl. O fewn cwmpas ei phedair llinell fer mae'n llwyddo i gonsurio teimlad o dristwch a hiraeth a dygnwch ac mae'n ddarlun o unigrwydd enbyd heb ddihangfa. Ond mae amwyster yn perthyn i'r llinell olaf; mae gallu'r bardd i oroesi yn ddirgelwch iddo – neu iddi.

~

It has been said that the 'Hen Benillion' (folk verses) are 'great poems on a small scale'. This example, by an anonymous poet, is a masterpiece – if that word has any meaning. Within the confines of its four short lines the poet succeeds in conjuring a feeling of sadness, longing and perseverance and it's a picture of awful loneliness without escape. But the last line is ambiguous – the poet's ability to survive is a mystery to him – or her.

Rhif 148

Gwynt ar fôr a haul ar fynydd,
Cerrig llwydion yn lle coedydd,
A gwylanod yn lle dynion;
Och Dduw! pa fodd na thorrai 'nghalon?

Anon.

Hen Benillion, ed. T. H. Parry Williams (Gwasg Gomer, 1956)

Moc Morgan

Fy hoff gerdd yw 'Teifi' gan Cynan yn cael ei chanu gan Hogiau'r
Wyddfa.

Mae fy nghariad at yr afon Teifi – 'Brenhines afonydd Cymru' – yn
mynd nôl dros hanner canrif ac mae'r cariad yma yn tyfu fel yr wyf
yn teithio dros y byd i bysgota afonydd eraill.

Yr wyf hefyd yn hoffi'r gân gan mai Cynan oedd wedi ei
hysgrifennu. Yr oedd Cynan yn bysgotwr ac yn hoffi cwrsio'r sewin
yn ardal Llandysul. Yr wyf yn cofio cymryd rhan mewn rhaglen
radio am y sewin gyda Cynan yn y pumdegau. Yr oedd yn gymeriad
mawr ac yn medru rhoi i'r sewin y mawredd a'r clod a haeddai, ac
yr oedd yn fraint cael rhannu rhaglen ganddo. Mae'r gân am yr afon
Teifi yn dangos fod Cynan wedi bod yn pysgota yr afon ar ei hyd – a
dyna hyfryd pe bai ef wedi pysgota gyda Dewi Emrys a oedd yn dod
i Bontrhydfendigaid bob blwyddyn i fwynhau'r pysgota yno.

Bob tro clywaf Hogiau'r Wyddfa – hogiau gyda llaw sy'n hoffi
pysgota – yr wyf yn ail-fyw y gwefr a gaf wrth bysgota ac mae'r gân
bob amser yn fy nhywys i byllau enwog yr afon Teifi. Mae'r afon
Teifi yn un o afonydd prydferthaf Cymru ac mae Cynan wedi dal ei
phrydferthwch yn ei gân i'r afon.

~

My favourite poem is 'Teifi' by Cynan, sung by Hogiau'r Wyddfa.

My love for the Teifi – 'the Queen of the rivers of Wales' – goes
back over half a century and this love grows as I travel all over the
world to fish in other rivers.

I also like the poem because it was written by Cynan. Cynan was a
fisherman and enjoyed pursuing the sewin in the Llandysul area. I
remember taking part in a radio programme about the sewin with
Cynan in the fifties. He was a great character and able to give the
sewin the praise and majesty it rightly deserved and it was an
honour to share a programme with him. The poem about the Teifi
shows that Cynan had fished the length of the river – and how
wonderful it would be if he had fished with Dewi Emrys who came
to Pontrhydfendigaid every year to enjoy the fishing there.

Every time I hear Hogiau'r Wyddfa – lads who incidentally enjoy
fishing themselves – I relive the thrill I get whilst fishing and the
song always leads me to the famous pools of the River Teifi. The
Teifi is one of the most beautiful rivers in Wales and Cynan has
captured her beauty in his song to the river.

Teifi

(I'm cyfaill a'm cyd-bysgotwr, Wilbert Lloyd Roberts)

Mae afon sy'n groyw a gloyw a glân,
A balm yn addfwynder a cheinder ei chân.
Pob corbwll fel drych i ddawns cangau'r coed cnau,
Pob rhyd fel pelydrau mewn gwydrau yn gwau;
A'i thonnau, gan lamu yn canu'n un côr
Ym Mae Aberteifi ger miri y môr.

Er dod o Gors Caron, a'i llarpio'n y llaid,
Mae'n llamu i'w glendid, – gweddnewid ar naid.
Ar ol pasio Llanbed' – a theced ei thŵr –
Pont Henllan sy'n estyn ei darlun i'r dŵr;
Toc Rhaeadr Cenarth sy'n daran drwy'r fro,
Ond rhowch i mi Deifi Llandysul bob tro.

Mae'r llif yno'n ddiog, a'r dolydd yn las,
A'r brithyll, a'r sewin a'r samon yn fras;
A dau o enweirwyr, heb ofal is nen
Yn disgyn i'r afon o Blas Gilfach Wen,
A thoc bydd Coch Bonddu yn llamu'n ei lli' –
Rhowch Deifi Llandysul i Wilbert a mi.

Ar ba sawl blaen llinyn caed sewin yn saig
A'r sêr yn rhoi tro uwchlaw gro Tan-y-Graig?
Sawl samon a fachwyd, chwaraewyd i'r rhwyd
Yn 'ffedog Pwll Henri, a'r lli' braidd yn llwyd?
A sawl brithyll ëon fu'n ffustio'n rhy ffôl
A chyrch y cyflychwr ar ddŵr Pwll-y-Ddôl?

O'r bore tra thirion hyd hinon brynhawn
Crwydrasom ein deuwedd un duedd, un dawn.
Pysgota tan fangoed a glasgoed y glyn,
A dal i bysgota a'r nos ar y bryn.
A pha sawl cyfrinach cyfeillach a fu
Ar bulpud o greigan ar dorlan Pwll Du?

Fy nghyfaill genweirig, caredig dy ryw,
Faint gawn ni'n dau eto o hafau i fyw?
Os byddi dy hunan wrth bwll Gilfach Wen
Un noson, a chlywed sŵn rîl wrth lein den,
Nac ofna, myfi fydd yn llithro drwy'r gro
O erddi Paradwys i Deifi am dro.

Cynan

Cerddi Cynan: Y Casgliad Cyflawn (Gwasg Gomer, 1987)

Rhodri Morgan

My choice is 'Pwllderi' by Dewi Emrys.

My reasons for choosing it are that Pwllderi is also one of my favourite places anywhere in the world. There is a memorial column to Dewi Emrys at Pwllderi. If you stand next to that memorial column you can look down the Pembrokeshire coastal footpath and coast for about ten miles, all the way down to St David's. The view is absolutely unbelievable. If you want a place to be inspired to write a poem, then undoubtedly Pwllderi is the place.

The poem is written in Pembrokeshire dialect Welsh. It won the equal First Prize in the Dialect Poem at the 1926 Swansea National Eisteddfod, so that makes it particularly suitable for the Swansea Year of Literature. It is perhaps notable that dialect verse gets treated more seriously in Wales than elsewhere. Within the Welsh language, dialects seem to be more important relative to standardized Welsh than would be the case in English, for example.

At a time as well when gradually dialects are weakening in Wales and we will all, no doubt, not long after the year 2000, finish up speaking the Milton Keynes Welsh that is now being taught in Welsh-medium schools, it is of great interest to note how Dewi Emrys resolves the conflicts between writing in dialect and writing serious poetry.

In the Swansea Year of Literature, it is also worth noting that both in the Welsh and in the English language, two of the greatest exponents of the twentieth century, Dewi Emrys and W. H. Davies (of 'We Have No Time to Stand and Stare' fame) were tramps for large parts of their lives. I don't know whether anyone has done a comparison of their poetry as well as their lifestyles, but it is certainly a long way away from the medieval traditions where poets were employed by princes to act as 'muses' at their court!

Apparently, Dewi Emrys was very fond of reciting Pwllderi himself to his fellow tramps whose society, called Fforddolion Dyfed, would meet at Pwllgwaelod. It is hard to imagine that there would be well-recognized poets now tramping the back roads and cart tracks of Pembrokeshire with their rear ends coming out of their trousers and meeting for a poetry recitation get-together on a beach. It seems more like 600 years ago than 60!

Pwllderi
(Yn nhafodiaith Dyfed)

Fry ar y mwni mae nghatre bach
Gyda'r goferydd a'r awel iach.
'Rwy'n gallid watwar adarn y weunydd, –
Y giach, y nwddwr, y sgrâd a'r hedydd;
Ond sana i'n gallid neud telineg
Na nwddi pennill yn iaith y coleg;
A 'sdim rhocesi pert o hyd
Yn hala goglish trwyddw'i gyd.
A hinny sy'n y'n hala i feddwl
Na 'sdim o'r awen 'da fi o gwbwl;
Achos ma'r sgwlin yn dala i deiri
Taw rhai fel 'na yw'r prididdion heddi.

'Rown i'n ishte dŵe uwchben Pwllderi,
Hen gatre'r eryr a'r arth a'r bwci.
'Sda'r dinion taliedd fan co'n y dre
Ddim un llefeleth mor wyllt yw'r lle.
'All ffrwlyn y cownter a'r brethin ffansi
Ddim cadw'i drâd uwchben Pwllderi.
'Ry'ch chi'n sefill fry uwchben y dwnshwn,
A drichid lawr i hen grochon dwfwn,
A hwnnw'n berwi rhwng creige llwydon
Fel stwceidi o lâth neu olchon sebon.
Ma' meddwl amdano'r finid hon
Yn hala rhyw isgrid trwy fy mron.

Pert iawn yw'i wishgodd yr amser hyn, –
Yr eithin yn felyn a'r drisi'n wyn,
A'r blode trâd brain yn batshe mowron
Ar lechwedd gwyrdd, fel cwmwle gleishon;
A lle mae'r gwrug ar y graig yn bwnge,
Fe dingech fod rhywun yn tanu'r llethre.
Yr haf fu ino, fel angel ewn,
A baich o ribane ar ei gewn.
Dim ond fe fuse'n ddigon hâl
I wasto'i gifoth ar le mor wâl,
A sbortan wrth hala'r hen gropin eithin
I allwish sofrins lawr dros y dibyn.
Fe bange hen gibidd, a falle boddi
Tae e'n gweld hinny uwchben Pwllderi.

175

'Pwllderi'. Graphics by Anthony Evans.

Mae ino ryw bishyn bach o drâth –
Beth all e' fod? Rhyw drigen llâth.
Mae ino dŵad, ond nid rhyw bŵer,
A hwnnw'n gowir fel hanner llŵer;
Ac fe welwch ino'r crechi glas
Yn saco'i big i'r pwlle bas,
A chered bant ar 'i fagle hir
Mor rhonc bob whithrin â mishtir tir;
Ond weles i ddim dyn eriŵed
Yn gadel ino ôl 'i drŵed;
Ond ma' nhw'n gweid 'i fod e', Dai Beca,
Yn mento lawr 'na weithe i wreca.
Ma'n rhaid fod gidag e' drâd gafar,
Neu lwybir ciwt trwy fola'r ddeiar.
Tawn i'n gweld rhywun yn Pwllderi,
Fe redwn gatre pentigili.

Cewch ino ryw filodd o dderinod –
Gwilanod, cirillod a chornicillod;
Ac mor ombeidus o fowr yw'r creige
A'r hen drwyn hagar lle ma' nhw'n heide,
Fe allech wrio taw clêrs sy'n hedfan
Yn ddifal o bwti rhyw hen garan;
A gallech dingi o'r gribin uwchben
Taw giar fach yr haf yw'r wilan wen.

A'r mowcedd! Tina gimisgeth o sŵn! –
Sgrechen hen wrachod ac wben cŵn,
Llefen a whiban a mil o regfeydd,
A'r rheini'n hego trw'r ogofeydd,
A chithe'n meddwl am nosweth ofnadwi,
A'r morwr, druan, o'r graig yn gweiddi –
Yn gweiddi, gweiddi, a neb yn aped,
A dim ond hen adarn y graig yn clŵed,
A'r hen girillod, fel haid o githreilied,
Yn weito i'r gole fynd mâs o'i liged.
Tina'r meddilie sy'n dwad ichi
Pan foch chi'n ishte uwchben Pwllderi.

Dim ond un tŷ sy'n agos ato,
A hwnnw yng nghesel Garn Fowr yn cwato.
Dolgâr yw ei enw, hen orest o le,

Ond man am reso a dished o de,
Neu ffioled o gawl, a thina well bolied,
Yn gennin a thato a sêrs ar 'i wmed.
Cewch weld y crochon ar dribe ino,
A'r eithin yn ffaglu'n ffamws dano.
Cewch lond y lletwad, a'i llond hi lweth,
A hwnnw'n ffeinach nag un gimisgeth;
A chewch lwy bren yn y ffiol hefyd
A chwlffyn o gaws o hen gosin hifryd.

Cewch ishte wedyn ar hen sgiw dderi.
A chlŵed y bigel yn gweid 'i stori.
Wedith e' fowr am y glaish a'r bŵen
A gas e' pwy ddwarnod wrth safio'r ŵen;
A wedith e' ddim taw wrth tshain a rhaff
Y tinnwd inte i fancyn saff,
Ond fe wedith, falle, a'i laish yn crini,
Beth halodd e' lawr dros y graig a'r drisi;
Nid gwerth yr ŵen ar ben y farced,
Ond 'i glwed e'n llefen am gal 'i arbed;
Ac fe wedith bŵer am Figel Mwyn
A gollodd 'i fowyd i safio'r ŵyn;
A thina'r meddilie sy'n dwad ichi
Pan foch chi'n ishte uwchben Pwllderi.

Dewi Emrys

Cerddi'r Bwthyn (Gwasg Gomer, 1948)

Jan Morris

I have chosen this well-known and out-of-fashion poem for three reasons. The first is that I have always loved it. The second is that if there is one thing I don't much like about Welshness, it is the tendency towards introspection that keeps so many of our people for ever looking inwards – the exact opposite of the poem's flaming embracement of far horizons, distant times, exotic colours and suggestions. And the third reason is that I have Old Ships of my own: for when I look out to sea from my window at Llanystumdwy, sometimes I seem to see the Porthmadog slate schooners sailing by beneath their taut white sails – the Western Ocean Yachts which Welshmen once navigated to the far corners of the earth, and which excite me as grandly in the imagination as ever the ancient vessels of the Mediterranean excited James Elroy Flecker.

The Old Ships

I have seen old ships sail like swans asleep
Beyond the village which men still call Tyre,
With leaden age o'ercargoed, dipping deep
For Famagusta and the hidden sun
That rings black Cyprus with a lake of fire;
And all those ships were certainly so old
Who knows how oft with squat and noisy gun,
Questing brown slaves or Syrian oranges,
The pirate Genoise hell-raked them till they rolled
Blood, water, fruit and corpses up the hold.
But now through friendly seas they softly run,
Painted the mid-sea blue or shore-sea green,
Still patterned with the vine and grapes in gold.

But I have seen
Pointing her shapely shadows from the dawn
And image tumbled on a rose-swept bay
A drowsy ship of some yet older day;
And, wonder's breath indrawn,
Thought I – who knows – who knows – but in that same

179

(Fished up beyond Aeaea, patched up new
– Stern painted brighter blue –)
That talkative, bald-headed seaman came
(Twelve patient comrades sweating at the oar)
From Troy's doom-crimson shore,
And with great lies about his wooden horse
Set the crew laughing, and forgot his course.

It was so old a ship – who knows, who knows?
– And yet so beautiful, I watched in vain
To see the mast burst open with a rose,
And the whole deck put on its leaves again.

James Elroy Flecker

Collected Poems (Martin Secker, 1916)

Twm Morys

Un o bleserau mawr fy mywyd i, ers gwell na deng mlynedd bellach, ydi mynd am dro i ganol Llyfr Coch Hergest, a sgwennwyd rywbryd yn niwedd y bedwaredd ganrif ar ddeg. Mae rhai o'r hen feirdd a fi yn hen lawiau erbyn hyn. Un ohonyn nhw ydi yr Ustus Llwyd. Mae'r *Cydymaith i Lenyddiaeth Cymru* yn dweud amdano, mewn tair brawddeg fach swta, guwch yn uwch na ffroenuchel, ei fod yn un o'r glêr, neu'r 'ofer-feirdd', a'i fod yn canu'n fras a sarhaus. Ond mae ymgolli yn ei gerddi o, ar ôl yr holl ganu mawl, yn debyg i gyrraedd y dafarn yn y Dociau o'r diwedd, ar ôl rhyw noson wobrwyo fawr. Dyma ichi ddarn o awdl wnaeth yr Ustus i Madog 'Gwyncu' Offeiriad, gŵr eglwysig oedd yn gwneud pethau drwg iawn iawn ar ganol y gwasanaeth yn ei eglwys dywyll. A noddwr cybyddlyd, oedd wedi gaddo rhoi ei gôt yn rhodd i'r bardd. Roedd yr holl sôn am hen arwyr a chwedlau'r Cymry, wrth ddweud mor uffernol o hen oedd y racsyn côt 'ma, yn codi chwerthin mawr, mae'n siŵr gen i.

Detholiad o Lyfr Coch Hergest

Hawdd ganthaw addaw eddystyr – pe'i herchid,
A phyth ni ceffid odid edau.
Eddewis is mis, a mwy – no blwyddyn,
Im ei gedechyn, cefndedyn cul,
Sorrais nas cefais, cyfyng offeiriad,
A'i dad oedd reiniad taergad dyfrgwn . . .
Swrcodan druan, adrywedd noethi,
A fu am Benlli, yn hen fonllawdr.
Hi a fu yng ngwydd llu fab Llŷr – Llediaith,
Hi a fu ganwaith yn hen Gonacht.
Hi a fu'n ny yn achaws – ei haint,
Hi a fu am Eraint ac am Arwy,
Hi a fu'n gwasgu gweisgon – ar fara,
Hi a fu yn Sacsonia i mewn senedd,
Hi a fu'n mygu ynghylch megin – ledr,
Hi a fu am fam Bedr, cyn cael bedydd,
Hi a fu'n cyrchu ceirch ebawl – Catus,
Hi a fu am Frutus yn hen fretyn,
Hi a fu'n malu ym Melin – Rheinallt,
Ar ryd Cae Llugallt yn rhwyd llygod.

Hi a fu'n llechu lluwch eiry – mynydd,
Bellach yam gybydd y mae'n gebystr,
Hi a fu'n tarnu turnen – wraig fab Pyll,
Hi a fu'n bebyll i hen Babo,
Hi a ddoeth yn noeth o neithiawr – Franwen,
Hyd yn llys Facsen, nid lles focsach,
Hi a dynnwyd yn rhwyd ar hyd – Cwm Safn Ast
I geisiaw dyfrast yn ei dwyfron.
Hi ni chaad, drwy frad, mae'n fradw – ei llun,
Gan berchen corun, byth ni'm ciried.
Madawg yw hwnnw, meudag llwy haearn,
Calon culfaen sarn carn, corn iyrchell . . .
Byth o'i fodd yn rhodd, nid Rhydderch – gampau,
Noeth fy ysgwyddau anosgeiddig,
Ni welir am ddyn eddewid – ganthaw,
Ni ddaw o'i ddurlaw, Fadawg ddyfrllyd,
Madyn, gi gelyn, go galed – Wyncu,
Oni ddêl esgob du o din dyfrgi.

~

In the fourteenth-century manuscript, the Red Book of Hergest, there's a large body of satirical verse, hardly touched even now by Welsh scholarship, because it's very bawdy. An extremely prominent Welsh academic warned others away from it when I was in college, because it would 'do damage to their soul'. Nevertheless, about ten years ago I started to edit some of it for the University of Wales. And though my interest in MAs and Ph.D.s lapsed long ago, my interest in these gaudy, bawdy bards did not. Their outrageous, largely bestial, imagery; their pictures of the smoky, half-ruinous halls where miserly patrons glower over bare tables, and of crafty beggars, and blasphemous thieves, and lascivious priests; their impudence in calling on the saints, and even on Mary, and Jesus, and God Himself, to help in the downfall of the object of their satire; and most of all their love of words, and the sound of them – all these things have made these poets of long ago into friends and familiars of mine. Here is a part of an *awdl* by Yr Ustus Llwyd (The Grey Justice) to a niggardly priest, Madog 'Gwyncu' Offeiriad, who promised to give his coat to the poet, but never did. The references to the heroes of Welsh mythology are very involved – even the 'mountain snow' calls to mind a famous, much older poem kept in the same manuscript, each verse of which begins 'mountain snow'.

Easy for him to promise a horse, if it were asked for, but you'd be lucky to get a piece of thread. He promised me a month and more than a year ago, his rag. It's like a strip of sweetbread, but I'm angry that I didn't get it, tight priest. His father was the leader of a yapping pack of otters . . . Wretched surcoat, track of nakedness, which Benlli wore as old breeches. It was in the presence of the hosts of Llyr Llediaith. It was a hundred times in old Connaught. It has wasted away in its disease. Geraint wore it, and Garwy. It has pressed the husks on bread. It has been in Sacsonia in a senate. It has been smoking around a leather bellows. Peter's mother wore it before the baptism. It has taken oats to Catus's foal. Brutus wore it as an old pinafore. It frayed in Rheinallt's mill. Across the field of Llugallt it was a mousenet. It has lurked in a drift of mountain snow. Now it's a truss about a miser. It has polished the spinning-wheel of Pyll's daughter-in-law. It was a tent to old Pabo. It came bare from Branwen's wedding-feast, to the court of Macsen. Nothing to boast about. It was stretched as a net across the Valley of Safn Ast, to catch an otter. And because of treachery, it was not forthcoming from that owner of a tonsure. It's all tattered. He will never give it to me. Madog, that is – Adam's apple like an iron spoon, heart like the narrow stone of a ruined cairn, horn like a roebuck. My ungainly shoulders are bare. This is not Rhydderch's style! The thing he promised will never be seen on anyone, as a gift of his free will. It will not come from his steely hand – false Madog, fox, hateful dog, hard Gwyncu – until a black bishop comes out of an otter's arse.

Yr Ustus Llwyd

Llyfr Coch Hergest, translated by Twm Morys

Daniel Mullins

Ers dwy fil o flynyddoedd, mae'r un dewis yn wynebu pob dyn. Yn ein canrif ni, fel yng nghyfnod Crist, ffolineb yw'r Groes, a threfn yr uned fawr yw camp a delfryd dynoliaeth. Bardd yn unig sy'n gallu gosod y dewis sylfaenol a thyngedfennol mor gryno ac mor ddifloesgni.

Mae'r ddelwedd yn hen ac yn gyfoes. Mae doethineb llywodraethau a gwleidyddion yn cynnig atebion i broblemau'r presennol a'r dyfodol. Ond dros y cyfan, mae cysgod y Groes yn herio atebion parod doethion byd.

Ystyrir Saunders Lewis gan lawer yn brif lenor Cymraeg y ganrif. Fy mraint oedd ei adnabod a chael croeso a chyfeillgarwch ar ei aelwyd.

~

For two thousand years the same choice has faced every man. In our century, as in the time of Christ, the Cross is folly, and the order of the great unit is mankind's feat and ideal. Only a poet can set out the basic and fateful choice so concisely and unfalteringly.

The image is old and modern. The wisdom of governments and politicians offers answers to the problems of the present and the future. But over it all, the shadow of the Cross challenges the ready answers of worldly wisdom.

Saunders Lewis is considered by many to be the greatest Welsh literary writer and critic of this century. It was my honour to know him and to be welcomed as a friend at his home.

Y Dewis

Darfu'r gyflafan olaf. Unwyd y byd.
Terfysg nac un gwrthryfel mwy ni chaed,
Ond trefn fel rheilffordd lle bu gynt y gwaed,
Pob glin yn plygu'n ddof a dof pob bryd.
Cododd yr Unben o'i filwriaeth ddrud;
A phum cyfandir ufudd dan ei draed,
Câi ymddigrifo yn y gamp a wnaed,
A rhodio'n dawel rhwng ei ddeiliaid mud.

A daeth at fryn oedd ddisathr, lle'r oedd croes
Ac arni un yn marw. Chwarddai'r teyrn,
'Os Mab Duw wyt ti, tyrd i lawr o'th loes,
Dewised y byd rhyngom; achub dy hun.'
A meddai'r Aberth dan yr hoelion heyrn,
'Yma y byddaf tra bydd na byd na dyn.'

Saunders Lewis

Byd a Betws (Gwasg Aberystwyth, 1941)

Paul Murphy

This is 'Slagtips' written this year by my father, Ronald Murphy.

It might seem strange that I should offer this poem, considering it is not written by any of the great poets, but it is, to me, a highly personal and evocative description of our south Wales valleys. In another way, it shows how good poetry can be written by those who have not had any formal further education. My father left school at fourteen to work underground at the Llanarch Colliery, in Abersychan, in my constituency. He remained a miner, like his father, for twenty-five years, before working at ICI Fibres, Pontypool, where he was a TGWU shop steward.

I hope the poem will not only evoke memories of valley life, but will also remind generations to come of the hardship our people endured over the years.

Slagtips

Like sentinels sombre and gray, grim reminders of bygone days,
of pits whose shiny seams of coal first gave men work and then
the dole. Of men and boys, slag and stone, early graves and
broken bones.

Sweat and toil in headings, stalls, feared of gas and dread of falls,
Working hidden out of sight in another world where it's always
night.

No moon nor stars are seen down there, just total darkness
everywhere.
No city lights to show the way, no sign to tell if it's night or day.

No birds there sing or fly on wing, no crocus grow to welcome
spring.
No scented rose on the summer breeze, no autumn leaves to fall
from trees.

No winter snow or sun or sky, the changing seasons pass them by.

Their world of darkness underground where nothing changes all
year round.

186

Where nature's beauty never treads, they spend their lives in fear
and dread.

Oil lamps dim with tiny flame, lifeline, numbered, miner's name.
Spikes and chalk, moleskins, yorks, bread and cheese, tea-jack,
corks.

Mandrills, shovels, clamps and nedge, hatchet, bar and heavy
sledge.
Pairs of timber, props and flats, hornets, black-pats, hungry rats.

Horses with impressive names like Royal, Roman, Easter Flame.
Windroads, airways, double doors, brattice sheets draped to the
floor.

Big vein, black vein, drams raced high, journey ropes that kick
and fly.
Rippings, slag and drams of much go up the pit to waiting trucks.

Engines, hooters, whistles blow, trucks are full and off they go,
down the line for slag tip bound, carrying muck from under-
ground.

Bloodstained stones, and slag and shale, broken timber, bent up
nails, brattice sheets all torn and ripped all went hurtling down
the tips.

Waiting there in bitter cold, men and women, young and old,
fingers, bodies numb to bone, picking coal from slag and stone.

But now the tips are grassed and green, its slag and stone by them
unseen.
No sign of blood, of pain, or grief, that lies there buried
underneath.

Nothing. Nothing to show unless you know of those sad days so
long ago.

Ronald Murphy

187

Mavis Nicholson

Love it – because it reminds me of the past when there were steam trains. It is pure romance. A mysterious, ordinary moment. A train journey that temporarily suspends you from the rest of your life.

It is so powerful that you can read it just as it is – the words and the punctuation are very satisfying.

Or you might find yourself playing around a bit with it for it's suggestive of a bigger plot. Well, train journeys are like that, somehow. You are alighting at that station and walking into that countryside . . .

To whom? To what? Or, you are willing someone to board the train at that bare station. A stranger who will change the whole course of your life . . .

It's a straightforward poem of wonderful British summer seen and heard from a train . . . and there are no mobile phones.

Adlestrop

YES. I remember Adlestrop –
The name, because one afternoon
Of heat the express-train drew up there
Unwontedly. It was late June.

The steam hissed. Someone cleared his throat.
No one left and no one came
On the bare platform. What I saw
Was Adlestrop – only the name.

And willows, willow-herb, and grass,
And meadowsweet, and haycocks dry,
No whit less still and lonely fair
Than the high cloudlets in the sky.

And for that minute a blackbird sang
Close by, and round him, mistier,
Farther and farther, all the birds
Of Oxfordshire and Gloucestershire.

Edward Thomas

Poems (Selwyn & Blount, 1917)

George Noakes

Ymhlith aelodau ffyddlon Eglwys Dewi Sant, Caerdydd, pan euthum yn ficer yno yn y chwedegau, oedd y darlledydd, llenor, bardd a diwinydd Aneirin Talfan Davies. Ni chafodd yr un ficer gyfaill mwy cywir na chefnogwr mwy brwd ac nid anghofiaf y seiadu yn ei gartref a ehangodd fy ngorwelion gymaint.

Yn haf 1970, aeth ef a'i briod Mari am wyliau i Iwgoslafia. Roedd iechyd y ddau yn dirywio – Mari yn diodde o ganser ac Aneirin o glefyd y galon. Dyma eu gwyliau olaf gyda'i gilydd. Efallai y clywir tinc o hynny yn y soned yma a gyfansoddodd tra ar ei wyliau. Danfonodd y drafft cyntaf ata i ar gerdyn post. Mae seld yn gelficyn cyfarwydd i ni Gymry cefngwlad – yn symbol o dreftadaeth – a'r llestri amhrisiadwy arni yn etifeddiaeth a ddaeth lawr i ni o genhedlaeth i genhedlaeth. Beth am ein treftadaeth fel cenedl? Faint o lestri a chrac ynddynt sydd ar y seld genedlaethol? Fel unigolion gwyddom nad ydym yn llestri heb nam arnynt. Ac fe ŵyr pob gweinidog yr efengyl sy'n bugeilio ymhlith pobl sy wedi colli eu ffydd am yr ofn dychrynllyd y gall yntau golli ei ffydd a mynd yn llestr a chrac ynddo. Diolch am drugaredd ac amynedd y Crochennydd Mawr ac am addewid ei Fab, 'Ni fwriaf allan byth mo'r sawl sy'n dod ataf fi'.

Rwy'n diolch i Dduw am Aneirin a Mari ac am y seiadau a ddyfnhaodd fy ffydd.

~

Amongst the faithful members of St David's Church, Cardiff, when I went there as vicar in the sixties was Aneirin Talfan Davies, the broadcaster, writer, poet and theologian. No vicar had such a true friend or such a keen supporter and I will never forget the religious discussions in his home that so greatly widened my horizons.

In the summer of 1970 he and his wife Mari went on holiday to Yugoslavia. Both were in failing health – Mari suffering from cancer, Aneirin from heart disease. This was their last holiday together. Maybe one hears a note of that in this sonnet he composed whilst on holiday. He sent me the first draft on a postcard. A dresser is a familiar piece of furniture to us Welsh country folk – a symbol of heritage – and the priceless crockery on it an inheritance that was handed down to us from generation to generation. What about our heritage as a nation? How many cracked pieces of crockery are there on the national dresser? As individuals we know we aren't perfect

189

vessels. And every minister of religion who works amongst people who have lost their faith knows of the awful fear that he too could lose his faith and become a cracked vessel. Thanks for the mercy and patience of the Great Potter and for his Son's promise, 'I will never disregard he who cometh unto me'.

I thank God for Aneirin and Mari and for the religious discussions that strengthened my faith.

Y Seld

Bu chwilio dyfal am y llestri hyn
    Ar hyd disberod lwybrau'r byd, cyn gweld
Dwyn gwyrth eu holl dreuliedig liwiau syn
    I drefnus ddiogelwch rhesi'r seld.
Ba luniaidd odidowgrwydd gynt a fu
    Yn llathru priddyn rhain, eu llun a'u lliw;
Y coch, y glas, y melyn mwyn, y du
    A'r aur brenhinol ar eu godre gwiw?
Pan ddôi i hulio bwrdd yr hyfryd wledd,
    A thynnu'r llestri fesul un o'r rhac:
Rhoi tinc â'th ewin gwyn a barnu'u gwedd
    Rhwng golau deufyd, a weli yno'i 'r crac,
A'm taflu, O Gasglwr diflin, lwr' dy gefn
Trwy ddrws y bac i'r pentwr chwâl, di-drefn?

Aneirin Talfan Davies

Diannerch Erchwyn a Cherddi Eraill (Christopher Davies, 1975)

Roy Noble

This comes from a teacloth picked up in Portree on the Isle of Skye in Scotland, whilst filming one of the *Celtic Trail* programmes. I had just had an interview with a writer who lived in a croft on the island and he was explaining to me how the 'clearances' of the Highlands still ran deep within the souls of the Highland and Island people. It was an extreme form of forced homelessness and the enormity of the unjust decision by the authorities, so that the land could be given over to sheep runs, still rankled. Sitting with this gentleman in his croft with the snow coming down outside brought home to me the extreme weather conditions of a hard land and the trauma of the clearances could clearly be understood. It is a poem I know off by heart.

Canadian Boat Song

From the lone shieling
Of the misty island,
Mountains divide us, and
A waste of seas; yet
Still the blood is strong
The heart is highland
And we in dreams
Behold the Hebrides.
The bold kindred, in time
Long vanished, conquered
The soil and fortified the
Keep, no seer foretold the children
Should be banished that a
Noble lord can boast his sheep.

Anon.

(1829)

Leslie Norris

I have so many favourite poems that it has been a task to decide on one; for example, not a day goes by that I do not read some of Yeats's later poems. Every summer I read every line in Thomas Hardy's *Collected Poems*, and I also read often in Henry Vaughan. I would not like to be without nearly all of Dylan Thomas. Keats's odes and the great Wordsworth poems are part of my life. But if I have to decide on one poem then it has to be Coleridge's 'Frost at Midnight'.

The poem is so well-known that I can't imagine other people will not choose it. I have taught it many times in courses at the university and do not want to offer any academic opinion now. It is enough to say that I never fail to admire the organic unity of the poem, the clarity of Coleridge's meditation, the ordering of his images, and the lovely optimism of his promise to his child. It's also a winter poem, the season when things are at their most clear; even at midnight the ice reflects any grain of light there is.

I'm grateful too that 'Frost at Midnight' so affected Keats that its influence is clearly to be seen in the younger poet's great last poem 'To Autumn'. And that might well have been my second choice.

('Frost at Midnight' was also chosen by Robert Minhinnick and appears on page 162)

John Ogwen

Ar y wal yn y stafell fyw mae ffrâm ac ynddi gopi llawysgrifen gain o gerdd Gerallt Lloyd Owen 'Etifeddiaeth'. Nid gormod yw dweud petai 'Oscar' ar y silff-ben-tan hefyd mai'r gerdd fyddai fy nhrysor i.

Rhoddwyd y copi i mi am fod yn aelod o dîm Talwrn y Beirdd Penrhosgarnedd a gyrhaeddodd ffeinal y gystadleuaeth yn Aberystwyth yn 1992. Gan fod y gerdd yn un o'm ffefrynnau a'i hawdur yn un o'm harwyr mae'n werth ffortiwn.

Gyda balchder un yn cael gwireddu uchelgais y cerddwn tua'r Babell Lên y diwrnod hwnnw. Fy nhasgau wedi'u cwblhau ac yn nwylo y Meuryn. Beth bynnag fyddai canlyniad y ffeinal roeddwn yn mynd i fwynhau'r achlysur.

Fel yr oeddwn yn mynd i adrodd fy englyn, dyma'r Meuryn gyda'i amseru perffaith arferol yn cyflwyno pennill i mi . . .

> Peth digri iawn yw berfa
> Sydd isio bod yn dractor,
> Peth trist yw isio bod yn fardd
> A chitha ddim ond actor!

Mae bardd 'Etifeddiaeth' yn deall ei genedl a'i phobol.

~

On the wall of the sitting-room there is a frame containing a beautifully handwritten copy of Gerallt Lloyd Owen's poem 'Etifeddiaeth'. It wouldn't be an exaggeration to say that if there was also an Oscar on the mantlepiece, it's the poem that I would treasure.

The copy was given to me for being a member of the Penrhosgarnedd 'Talwrn y Beirdd' (poetic contest) team which reached the final of the competition in Aberystwyth in 1992. As the poem is one of my favourites and its author one of my heroes it is worth a fortune to me.

I walked towards the Literary Pavilion that day full of the pride of one realizing an ambition. My tasks completed and in the hands of the Adjudicator. Whatever the outcome of the final I was going to enjoy the event.

As I was going to recite my *englyn*, the Adjudicator with his usual perfect timing dedicated a verse to me . . .

Highly amusing is a wheelbarrow
That wants to be a tractor,
It's sad to want to be a poet
And you only an actor!

The composer of 'Etifeddiaeth' understands his nation and its
people.

Etifeddiaeth

Cawsom wlad i'w chadw
darn o dir yn dyst
ein bod wedi mynnu byw.

Cawsom genedl o genhedlaeth
i genhedlaeth ac anadlu
ein hanes ni ein hunain.

A chawsom iaith, er na cheisiem hi,
oherwydd ei hias oedd yn y pridd eisioes
a'i grym anniddig ar y mynyddoedd.

Troesom ein tir yn simneiau tân
a phlannu coed a pheilonau cadarn
lle nad oedd llyn.
Troesom ein cenedl i genhedlu
estroniaid heb ystyr i'w hanes,
gwymon o ddynion heb ddal
tro'r trai.
A throesom iaith yr oesau
yn iaith ein cywilydd ni.

Ystyriwch: a oes dihareb
a ddwed y gwirionedd hwn:
Gwerth cynnydd yw gwarth cenedl,
a'i hedd yw ei hangau hi.

Gerallt Lloyd Owen

Cerddi'r Cywilydd (Gwasg Gwynedd, 1977)

John Osmond

John Tripp spoke directly to me, from my own Welsh wilderness that is Whitchurch in Cardiff, in terms I could readily understand and be amused by, and generally on subjects of immediate, poignant concern.

Nigel Jenkins opens his short, brilliant biography (in the University of Wales *Writers of Wales* series) with a typical comment from John: 'I was born in Bargoed in 1927', he used to say, 'and I want to know why.' Inside the front cover of my copy of his *Collected Poems 1958–78*, John hastily scribbled the words 'To John O. What is the Welsh problem? Let me know . . .'

John's life was about searching for answers to such questions and, of course, he found it in Wales, not withstanding that it was a Wales that brought him to continual despair. The Wales he knew and spoke up for never lived up to *his* expectations.

He, however, never gave up. He continued his anarchic, unpredictable swathe through life, here a touch of warmth, there a sardonic smile. It seems that all who knew and were touched by him, and are also known to me, are my friends too.

The poem I have chosen is not his best, and certainly not his best known. But it is personal to me. Like so much of John's poetry, it has sustained me through the hard years of keeping Wales on the straight and narrow towards autonomy.

1.III.79

There comes a day
to leave the trench,
to go back for a rest
and the bandages and ointment.

'Enough is enough'
as the captain muttered
after years of it.
'Let's fall back, boys'.

Old gunfire fades
but the shock does not.
In their faces I could read
dismay, the malady of defeat.

I met the 'cynics', victims
of collapse and fatigue
who asked me the time
of the next train out.

But some tired old valiants
come limping through the smoke,
get patched up and mended,
then go back up the line again.

John Tripp
Planet, No. 48 (May 1979)

Lord Parry

Among several poems on my short-list, I would choose 'On Death' by Keats. It was written by Keats when he realized that he would not recover from tuberculosis and that he would be parted from Frances Brawn, his lady love.

It certainly seems a pessimistic theme, but the verse is triumphant. The choice is not simply because of my sixty-eight years. I learned this poem for Central Welsh Board examinations when I was fifteen. It even seemed relevant then!

On Death

I

Can death be sleep, when life is but a dream,
   And scenes of bliss pass as a phantom by?
The transient pleasures as a vision seem,
   And yet we think the greatest pain's to die.

II

How strange it is that man on earth should roam,
   And lead a life of woe, but not forsake
His rugged path; nor dare he view alone
   His future doom which is but to awake.

John Keats
Poetical Works, ed. H. W. Garrod (Oxford University Press, 1956)

Phil Parry

My selection is 'The Second Coming' by W. B. Yeats.

I'm not especially religious but the language is wonderful. I try to write stirring television scripts but nothing can compare to the beauty and strength of this writing. It's frightening but somehow inspiring at the same time. I do my best to find and tell good stories in my job – but the second coming, now that would be the exclusive of a lifetime!

The Second Coming

Turning and turning in the widening gyre
The falcon cannot hear the falconer;
Things fall apart; the centre cannot hold;
Mere anarchy is loosed upon the world,
The blood-dimmed tide is loosed, and everywhere
The ceremony of innocence is drowned;
The best lack all conviction, while the worst
Are full of passionate intensity.

Surely some revelation is at hand;
Surely the Second Coming is at hand.
The Second Coming! Hardly are those words out
When a vast image out of *Spiritus Mundi*
Troubles my sight: somewhere in sands of the desert
A shape with lion body and the head of a man,
A gaze blank and pitiless as the sun,
Is moving its slow thighs, while all about it
Reel shadows of the indignant desert birds.
The darkness drops again; but now I know
That twenty centuries of stony sleep
Were vexed to nightmare by a rocking cradle,
And what rough beast, its hour come round at last,
Slouches towards Bethlehem to be born?

W. B. Yeats

Selected Poetry (Macmillan, 1962)

'Silicosis'. Graphics by Paul Peter Piech.

198

Paul Peter Piech

This poem 'Silicosis' by the English poet, John Gurney, epitomizes all the stories that my father-in-law John Tomkins, an ex-miner who died from silicosis, used to relate to me when I courted his daughter in the Cynon Valley town of Abercwmboi. I was very fortunate to be selected by John Gurney to illustrate his collection of sonnets, *Coal*, since this was a golden opportunity to say 'graphically' and visually my 'thanks' for the great friendships and comradeship encountered with so many of the Cynon Valley miners and in some way record the history of the miners' lives and hardships throughout the years here in south Wales.

The entire graphic collection of prints from the *Coal* poetry book will become a permanent exhibition at the Rhondda Heritage Park Miners' Museum, near Pontypridd, as a visual memorial to all the miners, not only from the valleys of Wales, but from all the other pits throughout Britain. Long live their contribution to society and never let the coming generations forget this honour due every digger of Coal.

Silicosis

The dust had got him. Filled his lungs with grit.
He sat up nights, coughing like a pick
at the soft coal. Each wheeze a wound. The pit
still gassed him, and the mucus bubbled, thick
as a black stew. Clouds hung like punctured lungs
on the dark tips. But sometimes, in the day,
he'd sit out in his pit-clothes, watch the tongues
of smoke lick from the stack. At times he'd say
the hill had turned transparent. He could see
the far end of the mine, the curving roads
that bent beneath the mountain, every
dead horse, and boy and collier. Or explode
with sudden gusts of dread. In night attire
would shout into the street, 'The pit's on fire!'

John Gurney

Coal (Taxus Press, 1994)

Clive Ponting

I first became attracted to Wilfred Owen's poems after hearing Britten's *War Requiem* in the early 1960s, although I now think that Britten's settings detract from rather than enhance the poetry. Owen is the voice of those who were given no choice by the ruling élites of Europe during the slaughter of the First World War – the voice of those condemned to die without understanding why they had to fight and who were sacrificed by those who knew little of the realities of trench warfare. Owen was a man who became disillusioned by the platitudes and the propaganda about the war and 'Dulce et Decorum Est' encapsulates that disillusionment at its most bitter. For me it is the voice of the countless millions across the world who have been asked to suffer and die for meaningless slogans and for the benefit of others during the twentieth century.

Dulce et Decorum Est

Bent double, like old beggars under sacks,
Knock-kneed, coughing like hags, we cursed through sludge,
Till on the haunting flares we turned our backs
And towards our distant rest began to trudge.
Men marched asleep. Many had lost their boots
But limped on, blood-shod. All went lame; all blind;
Drunk with fatigue; deaf even to the hoots
Of tired, outstripped Five-Nines that dropped behind.

Gas! GAS! Quick, boys! – An ecstasy of fumbling,
Fitting the clumsy helmets just in time;
But someone still was yelling out and stumbling,
And flound'ring like a man in fire or lime . . .
Dim, through the misty panes and thick green light,
As under a green sea, I saw him drowning.

In all my dreams, before my helpless sight,
He plunges at me, guttering, choking, drowning.

If in some smothering dreams you too could pace
Behind the wagon that we flung him in,
And watch the white eyes writhing in his face,
His hanging face, like a devil's sick of sin;
If you could hear, at every jolt, the blood
Come gargling from the froth-corrupted lungs,
Obscene as cancer, bitter as the cud
Of vile, incurable sores on innocent tongues, –
My friend, you would not tell with such high zest
To children ardent for some desperate glory,
The old Lie: Dulce et decorum est
Pro patria mori.

Wilfred Owen

The Poems of Wilfred Owen, ed. Jon Stallworthy
(Chatto and Windus, 1990)

Dewi Watkin Powell

Mae'r englyn hwn o 'Gân yr Henwr', lle y cyffelybir ffawd henwr siomedig a thrist i ddeilen, yn enwog.

Nid am ei enwogrwydd ac, yn sicr, nid oblegid mai mynegi tristwch henaint y mae, y'i dewisais.

Bob tro y'i darllennaf neu y clywaf yn cael ei adrodd, ni allaf ond rhyfeddu at geinder a chynildeb soffistigedig y mynegiant, a hynny'n dod o'r nawfed ganrif. Gyda'r rhyfeddu, daw syndod fy mod i, ddeuddeg canrif yn ddiweddarach, yn gallu ei ddeall, balchder mod i'n perthyn i genedl a feddai ar ddigon o warineb i allu llunio'r fath geinder mewn geiriau a'u gwerthfawrogi, a llawenydd bod y genedl Gymreig, er gwaethaf pawb a phopeth, yma o hyd ac yn ymfalchïo yn ei threftadaeth wâr.

~

This *englyn* from 'Cân yr Henwr', which likens the fate of a disappointed and sad old man to a leaf, is famous.

I did not choose it because it is well known and certainly not because it expresses the sadness of old age .

Every time I read it or hear it being recited, I cannot but wonder at the elegance and sophisticated economy of expression of this ninth-century work. With the wonder, comes surprise that I, twelve centuries later, am able to understand it, pride that I belong to a nation that was civilized enough to be able to compose such elegance in words and appreciate them, and happiness that the Welsh nation, in spite of everybody and everything, is still here and taking pride in her civilized heritage.

Cân yr Henwr

(detholiad / an extract)

Y ddeilen hon, neus cynired gwynt,
  Gwae hi o'i thynged!
Hi hen; eleni ganed

Anon.

The Oxford Book of Welsh Verse, ed. Thomas Parry
(Oxford University Press, 1962)

Jonathan Pryce

It's not exactly a poem, but a passage of Shakespeare.

My mother died not long before I played Macbeth at Stratford. I wanted these words read at her funeral – but it would have been too painful.

But some of that pain and sorrow was present during this speech of Macbeth's when he learnt of his Queen's death – and I thought of the loss of all our loved ones.

Seyton: The Queen, my lord, is dead.

Macbeth: She should have died hereafter;
            There would have been a time for such a word.
            To-morrow, and to-morrow, and to-morrow,
            Creeps in this petty pace from day to day,
            To the last syllable of recorded time;
            And all our yesterdays have lighted fools
            The way to dusty death. Out, out, brief candle!
            Life's but a walking shadow, a poor player
            That struts and frets his hour upon the stage
            And then is heard no more: it is a tale
            Told by an idiot, full of sound and fury,
            Signifying nothing.

William Shakespeare

Macbeth, Act V, Scene V, ll.16–28

Sheenagh Pugh

I can't understand people who have one favourite poem all their lives. Mine changes constantly, with my personal circumstances and preoccupations. Just now I am preoccupied with mortality, having reached an age where you have to admit they aren't going to find an antidote to death, at least not in your lifetime.

This poem, by the great George Mackay Brown, was written in 1990 when he was a patient at the Aberdeen Royal Infirmary. He passed time by writing a sequence in which he imagined a medieval monastic beginning for the hospital. 'Homily' is a bleak, aching, beautiful vision of the journey of life; its delight, its essential loneliness in the end; the small ways in which that loneliness can be rendered slightly less painful. I love it for its images – the snow, the broken bridge – which acquire a life beyond themselves, and its honesty. It makes me feel like crying my eyes out, which is part of what I want from a poem. I've no time for what Gillian Clarke calls 'clever young man poems', which make you think 'how clever that poet is', rather than 'how profound', or 'how moving'.

Homily

We go into distances, near or far, each man to his own bourne.

In childhood, all is green and good,
Trees, horses, stones, stars, flowers.
                (There is only the garden,
                    never gate or a road
                    beyond the garden.)

There comes a call in the night, in youth, a summons
                    purer than music,
               deeper than truth itself.
We go out into wind and a few stars.

In the morning we are on a desolate road
(Where is the woman, keeper of fire, the children,
The house on its firm rock, the flock on the hill?
There and not there: shadows.)

The voice is all delight to us still
In the first lingering flakes of age.

The sun sets on our labouring urgency.
We hurry to find an inn
With fire and bottle, fish and bread.
It thickens to black snow.
Breath, heart are snagged with nets of blizzard.
But there is no lamp of welcome at midnight.

Cry of a torrent under a broken bridge, far on.
What will the dayspring show?

Look for no company of goodly folk
No fellow pilgrims on that road.
Loneliness is all
And the bitter fruit of the selfhood of each man –
Shame, regret, fear, sorrow, rage.

We are beyond the last scars of snow
And there the fires begin.

*

We brothers put ourselves here, at the door
And in the choir, with music
And at the board with a few loaves
And at the beds with candles
And one on the road outside, at midnight, with a lantern

Should a soul go past bereft and weeping.

George Mackay Brown

Foresterhill (Babel Press, 1992)

John Puzey

I cannot divorce writing from the writer. I need to have some empathy with the outlook and the 'persuasion' of the poet in order really to enjoy the poetry.

I have many things in common with John Hegley. He is pre-occupied with dogs, garden sheds, spectacles, the Romans – and injustice. (I spoke with him once and confirmed all this.)

He also entertains – he jokes and sings his way through his work. He believes poetry is an everyday common occurrence that we all take part in. He writes: 'there's poetry that you can see in the life of everybody . . . poetry is good for me, I think I'll have some for my tea.' Me too.

I have chosen 'Eddie don't like furniture' – the kids like this too – try singing it.

Eddie don't like furniture

Eddie don't go for sofas or settees
or those little tables that you have to buy in threes
the closest thing that Eddie's got to an article of
    furniture's
the cheese board
Eddie doesn't bolster the upholstery biz
there's a lot of furniture in the world but none of it's
    Eddie's
he won't have it in the house however well it's made
Eddie's bedroom was fully furnished
when the floorboards had been laid
and Eddie played guitar
until he decided that his guitar was far too like
an article of furniture
Eddie offers visitors a corner of the room
you get used to the distances between you pretty soon
but with everyone in corners though
it isn't very easy when your trying to play pontoon
he once got in a rowing boat and they offered him a
    seat

'Eddie don't like furniture'. Graphics by William Brown.

it was just a strip of timber but it wasn't up his street
he stood himself up in the boat and made himself feel
    steady
then he threw the plank onto the bank and said
furniture?
no thank you
when it's on a bonfire furniture's fine
any time that Eddie gets a number twenty-nine bus
even if there's seats on top and plenty down below
Eddie always goes where the pushchairs go
does Eddie like furniture?
I don't think so
if you go round Eddie's place and have a game of
    hide and seek
it isn't very long before you're found
and in a fit of craziness Eddie took the legs off his dash
    hound
that stopped him dashing around
Eddie quite likes cutlery
but he don't like furniture
if you give him some for Christmas
he'll returniture

John Hegley

Can I Come Down Now Dad? (Methuen, 1991)

Ioan Bowen Rees

Yn naturiol, nid hoff gerdd sydd gennyf ond ugeiniau o hoff gerddi mewn pedair neu bum iaith wahanol. Sut y gellwch chwi gymharu cywydd serch gan Ddafydd ap Gwilym (er gwaethaf fy oedran, bûm yn ystyried 'Y Deildy') â 'Chywydd Berwyn' Cynddelw neu 'Y Lluwch' gan Ieuan Wyn, 'Caniad y Gog i Feirionnydd' gan Lewis Morris â 'Drudwy Branwen' Williams Parry neu 'Caniad Ehedydd' Waldo; 'Ffarwel yr Orsaf Lanio' Alun Llywellyn-Williams â cherdd Gareth Alban Davies i un o gefnogwyr Allende neu 'Clochdy Bangor' Ifor ap Glyn?

Y tro hwn, bodlonaf ar gerdd sy'n dangos fod y gynghanedd yn ddigon ynddo ei hun i gyfiawnhau'r iaith Gymraeg, sy'n coffáu dawn lleiafrif sylweddol o ffermwyr a gwragedd fferm Cymru – a'i gweithwyr diwydiannol a'i chyfreithwyr – i fyw 'bywyd gwâr mewn byd gerwin'. Cerdd sy'n dathlu 'parhad y cyffredin', yn yr ystyr cymunedol, brawdol, yr ystyr cydraddol, a'r ystyr sy'n cyfateb i 'culture is ordinary' Raymond Williams a'r 'diwylliant cefn gwlad' a ysbrydolodd Gwynfor. Ac er bod pob moel a mawnog yn y 'tir crintach' yn 'odidog' i mi hefyd, sicrhau 'aelwyd' i bawb yw'r flaenoriaeth, fel y gŵyr Shelter mor dda. Ystyriaf fod yr englynion hyn lawn cystal ag englynion coffa adnabyddus Williams Parry ond bu farw Bili Puw dros well achos na Hedd Wyn.

~

Naturally I haven't got one favourite poem but numerous favourite poems in four or five different languages. How can one compare a love poem by Dafydd ap Gwilym (in spite of my age I considered 'Y Deildy') with Cynddelw's 'Chywydd Berwyn' or 'Y Lluwch' by Ieuan Wyn, 'Caniad y Gog i Feirionnydd' by Lewis Morris with Williams Parry's 'Drudwy Branwen' or Waldo's 'Caniad Ehedydd'; Alun Llewelyn-Williams's 'Ffarwel yr Orsaf Lanio' with Gareth Alban-Davies's poem to one of the supporters of Allende or 'Clochdy Bangor' by Ifor ap Glyn?

This time I shall be content with a poem that shows that *cynghanedd* is enough in itself to justify the Welsh language. A poem which commemorates the ability of a substantial minority of the farmers and farmers' wives of Wales – and her industrial workers and lawyers – to live 'a civilized life in a harsh world'. A poem which celebrates 'the continuation of the ordinary' in the community, brotherly sense, the equative sense and the sense which corresponds to Raymond Williams's 'culture is ordinary' and the 'culture of the hinterland' which inspired Gwynfor. And although every hill and marsh in the 'mean land' is 'splendid' to me also, ensuring a 'home' for all is the priority, as Shelter Cymru knows so well. I consider these *englynion* to be just as good as Williams Parry's well-known *englynion* in memory of Hedd Wyn but Bili Puw died for a better cause than he did.

Bili Puw, Cynythog Bach

(Bu farw mewn damwain ar y ffordd o Ddolgellau i Benllyn yn hwyr y nos, ar ôl bod yn cystadlu mewn cwrdd cystadleuol yno.)

Troist eilwaith tros y dalar, – a hwyrnos
    ar dalyrnau'r ddaear,
    ac fel o'r blaen o'r braenar,
    troist dy drem tros dy dir âr.

Sawl gwaith, â'th ddyddgwaith o'th ôl, – y cerddaist
    tua'r cwrdd nosweithiol,
    cyn dod, o'th gyrch 'steddfodol,
    eilwaith at ddyddgwaith y ddôl?

Pe medrwn, cofnodwn i – dy hanes
    â pheth dawn artistri,
    ond heb ddiweddglo'r stori
    mor anodd ei hadrodd hi.

Fe'th aned i galedi – ar dalar
    dy hil ym mro'r tlodi;
    digonedd yn dy gyni
    ni chefaist, ond heuaist hi.

Dwrdiaist dir sofl Llidiardau – a'i edliw
    am adladd ei erwau;
    ofer, rhy ofer ei hau
    a'r drain ar hyd ei rynnau.

'Roedd ffridd lom ar dy gomin – mieri'n
    ymyrryd â'th g'nefin;
    llociau'r ŵyn dan ysgall crin
    a'th Gynythog yn eithin.

Tir crintach, tir corwyntoedd, – a thir heth
  yr hil o'r mynyddoedd;
 y llain o dir lle nad oedd
 eginyn yn troi'n gannoedd.

Eto gwnaethost Gynythog – yn aelwyd,
  anwylaist ei mawnog;
 anwylo'i hâr prin ei log,
 maldodi'i moel odidog.

Llwyn dy ros yn llawn drysi, – hithau'r waun
  dan ei thrwch mieri,
 ond â'th oged, i'w medi,
 lluniaist drefn o'i llanastr hi.

Troi, wrth drin fel dy linach – â phladur,
  bamffledyn y gweiriach;
 gyfair hen! Ce'st gyfrinach
 fawr ein byw'n ei llyfryn bach.

Anhygyrch dy fawnogydd, – anhygyrch
  unigedd y mynydd;
 tir y gaeaf tragywydd,
 tir crintach heb decach dydd.

Ond deuit ar bob tywydd – drwy lidiart
  dreuliedig y mynydd
 i'r cyrddau, ar frig hwyrddydd,
 ym Mro Penllyn derfyn dydd.

Â llais taer, enillaist ti – yn fynych
  ar lwyfannau'i phlwyfi;
 curaist bob un o'r cewri,
 ysgubo'i rhes gwobrau hi.

Bywyd gwâr mewn byd gerwin – a gefaist
  er gaeafau'r ddrycin;
 ceraist hen bethe'r werin,
 drachtiaist ac yfaist o'i gwin.

Erys yn fyw dy stori – nad enwog
na dinod mohoni,
a heb fedd, byw a fyddi
ym Myth dy wehelyth di.

Tra bo dy epil, Bili, – yn cywain
y caeau wrth fedi,
bydd cân yn boddi cyni,
bydd parhad i'n henwlad ni.

Parhad symlder y werin, – a pharhad
cyff yr hen gynefin;
parhad y brawdgarwch prin,
a pharhad y cyffredin.

Alan Llwyd

Rhwng Pen Llŷn a Phenllyn (Christopher Davies, 1976)

Lord Merlyn-Rees

A part of a poem that is a favourite of mine.

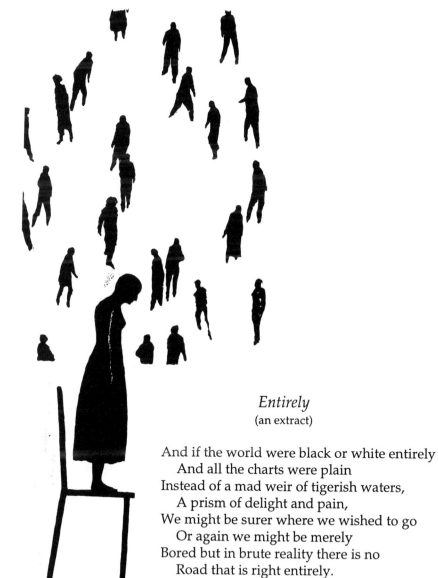

Entirely
(an extract)

And if the world were black or white entirely
    And all the charts were plain
Instead of a mad weir of tigerish waters,
    A prism of delight and pain,
We might be surer where we wished to go
    Or again we might be merely
Bored but in brute reality there is no
    Road that is right entirely.

Louis MacNeice

Collected Poems 1925–48, ed. E. R. Dobbs
(Faber & Faber, 1949)

Graphics by Deborah Jones.

213

Maureen Rhys

Nid ar chwarae bach y mae bardd yn cael yr anrhydedd o gael ei alw'n 'fardd y bobol'. Fe ddigwyddodd hynny i R. Williams Parry – a pha ryfedd. Ond ydi o'n sgrifennu mewn iaith ddealladwy am bethau sy'n ein cyffwrdd ni i gyd?

Oherwydd hynny mae dewis un gerdd o'i waith yn dasg anodd – ond at 'Dinas Noddfa' yr ydw i'n dod yn ôl o hyd ac o hyd – cerdd o obaith os bu un erioed.

Mae yna reswm personol arall dros ddewis 'Dinas Noddfa'. Yn y nofel *Tywyll Heno* gan Kate Roberts mae Bet, gwraig y gweinidog, wedi 'cyrraedd y gwaelod', yn gofyn i'w gŵr, Gruff, ddarllen 'Dinas Noddfa' iddi – yn yr addasiad ffilm o'r nofel, a minnau'n chwarae rhan Bet, wna i byth anghofio gweithio ar yr olygfa honno.

~

It is not without effort that a poet receives the honour of being called 'a poet of the people'. That happened to R. Williams Parry – and little wonder. Doesn't he write in intelligible language about things that touch each and every one of us?

Because of that it is difficult to choose one of his works in particular – but it's to 'Dinas Noddfa' that I return time after time – a poem of hope if ever there was one.

There is another personal reason for choosing 'Dinas Noddfa'. In the novel *Tywyll Heno* by Kate Roberts, Bet, the minister's wife, having reached the depths of despair, asks her husband Gruff to read 'Dinas Noddfa' to her – I'll never forget working on that scene in the film adaptation of the novel in which I played the part of Bet.

('Dinas Noddfa' was also chosen by Menna Elfyn and appears on page 65)

Lord Richard

I am not at all sure that this should be called 'a dirge'. It deserves more than that and I don't think Shakespeare so entitles it. It is in fact the second song from *Cymbeline*, a somewhat under-performed play and one set partly in Wales.

The poem touches me mainly because of the last two lines:

> Quiet consummation have;
> And renownèd be thy grave!

That is surely as much as anyone can conceivably hope for.

The feeling of peace after struggle echoes perhaps those splendid words of Spenser:

> Sleep after toil, port after stormy seas,
> Ease after war, death after life does greatly please.

Either way the sentiment is profound, the language noble and I have treasured it for many years.

Dirge

> Fear no more the heat o' the sun
>   Nor the furious winter's rages;
> Thou thy worldly task hast done,
>   Home art gone, and ta'en thy wages;
> Golden lads and girls all must,
> As chimney-sweepers, come to dust.
>
> Fear no more the frown o' the great,
>   Thou art past the tyrant's stroke;
> Care no more to clothe and eat,
>   To thee the reed is as the oak:
> The sceptre, learning, physic, must
> All follow this and come to dust.

Fear no more the lightning-flash,
    Nor the all-dreaded thunder-stone;
Fear not slander, censure rash;
    Thou hast finish'd joy and moan:
All lovers young, all lovers must
Consign to thee and come to dust.

No exorciser harm thee!
    Nor no witchcraft charm thee!
Ghost unlaid forbear thee!
    Nothing ill come near thee!
Quiet consummation have;
And renownèd be thy grave!

William Shakespeare

Cymbeline, Act IV, Scene II, ll.259–82

Menna Richards

I first read 'Return to Cardiff' when I moved to the city in the mid-seventies. It was an exciting, vibrant place to be for someone who'd just left university and I was delighted to discover a poem which conveyed the affection I felt for Cardiff.

Indeed, I liked it so much that a poster of 'Return to Cardiff' was sellotaped to the kitchen wall of my first flat for many years. It was also an introduction to Dannie Abse, whose work I've enjoyed enormously ever since.

Return To Cardiff

'Hometown'; well, most admit an affection for a city:
grey, tangled streets I cycled on to school, my first cigarette
in the back lane, and, fool, my first botched love affair.
First everything. Faded torments; self-indulgent pity.

The journey to Cardiff seemed less a return than a raid
on mislaid identities. Of course the whole locus smaller:
the mile-wide Taff now a stream, the castle not as in some black,
gothic dream, but a decent sprawl, a joker's toy facade.

Unfocused voices in the wind, associations, clues,
odds and ends, fringes caught, as when, after the doctor quit,
a door opened and I glimpsed the white, enormous face
of my grandfather, suddenly aghast with certain news.

Unable to define anything I can hardly speak,
and still I love the place for what I wanted it to be
as much as for what it unashamedly is
now for me, a city of strangers, alien and bleak.

Unable to communicate I'm easily betrayed,
uneasily diverted by mere sense reflections
like those anchored waterscapes that wander, alter, in the Taff,
hour by hour, as light slants down a different shade.

Illusory, too, that lost dark playground after rain,
the noise of trams, gunshots in what they once called Tiger Bay.
Only real this smell of ripe, damp earth when the sun comes out,
a mixture of pungencies, half exquisite and half plain.

No sooner than I'd arrived the other Cardiff had gone,
smoke in the memory, these but tinned resemblances,
where the boy I was not and the man I am not
met, hesitated, left double footsteps, then walked on.

Dannie Abse

White Coat Purple Coat: Collected Poems 1948–1988
(Hutchinson, 1989)

Brynley F. Roberts

Y mae gennym bawb nifer o hoff gerddi a byddai'n amhosibl dewis un ohonynt i fod *yr* hoff gerdd. Maent yn apelio atom, neu'n dweud rhywbeth wrthym, bob un mewn ffordd arbennig yn ôl ein hamgylchiadau a'n hanghenion ar adegau gwahanol. Efallai fy mod wedi dychwelyd at y soned hon gan R. Williams Parry yn ddiweddar am fy mod newydd ymddeol ac felly'n fwy ymwybodol o dreigl y blynyddoedd – ac yn anorfod o'm hoedran – nag yr oeddwn gynt. Gall gweld cyfnod gwaith cyflogedig yn dod i ben fod yn newid byd ysgytwol sy'n peri ymdeimlad o ddiffyg hyder ac yn wir o bryder neu ofn: ac nid yw hynny ond un wedd ar yr ymboeni ynghylch mynd yn hen.

Ond nid wyf yn credu mai cerdd am heneiddio yw 'Cysur Henaint'. Gŵr yn nesu at ganol oed a heb ei gyrraedd oedd y bardd pan ysgrifennodd y soned hon, ac nid oedd eto wedi profi problemau henaint. Sôn y mae am rywbeth dyfnach na threfn amser a chyfnodau bywyd. Ym mha gyfnod neu gyflwr y byddwn mae'n demtasiwn inni ymlacio ac ymorffwys yn gysurus yn y cyfarwydd digyfnewid. Pechod parod yw glynu wrth batrwm cynefin, magu rhagfarnau a chau'r meddwl rhag profi llif bywyd. Nid oes a wnelo ymagwedd 'yr hen a ŵyr' ag oedran. Un o hanfodion byw yw canfod newydd-deb parhaus bywyd. Imi, sydd newydd ymddeol, mae'r her honno'n un amlwg, ond nid her heneiddio ydyw, oherwydd ymhob cenhedlaeth drachtio'r gwin newydd sy'n cadw'r esgyrn – a'r gobaith – rhag crino.

~

We all have a number of favourite poems and it would be impossible to choose one of them to be *the* favourite poem. They all appeal to us, or say something to us, each in a special way according to our circumstances and needs at different times. Maybe I have returned recently to this sonnet by R. Williams Parry as I have just retired and therefore am more aware of the passing of the years – and inevitably of my age – than I was previously. Seeing the end of paid employment can be a shocking change to one's world, causing a feeling of lack of confidence and indeed of anxiety or fear: and that is only one aspect of the worry regarding getting old.

But I don't believe that 'Cysur Henaint' is a poem about getting old. The poet was only nearing middle age when he wrote this sonnet and he hadn't as yet come across the problems of old age. He is referring to something deeper than the order of time and the stages of life. In whatever stage or condition we are it is tempting for us to relax and rest comfortably in the never-changing familiar. It's a ready sin to stick to the pattern of the familiar, adopt prejudices and close the mind from tasting of the flow of life. The attitude 'the old know best' has nothing to do with age. One of the essences of living is to perceive the continual newness of life. To me, who has recently retired, that challenge is an obvious one, but it is not the challenge of getting old, because in every generation it is the drinking deep of the new wine which keeps the bones – and the hope – from withering.

Cysur Henaint

Mae mewn ieuenctid dristwch, ac mewn oed
   Ddiddanwch, fel ar haul yr haf y trig
Y bore-ddydd yn dywyll yn y coed,
   A'r nawnddydd fel y nos o dan y brig;
Nes dyfod mis o'r misoedd pan fo'r gwynt
   Yn cychwyn crinddail ar eu hediad oer,
A thrwy'r di-nefoedd dywyll-leoedd gynt
   Yn chwythu llewych haul a llewych lloer.
Ninnau, pan syrth ein grawnwin, a phan dynn
   Dydd ein diddychwel haf hyd eitha 'i rawd,
Ni wyddom beth a fyddwn, onid hyn:-
   Mor druan nid yw Henaint nac mor dlawd
Nad erys yn ei gostrel beth o'r gwin
I hybu'r galon rhwng yr esgyrn crin.

R. Williams Parry

Yr Haf a Cherddi Eraill (Gwasg y Bala, 1924)

David Rowe-Beddoe

Apart from the poet himself, the person most closely associated with the performance of this poem was one Richard Jenkins of Pontrhydyfen, known from his late teens as Richard Burton – the Prince of Verse. The day we first met – some forty summers ago – he came unexpectedly to an outdoor music and drama evening which a group of students were organizing.

My involvement together with Brook, Emlyn Williams's son, was to introduce a significant Welsh element into the proceedings. It fell to me to recite 'Fern Hill'. Some five minutes before the event was due to start, the great man was spotted sitting on the grass. Convulsed with nervousness, I galloped through the verse – a dreadful performance. Nevertheless, it remains vividly in my memory as the start of a close and dear friendship, whilst the poem itself becomes even fresher each time it is read.

('Fern Hill' by Dylan Thomas was also chosen by John Humphrys and appears on page 114)

Ted Rowlands

One of my favourite poems is by Dylan Thomas. 'Poem in October' is a wonderful evocative poem capturing images very familiar to me.

The rhythm and sounds of the poem are very Welsh. They are part of my Welshness.

Poem in October

It was my thirtieth year to heaven
Woke to my hearing from harbour and neighbour wood
And the mussel pooled and the heron
Priested shore
The morning beckon
With water praying and call of seagull and rook
And the knock of sailing boats on the net webbed wall
Myself to set foot
That second
In the still sleeping town and set forth.

My birthday began with the water –
Birds and the birds of the winged trees flying my name
Above the farms and the white horses
And I rose
In the rainy autumn
And walked abroad in a shower of all my days.
High tide and the heron dived when I took the road
Over the border
And the gates
Of the town closed as the town awoke.

A springful of larks in a rolling
Cloud and the roadside bushes brimming with whistling
Blackbirds and the sun of October
Summery
On the hill's shoulder,
Here were fond climates and sweet singers suddenly
Come in the morning where I wandered and listened

To the rain wringing
Wind blow cold
In the wood faraway under me.

Pale rain over the dwindling harbour
And over the sea wet church the size of a snail
With its horns through mist and the castle
Brown as owls
But all the gardens
Of spring and summer were blooming in the tall tales
Beyond the border and under the lark full cloud.
There could I marvel
My birthday
Away but the weather turned around.

It turned away from the blithe country
And down the other air and the blue altered sky
Streamed again a wonder of summer
With apples
Pears and red currants
And I saw in the turning so clearly a child's
Forgotten mornings when he walked with his mother
Through the parables
Of sun light
And the legends of the green chapels

And the twice told fields of infancy
That his tears burned my cheeks and his heart moved in
mine.
These were the woods the river and sea
Where a boy
In the listening
Summertime of the dead whispered the truth of his joy
To the trees and the stones and the fish in the tide.
And the mystery
Sang alive
Still in the water and singingbirds.

And there could I marvel my birthday
Away but the weather turned around. And the true
Joy of the long dead child sang burning
In the sun.

It was my thirtieth
Year to heaven stood there then in the summer noon
Though the town below lay leaved with October blood.
O may my heart's truth
Still be sung
On this high hill in a year's turning.

Dylan Thomas

Collected Poems, 1934–1952 (Dent, 1952)

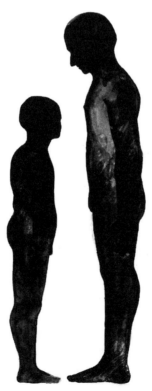

'It was my thirtieth year to heaven'. Graphics by Deborah Jones.

Michael Scholar

I have chosen 'The World' by Henry Vaughan. I like this poem for its genius and beauty. The first lines! I could well have chosen other poems by Henry Vaughan, of equal beauty. 'They are all gone into the world of light!'; or 'Happy those early dayes! When I/Shin'd in my Angell Infancy'; or even 'My Soul, there is a countrie/Far beyond the stars'.

This poem reminds me of nights near the River Usk which was Henry Vaughan's home: I like that too. I am not myself in any proper sense religious, but I feel at one with Henry Vaughan's religious vision, and his proper estimation of the world and its woes.

What is this religion in his poems and how should we live with it today? A religious awe, a religious fear: what do they mean? A sense of our insignificance, and of the mystery of that? Of the beauty and mystery of things? Or is what I am saying reductionist or dismissive?

I'm not sure:

> Ah! My soul with too much stay
> Is drunk, and staggers in the way.
> Some men a forward motion love,
> but I by backward steps would move.

The World

> I saw Eternity the other night
> Like a great Ring of pure and endless light,
>   All calm as it was bright;
> And round beneath it, Time, in hours, days, years,
>   Driven by the spheres,
> Like a vast shadow moved, in which the world
>   And all her train were hurled.
> The doting Lover in his quaintest strain
>   Did there complain;
> Near him, his lute, his fancy, and his flights,
>   Wit's sour delights;
> With gloves and knots, the silly snares of pleasure,
>   Yet his dear treasure
> All scattered lay, while he his eyes did pour
>   Upon a flower.

The darksome Statesman hung with weights and woe,
Like a thick midnight fog, moved there so slow
    He did nor stay nor go;
Condemning thoughts, like sad eclipses, scowl
    Upon his soul,
And clouds of crying witnesses without
    Pursued him with one shout.
Yet digged the mole, and, lest his ways be found,
    Worked under ground,
Where he did clutch his prey; but One did see
    That policy.
Churches and altars fed him, perjuries
    Were gnats and flies;
It rained about him blood and tears, but he
    Drank them as free.

The fearful Miser on a heap of rust
Sat pining all his life there, did scarce trust
    His own hands with the dust;
Yet would not place one piece above, but lives
    In fear of thieves.
Thousands there were as frantic as himself,
    And hugged each one his pelf.
The downright Epicure placed heaven in sense
    And scorned pretence;
While others, slipped into a wide excess,
    Said little less;
The weaker sort, slight, trivial wares enslave,
    Who think them brave;
And poor despisèd Truth sat counting by
    Their victory.

Yet some, who all this while did weep and sing,
And sing and weep, soared up into the Ring;
    But most would use no wing.
'Oh, fools,' said I, 'thus to prefer dark night
    Before true light,
To live in grots, and caves, and hate the day
    Because it shows the way,
The way which from this dead and dark abode
    Leads up to God,
A way where you might tread the sun, and be

More bright than he.'
But as I did their madness so discuss,
   One whispered thus,
This Ring the Bridegroom did for none provide
   But for his Bride.

Henry Vaughan

The New Oxford Book of English Verse, 1250–1950, ed. Helen Gardner
(Oxford University Press, 1972)

Sir Harry Secombe

This poem was one which I elected to recite at a school concert when I was about ten.

For weeks I did nothing but recite it to anyone who was daft enough to listen to me. I remember confronting our milkman with it one morning. He stood looking at me in complete bewilderment as I delivered the poem in my ear-piercing treble, whilst behind him, his horse ate his way through next door's privet hedge.

When the day of the concert dawned, I was beside myself with excitement and fear. The event was staged in the School Hall after morning assembly and the participants had to perform their individual pieces on the platform on which the Headmaster and various other members of staff were seated. My brother Fred who was Head Prefect was also up there.

My name was called and as I approached the platform I could hear muffled sniggers from the lads who knew my reputation as being a bit of a clown. My knees began to go as I mounted the platform and as I turned to face the assembly my spectacles started to steam up.

'Can I Forget The Sweet Days That Have Been' by W. H. Davies, I announced in a voice which was even higher than my normal register. I then launched into the poem.

'Can I Forget The Sweet Days That Have Been', I squeaked. And stopped. Nothing else came into my mind. I repeated the first line about five times until the dam burst as the boys out front erupted into laughter. Gently Fred came to me and, taking his by now babbling brother by the hand, led me from the platform.

That's why I have chosen this poem. Because, even now, whenever I wait to go on stage, that moment of dread comes back to me and I say a little prayer that it won't happen again.

Days That Have Been

Can I forget the sweet days that have been,
  When poetry first began to warm my blood;
When from the hills of Gwent I saw the earth
  Burned into two by Severn's silver flood:

When I would go alone at night to see
    The moonlight, like a big white butterfly,
Dreaming on that old castle near Caerleon,
    While at its side the Usk went softly by:

When I would stare at lovely clouds in Heaven,
    Or watch them when reported by deep streams;
When feeling pressed like thunder, but would not
    Break into that grand music of my dreams?

Can I forget the sweet days that have been,
    The villages so green I have been in;
Llantarnam, Magor, Malpas and Llanwern,
    Liswery, old Caerleon, and Alteryn?

Can I forget the banks of Malpas Brook,
    Or Ebbw's voice in such a wild delight,
As on he dashed with pebbles in his throat,
    Gurgling towards the sea with all his might?

Ah, when I see a leafy village now,
    I sigh and ask it for Llantarnam's green;
I ask each river where is Ebbw's voice –
    In memory of the sweet days that have been.

W. H. Davies

The Complete Poems of W. H. Davies (Jonathan Cape, 1963)

Ian Skidmore

My choice would be 'The Maimed Debauchee', the satire by the Earl of Rochester. As a reluctant teetotaller I have sympathy with the point of view of a man who admitted to spending his life – as I did – in a 'mist of perpetual revelry'.

My ancestor (John, 1st Viscount Scudamore (1601–1671) of Holme Lacy) would approve. He started the Hereford cider industry!

The Maimed Debauchee

As some brave admiral, in former war
    Deprived of force, but pressed with courage still,
Two rival fleets appearing from afar,
    Crawls to the top of an adjacent hill;

From whence, with thoughts full of concern, he views
    The wise and daring conduct of the fight,
Whilst each bold action to his mind renews
    His present glory and his past delight;

From his fierce eyes flashes of fire he throws,
    As from black clouds when lightning breaks away;
Transported, thinks himself amidst the foes,
    And absent, yet enjoys the bloody day;

So, when my days of impotence approach,
    And I'm by pox and wine's unlucky chance
Forced from the pleasing billows of debauch
    On the dull shore of lazy temperance,

My pains at least some respite shall afford
    While I behold the battles you maintain
When fleets of glasses sail about the board,
    From whose broadsides volleys of wit shall rain.

Nor let the sight of honourable scars,
   Which my too forward valour did procure,
Frighten new-listed soldiers from the wars:
   Past joys have more than paid what I endure.

Should any youth (worth being drunk) prove nice,
   And from his fair inviter meanly shrink,
'Twill please the ghost of my departed vice
   If, at my counsel, he repent and drink.

Or should some cold-complexioned sot forbid,
   With his dull morals, our bold night-alarms,
I'll fire his blood by telling what I did
   When I was strong and able to bear arms.

I'll tell of whores attacked, their lords at home;
   Bawds' quarters beaten up, and fortress won;
Windows demolished, watches overcome;
   And handsome ills by my contrivance done.

Nor shall our love-fits, Chloris, be forgot,
   When each the well-looked linkboy strove t' enjoy,
And the best kiss was the deciding lot
   Whether the boy fucked you, or I the boy.

With tales like these I will such thoughts inspire
   As to important mischief shall incline:
I'll make him long some ancient church to fire,
   And fear no lewdness he's called to by wine.

Thus, statesmanlike, I'll saucily impose,
   And safe from action, valiantly advise;
Sheltered in impotence, urge you to blows,
   And being good for nothing else, be wise.

John Wilmot

The Complete Poems of John Wilmot, Earl of Rochester, ed. David Vieth
(Yale University Press, 1968)

Victor Spinetti

This poem was written by me, whilst looking out of a bedsitter in London during a thunderstorm. The storm was so intense I felt I had to try to mark it down in some way.

Many years later, whilst working with Richard Burton in Rome, filming *The Taming of the Shrew*, he called for a poetry recital during a long wait on the set. He started the recital with a poem by Dylan Thomas; Cyril Cusack recited 'a bit of Yeats', I then spoke this poem.

When I had finished Richard said to me, 'Good God, Vic, that's Wales that is, write it down for me'. The next night at a party he was asked to recite; he must have learnt this poem overnight for he performed it magnificently. 'Who wrote that?' he was asked. He pointed to me and said, 'That Welsh bastard over there'. Richard, usually fondly, referred to me, in spite of me being born in Wales, as, 'You're not Welsh, you're a bloody Bracchi-shop, a bloody Eye-tie . . .'

I was now formally and finally, a fully fledged Welshman, dubbed by Richard Burton.

A very special poem indeed.

On Looking Out of a Bedsitter

This is a day
for gravestones
wet gravel paths
and high black ornamental railings.

This is a day
for the solidity
of non-conformist solidity
and heavy sided tombs
and wet carved angels
and rows and rows of R.I.P.'s.

This is a day
for mud
mud at the graveside

232

and umbrella'd cassock'd clergy
and mackintosh'd mourners
and dark wet windows
and all the purple trappings
of man's peaceful and ultimate
resting place.

This is a day
for the corpse to be left
in its deep and muddy cold resting place
with the rain
washing the deepest regrets off the cards
and the wind blowing the flowers
over the wet gravel paths.

In short,
descriptive passages put aside
this is a day
a God awful,
God almighty,
dank, dark day
for,
a funeral.

Victor Spinetti

Meic Stephens

I suppose most poets tend to admire in the work of others those poems they would themselves like to have written.

I am not an admirer of Philip Larkin's poetry as a whole. A good deal of it I rather dislike; nor do I warm much to what I know about the man. But there is one poem of his which I have carried around in my head ever since I came across it in Larkin's book, *High Windows*, about twenty years ago. I find 'The Explosion' unforgettable.

I suspect that one of the reasons why I like this poem is that it could very well be about a pit-disaster in Wales, and that it might have been written by a Welsh poet rather than by a very English one. Be that as it may, I can respond to 'The Explosion' on its own terms. I know nothing about the poem's provenance, but it seems to me closely observed, genuinely felt, and carefully constructed.

I am, of course, struck by the image of the unbroken eggs, upon which the poem's emotional charge depends for its effect. But I am also glad that it is capable of more than one interpretation. That it has an air of unresolved mystery is, for me, an essential part of its appeal. I shouldn't want anyone to explain to me which of the several interpretations is 'the right one'.

The Explosion

On the day of the explosion
Shadows pointed towards the pithead:
In the sun the slagheap slept.

Down the lane came men in pitboots
Coughing oath-edged talk and pipe-smoke,
Shouldering off the freshened silence.

One chased after rabbits; lost them;
Came back with a nest of lark's eggs;
Showed them; lodged them in the grasses.

So they passed in beards and moleskins,
Fathers, brothers, nicknames, laughter,
Through the tall gates standing open.

'Coughing oath-edged talk and pipe-smoke'. Graphics by Sarah Hopkins.

At noon, there came a tremor; cows
Stopped chewing for a second; sun,
Scarfed as in a heat-haze, dimmed.

The dead go on before us, they
Are sitting in God's house in comfort,
We shall see them face to face –

Plain as lettering in the chapels
It was said, and for a second
Wives saw men of the explosion

Larger than in life they managed –
Gold as on a coin, or walking
Somehow from the sun towards them,

One showing the eggs unbroken.

Philip Larkin

High Windows (Faber & Faber, 1974)

Vivienne Sugar

Just the last three lines of this extract from Shakespeare's *Hamlet* were written by a relative in my autograph book. I was eleven at the time, and didn't really come to understand it until many years later.

I've chosen it because of the contrast between then and now. Then, we had just moved into a brand new three-bedroomed council house (I had my own room!). My father worked in the steelworks and I and my brothers were children of the Welfare State, with good health care, free school milk (and the cod liver oil and malt which I hated). I went to the first comprehensive school in Wales and later became the first from our family to go to university (on a grant, not a loan). Teachers, family, all the adults I knew, encouraged me to believe that if you were prepared to work or study hard, you would always be able to better yourself.

Today's eleven-year-old is more likely to be in a family experiencing housing problems and even homelessness. She could be one of the 2,500 homeless families in Cardiff, or the 10,000 on our waiting list and living in poor or overcrowded conditions. She will see the impact of unemployment all around her and question whether it's worth studying when even graduates can't get work. She may have an elderly aunt or uncle waiting in pain for a knee or hip operation, she will be afraid to go out alone or leave the house unattended for fear of crime. At the school gates, she may be offered drugs or be taunted by racists if she is black.

I know that I've made the fifties sound better than they were, and the nineties sound worse, but I do believe that there was more hope around then and that the vision of society that lay behind telling an eleven-year-old 'to thine own self be true' is something worth holding on to.

> And these few precepts in thy memory
> Look thou character. Give thy thoughts no tongue,
> Nor any unproportion'd thought his act.
> Be thou familiar, but by no means vulgar;
> The friends thou hast, and their adoption tried,
> Grapple them to thy soul with hoops of steel;
> But do not dull thy palm with entertainment
> Of each new-hatch'd, unfledg'd comrade. Beware
> Of entrance to a quarrel; but, being in,

Bear't that th'opposed may beware of thee.
Give every man thine ear, but few thy voice;
Take each man's censure, but reserve thy judgement.
Costly thy habit as thy purse can buy,
But not expressed in fancy; rich, not gaudy;
For the apparel oft proclaims the man,
And they in France of the best rank and station
Are most select and generous, chief in that.
Neither a borrower, nor a lender be;
For loan oft loses both itself and friend,
And borrowing dulls the edge of husbandry.
This above all: to thine own self be true,
And it must follow, as the night the day,
Thou canst not then be false to any man.

William Shakespeare

Hamlet, Act I, Scene III, ll.58–79

Bryn Terfel

(Nesta Jones, mam Bryn Terfel, ar ei ran)

Newydd ddod yn ôl o Salzburg ddoe a thra yno daeth Doreen (asiant Bryn) i gyfarfod â Bryn ac wrth gwrs dyma pam 'rwyf yn anfon hwn ar ei ran, gan fod trafferth wedi dod ynglŷn â chael 'visa' i Bryn a'i amser yn brin iawn. Y gerdd ddaeth yn syth i'w feddwl oedd 'Eifionydd' gan R. Williams Parry gan fod y gerdd yn disgrifio mor fanwl ei fro mebyd – ac yntau yn teithio cymaint ar yr hen fyd yma!

~

(Bryn Terfel's mother, Nesta Jones, replying on his behalf)

I just returned from Salzburg yesterday and whilst there Doreen (Bryn's agent) came to meet Bryn and of course that's why I'm sending this on his behalf, as there is difficulty in getting him a visa and he has so little time. The poem that sprang instantly to his mind was 'Eifionydd' by R. Williams Parry as it describes in such detail the area of his youth – what with him travelling so much in this old world!

('Eifionydd' was also chosen by Arfon Haines Davies and appears on page 101)

Leslie Thomas

I only came across this Dannie Abse poem when it was published last season in *The Sunday Times*. I cut it out. It will give me pleasure and reflection in-and-out of season for as many summers as I have to come.

The poem gave me a glance, an insight, into a world I never knew, nor suspected. I was also a pre-war boy in Wales but cricket was a stranger in our street in Newport. Reading it made me realize what I had missed all those years ago, never having seen cricket and the prowess of Slogger Smart, who was wonderfully free from the disgrace of fame.

Welsh cricket, naturally, is a game apart, a special game, a game different from that played on flat green fields in England, a private game played behind the privacy of our borders. Slogger Smart hoisting the ball through the discreet windowpane of the posh Angel Hotel is something you can imagine being discussed and savoured in years of evenings at working men's institutes; not to mention the flight of Abse's fancy which took it around the globe via the heights of Caerphilly.

But for all that, it is the sheer sweet nostalgia of this lovely verse that captures me. The time is indeed late and under that failing Westgate Street sky, I too can smell cut grass and – ready to bowl from the Taff end – shine an apple on my thigh.

Cricket Ball

1935, I watched Glamorgan play
especially Slogger Smart, free
from the disgrace of fame, unrenowned,
but the biggest hit with me.

A three-spring flash of willow
and, suddenly, the sound of summer
as the thumped ball, alive, would leave
the applauding ground.

'Cricket Ball'. Graphics by Sarah Hopkins.

Once, hell for leather, it curled
over the workman's crane
in Westgate Street
to crash, they said, through a discreet
Angel Hotel windowpane.

But I, a pre-war boy,
(or someone with my name)
wanted it, that Eden day,
to scoot around the turning world,
to mock physics and gravity,
to rainbow-arch the posh hotel
higher, deranged, on and on, allegro,
(the Taff a gleam of mercury below)
going, going, gone
towards the Caerphilly mountain range.

Vanishings! The years, too, gone like change.
But the travelling Taff seems the same.
It's late. I peer at the failing sky
over Westgate Street
and wait. I smell cut grass.
I shine an apple on my thigh.

Dannie Abse

On The Evening Road (Hutchinson, 1994)

M. Wynn Thomas

Cerdd yw hon sy'n seiliedig ar ddarlun o ffoaduriaid gan yr Americanwr Ben Shahn. Yn y pictiwr hwnnw, gwêl R. S. Thomas ddrych o'n cyfnod ni – bywyd ar chwâl, a phobl nid yn unig yn ddi-gartref ond hefyd yn ddi-gyfeiriad. 'Slawer dydd, byddai arlunydd yn arwyddo patrwm ystyrlon y cyfanfyd drwy greu llun cryno, gyda'r Forwyn Fair, a'r baban dwyfol yn ei chôl, yn dwt yn y canol. Bryd hynny, 'roedd y nef fel petai'n agos iawn at y ddaear. Ond erbyn heddiw, mae'r gwerthoedd a gynhaliai'r fath weledigaeth wedi eu dryllio, a ninnau'n gorfod dygymod, gorau gallwn ni, â chreulondebau'n bywyd daearol. Mae ein hymwybyddiaeth euog o erchyllterau'n canrif ni – a awgrymir yn y gerdd gan y dref a fomiwyd – yn gosod bwlch dychrynllyd rhyngom a diniweidrwydd cred oesau a fu. Hyd yn oed pan geisiwn gysylltu â'r gorffennol, mae rhyw letchwithdod yn y berthynas bob amser – fel yr awgrymir yn y darlun wrth i'r fam gario llun *ei* mam â'i ben i waered. Ond er i R. S. Thomas fynegi ing a thrallod y ganrif hon, fe wêl ar yr un pryd fod grym cariad dynol yn dal i ymddangos ar ganol y darlun – wrth i'r tad ddal ei faban yn dyn yn ei gôl.

~

This poem is based on a painting of refugees by the American artist Ben Shahn. In that picture, R. S. Thomas sees an image of our times – of a shattered world, full of people who are at once homeless and disorientated. In past ages, an artist used to signify the meaningful pattern of the cosmos by creating a balanced design in which the Virgin Mary, with the Holy Babe in her lap, was set in the very middle of the painting. Heaven seemed reassuringly near earth in those days. But by today, the values that sustained such a vision have been shattered. Our guilty awareness of the barbarism of our century – suggested in the poem by the bombed town – has created a terrible gulf between us and the innocent belief of bygone times. Even when we try to connect with the past, an awkwardness invariably enters the relationship – just as the mother in the picture carries *her* mother's picture upside down. But although R. S. Thomas gives powerful expression to the suffering and devastation of this century, he at the same time acknowledges that the power of human love still survives at the very centre of the picture – as the father clutches his baby tightly in his arms.

Father and Child
Ben Shahn

Times change:
no longer the virgin
ample-lapped; the child fallen
in it from an adjacent heaven.

Heaven is far off, back
of the bombed town. The infant
is human, embraced dearly
like a human mistake.

The father presses, his face set,
towards a displaced future.
The mother has salvaged her mother's
portrait and carries it upside down.

R. S. Thomas
Ingrowing Thoughts (Seren Books, 1985)

'Father and Child, Ben Shahn'. Graphics by Paul Peter Piech.

244

Ned Thomas

Harri Webb made a deserved name for himself with satiric verse and political squibs, but I think his 'Dyffryn Woods' will outlast them. I first read it when his volume *The Green Desert* was published in 1969. It is that rare thing in contemporary English, a poem written in accessible language that dares to express deep emotion straight, without defensive irony.

It looks backwards and forwards, encompassing the whole industrial cycle in south Wales. The second verse recalls the anonymous Welsh poet whose 'Coed Glyn Cynon' lamented the despoiling by the early ironmasters of a wood that stretched from Penderyn to Abercynon. The verses that follow have proved all too prophetic. I like the identifications implied by Harri Webb's use of the word 'our' in the second and fourth verses.

Dyffryn Woods

(For Robert Morgan, who asks, from exile, How are the Dyffryn trees now?)

In perfect equipoise a moment
Between the green leaf and the brown
The Dyffryn trees still stand in beauty
About the mean and straggling town.

Last of the spreading woods of Cynon
Our nameless poet loved and sung
Calling a curse on their despoilers
The men of iron heart and tongue,

In stillness at the end of autumn
They wait to see the doom fulfilled,
The final winter of the townships
When the last pithead wheels are stilled.

Our earth, though plundered to exhaustion
Still has the strength to answer back,
In houses built above the workings
The roof trees sag, the hearth stones crack.

245

Soon the last truckload down the valley
Will leave the sidings overgrown
While through the streets of crumbling houses
The old men crawl with lungs of stone.

And now as in the long green ages
The Dyffryn trees stand full and tall,
As lovely as in exile's memory,
Breathless, a breath before the fall.

Harri Webb

The Green Desert (Gwasg Gomer, 1969)

Rachel Thomas

Cyfansoddwyd y gerdd hon gan Ceiriog yn y bedwaredd ganrif ar bymtheg, ac yntau'n laslanc yn ymadael â chartre am y tro cynta i ddinas ddiwydiannol Manceinion. Dinas yn llawn prysurdeb a mwg a budreddi ac yntau yn dod o awyr iach mynyddoedd y Gogledd a Dyffryn Clwyd. Roedd Ceiriog yn gweithio mewn gorsaf yng nghanol y ddinas, dim awyr las yn y golwg, ac yntau'n dyheu am gael mynd yn ôl i'w gynefin, a'r sefyllfa yn codi hiraeth dwys arno. Mae'n disgrifio'r grug a phenrhyddid yr adar a'r pennill olaf yw allwedd y gerdd.

Nid wyf yn credu imi ddysgu'r gerdd erioed yn ffurfiol felly, ond yn sicr y mae'n rhan o'm henaid i. Afraid sôn am gerddoriaeth i gerdd fel hon, y mae'n gerddoriaeth ynddi hi ei hun, perl fach yn ddi-os.

~

This poem was composed by Ceiriog in the nineteenth century when he was a young lad leaving home for the first time for industrial Manchester. A city full of bustle, smoke and filth to him coming from the fresh air of the mountains of north Wales and the Vale of Clwyd. Ceiriog worked in a railway station in the centre of the city where no blue sky was to be seen; the situation made him deeply homesick and he longed to go back to his familiar habitat. He describes the heather and the total freedom of the birds, and the final verse is the key to the whole poem.

I don't think I ever learnt the poem formally, but without a doubt it is a part of my soul. It's unnecessary to talk of music for a poem like this, it is a piece of music in itself, a little pearl without a doubt.

Nant y Mynydd

Nant y Mynydd groyw loyw,
Yn ymdroelli tua'r pant,
Rhwng y brwyn yn sisial ganu;
O na bawn i fel y nant!

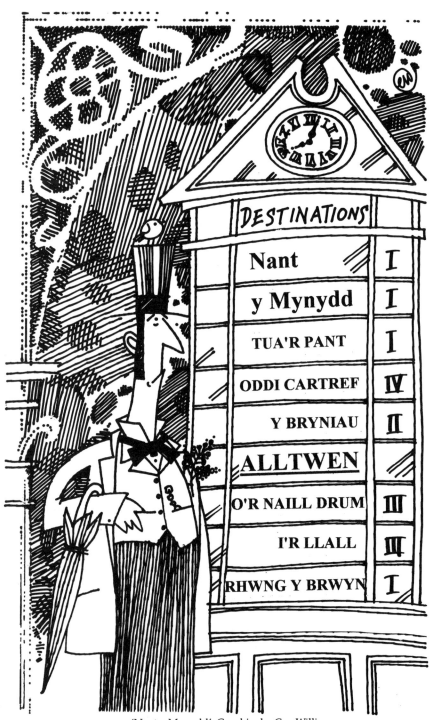

'Nant y Mynydd'. Graphics by Cen Williams.

Grug y mynydd yn eu blodau,
Edrych arnynt, hiraeth ddug
Am gael aros ar y bryniau
Yn yr awel efo'r grug.

Adar mân y Mynydd uchel,
Godant yn yr awel iach,
O'r naill drum i'r llall yn 'hedeg;
O na bawn fel deryn bach!

Mab y Mynydd ydwyf innau
Oddi cartref yn gwneud cân,
Ond mae 'nghalon yn y mynydd
Efo'r grug a'r adar mân.

Ceiriog

Oriau'r Hwyr Llyfr 1 (Hughes a'i Fab, 1872)

R. S. Thomas

Born Lost

It is a thicket;
the branches are bone.
Faces stare out at us,
human faces with mouths
wrenched on a wild cry:
'I am hungry, I am
alone'. To be born
lost – what greater misery
can befall? They offer
their plight and we nod
as we pass, dusting
them off our coat sleeves.
A coin is no key
to their enclosure, so why
waste one? The mind sheers
off the difficulty
they present: 'Neither this man
sinned, nor his parents . . .'
Who, then? Where did the road
fork, and who threw the genes'
dice? There is no answer
but that we are committed
to pursue it, they
with their mouths open,
we with the minds that
love grudges us closed.

R. S. Thomas

Siân Thomas

Un o gerddi'r canu cynnar yw un o fy hoff ddarnau o farddoniaeth. Pan yn fyfyriwr yn y brifysgol, cefais fy swyno gan symlrwydd y canu cynnar, a *Chanu Llywarch Hen*, a *Chanu Heledd* yn arbennig.

Yn ôl Syr Ifor Williams, lluniwyd y cerddi ym Mhowys i bortreadu cymeriadau o'r chweched a'r seithfed ganrif, ond fe berthyn eu hawdur i gyfnod diweddarach. Mae 'Canu Heledd' yn rhan o gylch o ganu a chwedlau am deulu Cyndrwyn. Y prif arwr yw Cynddylan ap Cyndrwyn o lys Pengwern yn Swydd Amwythig, ond prif gymeriad y canu yw Heledd ei chwaer, a'i galar ar ôl i'w brawd gael ei ladd mewn brwydr. Yn 'Stafell Gynddylan', mae'n cofio fel y bu pethau yn y llys – y cymeriadau, y bywyd hapus, y partïon, y gwmnïaeth, y croeso a'r cartref clud. Er bod iaith y canu bellach braidd yn ddieithr i ni, mae'r teimladau a fynegir yn y geiriau heb golli dim o'u hergyd. Yn ei symlrwydd, daw galar Heledd yn agos iawn i'r wyneb trwy'r gerdd – fe edrychir ar drychineb ac anobaith, ac fe gyfosodir yr hapusrwydd a fu gyda thristwch y presennol.

Yng 'Nghanu Heledd', a'r gerdd hon yn arbennig, dyn ni'n rhannu teimladau mwya' personol merch yn hiraethu am yr hyn a gollwyd. Mae modd i ni heddiw uniaethu â'r teimladau hynny – maent yr un mor berthnasol i ferch sy'n galaru am frawd neu gariad o filwr a laddwyd yn Fietnam neu'r Malvinas, yn y Gulf neu ar strydoedd Gogledd Iwerddon. Mae yma hiraeth am gymdeithas a fu, am ffordd o fyw a fu, ac am gariad a fu, ac mae yma hefyd alar am erchylltra rhyfel. Mae neges y gerdd yn apelio at bob oes, ac yn dweud rhywbeth wrth bob oes.

~

One of my favourite pieces of poetry is one of our earliest poems. Whilst a student in university I fell in love with the simplicity of our early Welsh verse, in particular *Canu Llywarch Hen*, and *Canu Heledd*.

According to Sir Ifor Williams, these poems were composed in Powys to portray characters from the sixth and seventh centuries, but their author belongs to a later period. 'Canu Heledd' is part of a cycle of poems and folktales about the Cyndrwyn family. The main hero is Cynddylan son of Cyndrwyn from the court of Pengwern in Shropshire, but the main character of the work is Heledd his sister, and her mourning after her brother is killed in battle. In 'Stafell Gynddylan', she remembers how things used to be in the court – the people, the happy life, the parties, the companionship, the welcome, the comfortable home. Although the language of the poetry is by now somewhat alien to us, the feelings expressed in the words have lost none of their force. In its simplicity, Heledd's mourning springs to the fore throughout the poem – one sees disaster and despair and the happiness that was is placed side by side with the sadness of the present time.

In *Canu Heledd*, and this poem especially, we share the most personal thoughts of a girl longing for that which was lost. It is perfectly possible for us today to appreciate these feelings – they are just as relevant to a girl mourning for a brother or lover killed whilst fighting in Vietnam, the Falklands, in the Gulf or on the streets of Northern Ireland. Here there is a longing for a past society, a former way of life, and for a former love, as well as grief concerning the atrocity of war. The message of the poem appeals to every age and has something to say to every age.

Stafell Gynddylan

Stauell Gyndylan ys tywyll heno,
  Heb dan, heb wely.
  Wylaf wers; tawaf wedy.

Stauell Gyndylan ys tywyll heno,
  Heb dan, heb gannwyll.
  Namyn Duw, pwy a'm dyry pwyll?

Stauell Gyndylan ys tywyll heno,
  Heb dan, heb oleuat.
  E[t]lit a'm daw amdanant.

Stauell Gyndylan ys tywyll y nenn,
  Gwedy gwen gyweithyd.
  Gwae ny wna da a'e dyuyd.

Stauell Gyndylan, neut athwyt heb wed,
  Mae ym bed dy yscwyt.
  Hyt tra uu, ny bu dollglwyt.

Stauell Gyndylan ys digarat heno,
  Gwedy yr neb pieuat.
  Wi a angheu, byr y'm gat?

Stauell Gyndylan, nyt esmwyth heno,
  Ar benn carrec hytwyth.
  Heb ner, heb niuer, heb amwyth.

Stauell Gyndylan, ys tywyll heno,
  Heb dan, heb gerdeu.
  Dygystud deurud dagreu.

Stauell Gyndylan ys tywyll heno,
  Heb dan, heb deulu.
  Hidyl [vyn neigyr] men yt gynnu.

Stauell Gyndylan a'm gwan y gwelet,
  Heb doet, heb dan.
  Marw vy glyw; buw mu hunan.

Stauell Gyndylan ys peithawc heno,
  Gwedy ketwyr bodawc,
  Eluan, Kyndylan, Kaeawc.

Stauell Gyndylan ys oergrei heno,
  Gwedy y[r] parch a'm buei.
  Heb wyr, heb wraged a'e katwei.

Stauell Gyndylan ys araf heno,
  Gwedy colli y hynaf.
  Y mawr drugarawc Duw, pa wnaf?

Stauell Gyndylan ys tywyll y nenn,
  Gwedy dyua o Loegyrwys.
  Kyndylan ac Eluan Powys.

Stauell Gyndylan ys tywyll heno,
  O blant Kyndrwyn[yn]
  Kynon a Gwiawn a Gwyn.

Stauell Gyndylan a'm erwan pob awr,
  Gwedy mawr ymgyuyrdan
  A weleis ar dy benntan.

Anon.

Canu Llywarch Hen, ed. Ifor Williams (University of Wales Press, 1935)

Alice Thomas Ellis

I had a little daughter who died when she was two days old. She was called Rosalind Mary.

Upon a Child That Died

Here she lies, a pretty bud,
Lately made of flesh and blood:
Who, as soone, fell fast asleep,
As her little eyes did peep.
Give her strewings; but not stir
The earth, that lightly covers her.

Robert Herrick

The Complete Poetry of Robert Herrick, ed. J. Max Patrick
(New York University Press, 1963)

Angharad Tomos

Mae yna lawer o'm hoff gerddi yn sôn am gariad a blodau a dyddiau braf, achos ar un olwg, gall barddoniaeth fod yn ddihangfa rhag anawsterau bywyd bob dydd.

Ond mae yna fath arall o farddoniaeth – yr un mor hardd – wedi ei wreiddio'n bendant yn y byd go iawn, sy'n cynnig gobaith i ddyfalbarhau. Dyna'r math o gerdd yw 'Porque Quiero la Paz', neu 'Dwi isio dal ati i gwffio' – fyddai'n deitl yr un mor addas.

Mae yna gymaint o bobl yn holi 'Pam ydych chi'n dal ati i gwffio?' yn hytrach na gofyn 'Pam ydych chi'n gorffwyso ar eich rhwyfau?' Nid cwffio er difyrrwch mae ymgyrchwyr, ond am fod yna achos i'w ymladd. Yma, mae'r bardd yn gosod y cyfan mewn iaith mor syml. Siŵr iawn mai dyna pam.

Nid yw heddwch yn golygu camu'n ôl o wres y frwydr – mae'n golygu bod reit yn ei chanol – dyna'r unig heddwch ystyrlon. Heddwch ymosodol os mynnwch chi.

Yn Nicaragua y ganed Claribel Alegria yn 1924, ond mae ganddi berthynas agosach at El Salvador. Ym mis Chwefror 1994, dyma gael cyfle i ymweld â Nicaragua ac ysgwyd llaw â'r rhai sy'n dal ati i gwffio yno. Er fod y gormes yn fwy milain, yr un yw egwyddorion y frwydr – a'r rhesymau pam ein bod eisiau heddwch.

~

Many of my favourite poems talk of love and flowers and fine days because in one sense, poetry can be an escape from the difficulties of everyday life.

But there is another kind of poetry – which is just as beautiful – and has its roots firmly in the real world, offering hope to persevere. 'Porque Quero la Paz', or 'I want to keep on fighting' – which would be just as appropriate a title – is that sort of poem.

So many people ask,'Why do you keep on fighting?', rather than asking, 'Why are you doing nothing?' Campaigners don't fight for pleasure but because there is a cause to be fought. Here the poet places everything in such simple language. Indeed that is why.

Peace doesn't mean stepping back from the heat of battle – it means being right in the middle of it – that's the only meaningful peace. Aggressive peace if you like.

Claribel Alegria was born in Nicaragua in 1924, but her relationship with El Salvador is closer. In February 1994 the opportunity arose to visit Nicaragua and shake hands with those who continue to fight there. Although the tyranny and oppression are more savage, the rudiments of battle are unchanged – as are the reasons why we want peace.

Am Mod i Eisiau Heddwch

Am mod i eisiau heddwch
Ac nid rhyfel
Am nad ydwi eisiau gweld plant heb fwyd
Merched mewn dillad carpiog
Dynion â'u tafodau wedi gorfod distewi
Mae'n rhaid i mi ddal ati i gwffio.
Am fod yna fynwentydd dirgel
Catrawdau marwolaeth
Llofruddwyr gwallgo –
Yn orffwyll – lawn cyffuriau –
Yn arteithio – bygythio –
Asasineiddio,
Dwi isio dal ati i gwffio.
Am fod ar gopa Guazapa,
Frodyr sy'n sbecian
O'u bwnceri
Tuag at dair carfan filwrol
O Carolina, ac o Georgia,
Mae'n rhaid i mi ddal ati i gwffio.
Am fod peilotiaid – profiadol –
Hofrenyddion Huey –
Yn dinistrio pentrefi gyda napalm,
Yn gwenwyno'r afonydd,
Ac yn llosgi'r cnydau
Sydd yn bwydo'r bobl,
Dwi isio dal ati i gwffio.
Am fod yna wledydd rhydd,
Lle mae pobl yn cael addysg,
Lle mae cleifion yn cael gwellhad
A lle mae ffrwythau'r tir yn berchen i bawb,
Mae'n rhaid i mi ddal ati i gwffio.
Am mod i eisiau heddwch
Ac nid rhyfel.

Claribel Alegria

'Porque Quero la Paz', *Adlais o America Ladin*, translated by Judith Humphreys, *Casgliad o Gerddi* (Grŵp Canolbarth America Môn/Arfon, 1994)

John Aloysius Ward

Lord,
daily we meet people
in our streets,
our homes, schools, offices,
workshops and churches . . .
and again and again I penetrate more deeply
into the mystery of life
which in countless ways
is ever being renewed in man.

Before my eyes
is a long line of the mysteries
of birth and death,
the courageous daring of youth
and the helplessness of old age,
the cheerfulness of the healthy
and the hard struggles of the sick,
the resentment of the godless
and the anxiety of humble,
neglected believers,
the mystery surrounding man's work,
his skill and his success,
the mystery of those who have bartered away their souls,
the homeless, the unemployed . . .

Lord,
is this an endless dream of destiny,
or the sacrifice of life itself
on the altar of unknown gods,
are we helplessly sacrificed
to the God who has no meaning?

Lord,
I believe in your Spirit
dwelling in silence
in the depths of our soul,
in the heart of this our world
and in the whole of our lives.
I believe in the Spirit
who sets us free from our lack of freedom,
transforming our infidelity into faith,

giving meaning to our meaningless days
and transforming
our blasphemous curses into prayer.
I believe in the Spirit
who gives firm support to all our sufferings
transforming
into a new heaven and a new earth
each atom of our mother-earth . . .

Lord,
through the power of your Spirit in me
I believe that the mystery of our life
is not unfathomable,
that our anxieties are not justified,
that the questions we ask
are not without an answer,
that human life is not just an accumulation
of pain and misery.

O God,
you are always with us, for us, in us.
You are our God and Father
even when we say that you are
absent,
non-existent,
inexpressible,
unknown . . .
You are, and always will be with us,
do not take your spirit from us,
for without you, O God,
man would be condemned
to misery and damnation,
he would be without redemption,
without a redeemer . . .

Lord,
save each and every man,
save contemporary man.
Lord, thank you for saving man.
Amen. Amen.

Drutmar Cremer

Sing me the Song of my World

Dafydd Wigley

Fy hoff gerdd yw 'A. E. Housman' gan R. Williams Parry.

~

My favourite poem is 'A. E. Housman' by R. Williams Parry.

A. E. Housman

Nid ofna'r doeth y byd a ddaw
   Ar ochor draw marwolaeth.
Ei ddychryn ef yw bod yn fyw:
   Angheuol yw bodolaeth.

Heb honni amgyffred – ow! mor rhwydd –
   Gwallgofrwydd creadigaeth,
Myfyria ar ei farwol stad,
   A brad ei enedigaeth.

Y doeth yn ei gadernid syrth
   Yn wyneb gwyrth ei gread,
Ond yn ei wendid cyfyd lais
   Yn erbyn trais dilead.

Ei fywyd mewn di-ddyddliw wig
   A fydd gaeadfrig yrfa:
Ni rydd ei hyder yn yr wybr,
   Ni rodia lwybr y dyrfa.

Bendith i ni dderbyn yn y llan,
   Nac yn y cwpan wynfyd;
Nid eistedd gyda'r union-gred,
   Na chyda'r anghred ynfyd.

Nid ardd, nid erddir iddo chwaith,
   Ond ar y daith ni phara,
Ei synfyfyrdod fe dry'n fwyd,
   Crea o'i freuddwyd fara.

259

A'r hwn ni ddaeth i'r byd o'i fodd
A dry o'i anfodd ymaith;
Oherwydd cyn ei ddifa a'i ladd
Ceisiodd, a chadd, gydymaith.

Hwnnw yw'r ansylweddol wynt
Sy oddeutu'r hynt yn mydru;
Ac ar y rhith y mae'n ei weu
Ni bydd dileu na phydru.

R. Williams Parry

Cerddi'r Gaeaf (Gwasg Gee, 1952)

Lord Williams of Elvel

The choice, of course, is difficult but in the end comes down to George Herbert's 'Love'.

The reason for my choice is that this poem sums up in the most elegant and beautiful way the essence of early seventeenth-century mystical Christianity. The message is simple but at the same time profound; the argument concise, without one word out of place; and the feeling conveyed goes to the heart of Christian belief. As I was brought up in this tradition – both my father and my grandfather were Welsh clergymen – nothing could be more special than that.

('Love' was also chosen by Joseph P. Clancy and appears on page 36)

J. P. R. Williams

I am not a big fan of poetry, but I do run a local village church choir and this song is one of my favourites. To hear the young children singing this with great enthusiasm is tremendous. I hope you like it too.

Autumn days when the grass is jewelled
And the silk inside a chestnut shell,
Jet planes meeting in the air to be refuelled,
All these things I love so well.

Chorus:
So I mustn't forget.
No, I mustn't forget,
To say a great big thank-you,
I mustn't forget.

Clouds that look like familiar faces,
And a winter's moon with frosted rings,
Smell of bacon as I fasten up my laces,
And the song the milkman sings.
Chorus

Whipped-up spray that is rainbow-scattered,
And a swallow curving in the sky.
Shoes so comfy though they're worn-out and
they're battered,
And the taste of apple-pie.
Chorus

Scent of gardens when the rain's been falling,
And a minnow darting down a stream,
Picked-up engine that's been stuttering and
stalling,
And a win for my home team.
Chorus

Estelle White

'Shoes so comfy though they're worn-out and they're battered'. Graphics by Sue Hunt.

Kyffin Williams

I have chosen 'Pied Beauty' by Gerard Manley Hopkins.

It is easy for me to give my reasons for choosing it. Even though it is not entirely comprehensible, it has nevertheless a very powerful presence. I believe it shows a very deep care and understanding of nature together with a feeling for the importance of little things. It is a very visual poem and consequently it must appeal to any artist.

Pied Beauty

Glory be to God for dappled things –
    For skies of couple-colour as a brinded cow;
      For rose-moles all in stipple upon trout that swim;
Fresh-firecoal chestnut-falls; finches' wings;
    Landscape plotted and pieced – fold, fallow, and plough;
    And all trades, their gear and tackle and trim.

All things counter, original, spare, strange;
    Whatever is fickle, freckled (who knows how?)
    With swift, slow; sweet, sour; adazzle, dim;
He fathers-forth whose beauty is past change:
                      Praise him.

Gerard Manley Hopkins

The Poetical Works of Gerard Manley Hopkins, ed. Norman MacKenzie
(Oxford University Press, 1990)

List of Contributors

Dannie Abse: Poet, novelist and dramatist

Leo Abse: Writer, former MP for Pontypool/Torfaen

Donald Anderson: MP for Swansea East

The Marquess of Anglesey: George Charles Henry Victor Paget, 7th Marquess of Anglesey, historian and writer

Graham Benfield: Director of the Wales Council for Voluntary Action

Clive Betts: Journalist

Michael Boyce: Chief Executive of Cardiff Bay Development Corporation

Noreen Bray: Equal Opportunities Commissioner

Rachel Bromwich: Scholar

Lord Callaghan of Cardiff: Former Prime Minister and MP for Cardiff South

Wyn Calvin: Broadcaster and entertainer

Alex Carlile: MP for Montgomery

Phil Carradice: Short-story writer, poet and historian

Harold Carter: Scholar

Pat Chown: Chair of the Welsh Federation of Housing Associations

Joseph P. Clancy: Poet and translator

Hafina Clwyd: Journalist and writer

Lord Crickhowell: Chairman of Cardiff Opera House Trust, former Secretary of State for Wales

Tony Curtis: Poet and academic

Cynog Dafis: MP for Ceredigion and Pembroke North

Sir Goronwy Daniel: Former Chairman of S4C, former Principal of University College of Wales, Aberystwyth

Alan Davies: Former Coach, Welsh Rugby Union

Gilli Davies: Cookery writer and broadcaster

Lyn Davies: Composer and academic

Father Deiniol: Priest, Russian Orthodox Church in Wales, Blaenau Ffestiniog

Steve Eaves: Poet and musician

Hywel Teifi Edwards: Literary historian and critic

Menna Elfyn: Poet

Islwyn Ffowc Elis: Novelist

Gwynfor Evans: Politician and historian

J. Wynford Evans: Chairman of SWALEC

Meredydd Evans: Academic and critic
Val Feld: Director of the Equal Opportunities Commission Wales and former Director of Shelter Cymru
Paul Ferris: Author and journalist
Peter Finch: Poet and short-story writer
Paul Flynn: MP for Newport West
Ken Follet: Novelist
Michael Foot: Writer and historian, former MP for Ebbw Vale and leader of the Labour Party
Karl Francis: Film and television producer
Raymond Garlick: Poet and academic
Huw Garmon: Actor
Beti George: Broadcaster
Tanni Grey: Para-olympic and world champion athlete
R. Geraint Gruffydd: Scholar and critic
Peter Hain: MP for Neath
Arfon Haines Davies: Television presenter
Patrick Hannan: Broadcaster and journalist
David Hanson: MP for Delyn
Lord Hooson: Former MP for Montgomery and President of the Llangollen International Eisteddfod
Lord Howe of Aberavon: Former Chancellor of the Exchequer and Foreign Secretary
Kim Howells: MP for Pontypridd
Emyr Humphreys: Novelist, poet and dramatist
John Humphrys: Presenter of the *Today* programme, Radio 4
Dafydd Hywel: Actor
Sir Geoffrey Inkin: Chairman of Cardiff Bay Development Corporation and the Land Authority for Wales
Nigel Jenkins: Poet and writer
Peter Johnson: Journalist and broadcaster, presenter of Radio Wales's *Good Morning Wales*
The Most Reverend Alwyn Rice Jones: Archbishop of Wales and Patron of Shelter Cymru
Barry Jones: MP for Alyn and Deeside
Bobi Jones: Scholar, critic, poet and author
Revd Derwyn Morris Jones: Secretary of the Union of Welsh Independents
Gwyn Jones: BBC National Governor for Wales, former Chairman of the Welsh Development Agency
Harri Pritchard Jones: Novelist and critic
Ieuan Wyn Jones: MP for Ynys Môn

John Elfed Jones: Chairman of HTV Cymru/Wales, former
 Chairman of the Welsh Language Board and of Welsh Water
R. Brinley Jones: Scholar and critic
R. Gerallt Jones: Poet, novelist and critic
Terry Jones: Film director and writer, former *Monty Python* star
Phyllis Kinney: Writer and critic
Glenys Kinnock: MEP for South Wales East
Neil Kinnock: European Commissioner, former MP for Islwyn and
 leader of the Labour Party
Elfyn Llwyd: MP for Meirionnydd Nant Conwy
Lionel Madden: Librarian, National Library of Wales
George Melly: Jazz musician, writer and art critic
Robert Minhinnick: Poet, writer and environmental campaigner
Owen Money: Comedian
Rupert Moon: Llanelli and Wales scrum-half and broadcaster
Eluned Morgan: MEP for Mid and West Wales
Mihangel Morgan: Poet and author
Moc Morgan: Angler and broadcaster
Rhodri Morgan: MP for Cardiff West
Jan Morris: Travel writer and historian
Twm Morys: Musician and poet
The Right Revd Daniel Mullins: Roman Catholic Bishop of Menevia
Paul Murphy: MP for Torfaen
Mavis Nicholson: Broadcaster and writer
George Noakes: Former Archbishop of Wales
Roy Noble: Television and radio presenter
Leslie Norris: Poet and short-story writer
John Ogwen: Actor
John Osmond: Journalist and television producer, Chairman of the
 Parliament for Wales Campaign
Lord Parry of Neyland: Writer and broadcaster, former Chairman of
 the Welsh Tourist Board
Phil Parry: Journalist and presenter of *Week In Week Out*
Paul Peter Piech: Graphic artist
Clive Ponting: Writer, academic and former civil servant
His Honour Judge Dewi Watkin Powell: Circuit judge
Jonathan Pryce: Actor
Sheenagh Pugh: Poet and translator
John Puzey: Director of Shelter Cymru
Ioan Bowen Rees: Writer
Lord Merlyn-Rees: Former MP for Leeds South, former Home
 Secretary

Maureen Rhys: Actress

Lord Richard of Ammanford: QC, former MP, former UK Permanent Representative to the United Nations, former EC Commissioner

Menna Richards: Director of Programmes, HTV Cymru/Wales

Brynley F. Roberts: Scholar and critic, formerly Librarian, National Library of Wales

David Rowe-Beddoe: Chairman of the Welsh Development Agency

Ted Rowlands: MP for Merthyr Tydfil and Rhymney

Michael Scholar: Permanent Secretary, Welsh Office

Sir Harry Secombe: Actor, comedian and singer

Ian Skidmore: Author

Victor Spinetti: Actor

Meic Stephens: Poet and editor

Vivienne Sugar: Chief Executive, County of Swansea, former Director of Housing, Cardiff City Council

Bryn Terfel: Opera-singer

Leslie Thomas: Novelist

M. Wynn Thomas: Scholar and critic

Ned Thomas: Literary critic and essayist, Director of University of Wales Press

Rachel Thomas (deceased): Actress

R. S. Thomas: Poet

Siân Thomas: Television presenter

Alice Thomas Ellis: Author

Angharad Tomos: Author and Welsh-language campaigner

The Most Revd John Aloysius Ward: Roman Catholic Archbishop of Wales

Dafydd Wigley: MP for Caernarfon

Lord Williams of Elvel: Politician, President of the Campaign for the Protection of Rural Wales

J. P. R. Williams: Doctor, former captain of the Welsh Rugby team

Kyffin Williams: Artist

Index of Poets

271

Acknowledgements

For permission to reprint copyright material, the editors and publishers are grateful to the following:

Dannie Abse for 'Cricket Ball' and 'Return to Cardiff';
John Murray (publishers) Ltd for 'Executive', 'Middlesex' and 'Myfanwy' from *Collected Poems* by John Betjeman;
Nic Blandford for 'Charity Begins at Home';
Bob Cobbing for 'WAN DO TREE' from *Kurrirrurriri*;
Christopher Davies Ltd. for 'Y Seld' from *Diannerch Erchwyn a Cherddi Eraill* by Aneurin Talfan Davies;
Pennar Davies for 'Disgyrchiant';
Gwyn Morris for 'Land of My Mothers' and 'The Sacred Road' by Idris Davies;
The Literary Trustees of Walter de la Mare, and The Society of Authors as their representative for 'The Ghost' by Walter de la Mare;
Eisteddfod Genedlaethol Frenhinol Cymru for 'Pwllderi' by Dewi Emrys and 'Y Briodas' by Caradog Prichard;
Random House UK Ltd. for 'The Road Not Taken' from *The Poetry of Robert Frost*, edited by Edward Connery Lathem;
J. Gwyn Griffiths for 'I'r Crwt a Ganai'r Piano';
John Gurney for 'Silicosis' from *Coal*;
John Hegley for 'Eddie don't like furniture' from *Can I Come Down Now Dad?*;
Faber and Faber Ltd. for 'Pike' from *Lupercal* by Ted Hughes;
Judith Humphreys for 'Am Mod i Eisiau Heddwch';
The Charisma Music Publishing Company for 'Before Death' from *Matters of Life and Death* by R. D. Laing;
The Marvell Press for 'Places, Loved Ones' from *The Less Deceived* by Philip Larkin;
Faber and Faber Ltd. for 'The Explosion' and 'The Whitsun Weddings' from *Collected Poems by Philip Larkin*, edited by Anthony Thwaite;
R. Geraint Gruffydd and Mrs Mair Jones for an extract from 'Buchedd Garmon', 'Eirin Gwlanog', 'I'r Lleidr Da', 'Mair Fadlen', 'Y Dewis' and 'Y Dilyw 1939' by Saunders Lewis;
Gwasg Gwynedd for 'Etifeddiaeth' from *Cerddi'r Cywilydd* by Gerallt Lloyd Owen;
Christopher Davies Ltd. for 'Bili Puw, Cynythog Bach' by Alan Llwyd;

About Shelter Cymru

Shelter Cymru is an independent Welsh-based charity (registered no. 515902). It works to prevent homelessness and improve housing conditions in Wales and for the right of everyone to a safe, suitable and affordable home.

Through its freefone Housing Helpline, a network of housing rights services, training, policy and campaigning work Shelter Cymru is able to help thousands of families and single people each year. The proceeds from this book are making an important contribution towards the continuation of this vital work.

A message from The Most Reverend Alwyn Rice Jones, Archbishop of Wales and Patron of Shelter Cymru

'Since becoming Patron of Shelter Cymru I have become increasingly aware of the tragic effects that homelessness and bad housing can have upon individuals and families, particularly young children.

The security and safety a decent home provides can make all the difference. Shelter helps to keep families together and gives them hope for the future. That is why I consider Shelter Cymru's work to be so important.

For further information please contact:

**Shelter Cymru, Freepost, 25 Walter Road, Swansea, SA1 1ZZ
Tel. (01792) 469400 Fax. (01792) 460050**

Registered Charity No. 515902